The Making and Breaking o
Soviet Lithuania

Appearing on the world stage in 1918, Lithuania suffered numerous invasions, border changes and large scale population displacements. The successive occupations by Stalin in 1940 and Hitler in 1941, mass deportations to the Gulag and the elimination of the Jewish community in the Holocaust gave the horrors of World War II a special ferocity. Moreover, the fighting continued after 1945 with the anti-Soviet insurrection, crushed through mass deportations and forced collectivization in 1948–1951. At no point, however, did the process of national consolidation take pause, making Lithuania an improbably representative case study of successful nation-building in this troubled region. As postwar reconstruction gained pace, ethnic Lithuanians from the countryside – the only community to remain after the war in significant numbers – were mobilized to work in the cities. They streamed into factory and university alike, creating a modern urban society, with new elites who had a surprising degree of freedom to promote national culture. This book describes how the national cultural elites constructed a Soviet Lithuanian identity against a backdrop of forced modernization in the fifties and sixties, and how they subsequently took it apart by evoking the memory of traumatic displacement in the seventies and eighties, later emerging as prominent leaders of the popular movement against Soviet rule.

Violeta Davoliūtė is a researcher and freelance journalist based at the Department of History, Vilnius University. She has published widely in the fields of memory, trauma and cultural studies in Eastern Europe. Her most recent book is *Maps of Memory: Trauma, Identity and Exile in Deportation Memoirs from the Baltic States.* Vilnius, 2012 (co-edited with T. Balkelis).

BASEES/Routledge Series on Russian and East European Studies

Series editor:
Richard Sakwa, Department of Politics and International Relations, University of Kent

Editorial Committee:
Roy Allison, St Antony's College, Oxford
Birgit Beumers, Department of Theatre, Film and Television Studies, University of Aberystwyth
Richard Connolly, Centre for Russian and East European Studies, University of Birmingham
Terry Cox, Department of Central and East European Studies, University of Glasgow
Peter Duncan, School of Slavonic and East European Studies, University College London
Zoe Knox, School of Historical Studies, University of Leicester
Rosalind Marsh, Department of European Studies and Modern Languages, University of Bath
David Moon, Department of History, University of York
Hilary Pilkington, Department of Sociology, University of Manchester
Graham Timmins, Department of Politics, University of Birmingham
Stephen White, Department of Politics, University of Glasgow
Founding Editorial Committee Member:
George Blazyca, Centre for Contemporary European Studies, University of Paisley

This series is published on behalf of BASEES (the British Association for Slavonic and East European Studies). The series comprises original, high-quality, research-level work by both new and established scholars on all aspects of Russian, Soviet, post-Soviet and East European Studies in humanities and social science subjects.

The Making and Breaking of Soviet Lithuania

Memory and modernity in the wake of war

Violeta Davoliūtė

Routledge
Taylor & Francis Group

LONDON AND NEW YORK

First published 2013
by Routledge

2 Park Square, Milton Park, Abingdon, Oxon OX14 4RN
711 Third Avenue, New York, NY 10017, USA

Routledge is an imprint of the Taylor & Francis Group, an informa business

First issued in paperback 2016

British Library Cataloguing in Publication Data
A catalogue record for this book is available from the British Library

Library of Congress Cataloging in Publication Data
Davoliūtė, Violeta, [date]
  The making and breaking of Soviet Lithuania : memory and modernity in the wake of war / Violeta Davoliūtė.
    pages cm. -- (BASEES/Routledge series on Russian and East European studies)
    Summary: "Appearing on the world stage in 1918, Lithuania suffered numerous invasions, border changes and large scale population displacements. The successive occupations of Stalin in 1940 and Hitler in 1941, mass deportations to the Gulag and the elimination of the Jewish community in the Holocaust gave the horrors of World War II a special ferocity. Moreover, the fighting continued after 1945 with the anti-Soviet insurrection, crushed through mass deportations and forced collectivization in 1948-1951. At no point, however, did the process of national consolidation take a pause, making Lithuania an improbably representative case study of successful nation-building in this troubled region. As postwar reconstruction gained pace, ethnic Lithuanians from the countryside--the only community to remain after the war in significant numbers--were mobilized to work in the cities. They streamed into factory and university alike, creating a modern urban society, with new elites who had a surprising degree of freedom to promote national culture. This book describes how the national cultural elites constructed a Soviet Lithuanian identity against a backdrop of forced modernization in the fifties and sixties, and how they subsequently took it apart by evoking the memory of traumatic displacement in the seventies and eighties, later emerging as prominent leaders of the popular movement against Soviet rule"-- Provided by publisher.
    Includes bibliographical references and index.
    1. Lithuania--History--1945-1991. 2. Lithuania--History--Autonomy and independence movements. 3. Elite (Social sciences)--Lithuania--History--20th century. 4. Collective memory--Lithuania. 5. Lithuanians--Ethnic identity. 6. National characteristics, Lithuanian. I. Title.
  DK505.77.D38 2013
  947.9308'5--dc23
                          2013024024

ISBN: 978-0-415-71449-5 (hbk)
ISBN: 978-1-138-20448-5 (pbk)

Typeset in Times New Roman
by Taylor & Francis Books

Contents

List of figures

List of tables

Preface

The story told in this book has been woven from a range of sources both private and public – memoirs, diaries and letters; speeches, newspapers and official documents; poems, novels, photographs and films – but a series of in-depth interviews with members of the Soviet Lithuanian cultural elite lies at its core. The interviews build upon the wealth of information recently made available in published and archival sources on the Soviet period in Lithuania, but they also, I believe, cast a new light on this growing body of knowledge.

I feel privileged to have been able to converse at length with so many writers, artists and thinkers whose very lives incorporate the complexities and contradictions of that age. Some of them were cultural icons during my school years in the Lithuanian Soviet Socialist Republic and in the post-Soviet period as well. The intensity of their experience and their storytelling mastery gives each of their life narratives a gravity that was difficult to resist. It was no simple matter to construct my own narrative out of theirs.

To maintain a sense of direction, I kept returning to two basic questions. The first was to describe the experience of moving from the village to the city – foundational for the majority of my interlocutors. The second was to recall the details of everyday life: the ambitions and disappointments of youth, friends, family, social circles and activities, professional achievements and failures. I wanted above all to understand their individual motivations, their subjective perceptions during the years of profound social transformation after World War II.

This approach may seem naïve, focussed on trivial, non-political questions, but I believe it afforded me a degree of access to a sphere of private recollection that is more often shielded from public scrutiny and criticism. The difficult post-war years and the Soviet period remain intensely controversial in Lithuania today. It is easier and safer to leave them cloaked in silence, or to recall and retell them only through tried and tested formulas.

My concentration on the experience of the Soviet Lithuanian cultural elite is rather exclusive. This was a conscious choice and, I hope, a conscientious one. The experiences of the Polish and Jewish communities of Vilnius, for example, are presented only to the extent necessary to understand the social and cultural context in which the new and self-consciously Lithuanian elites emerged in the cities after World War II. I have tried to provide references to other works that discuss the fates of the Polish and Jewish communities in the detail they deserve.

By the same token, my discussion of the Lithuanian victims of Stalinist repression is limited to the social and demographic consequences of the deportations and collectivization, and meant primarily to set the stage for the account of the last chapter on how the traumatic memory of repression was woven back into mainstream public consciousness during the popular movement. And if I say little about women writers, artists and thinkers, it is because they remained in the shadow of their male peers and were generally not perceived as public figures.

The justification for these exclusions is my belief that the story of the Soviet Lithuanian cultural mainstream needs to be told. It has been obscured by the narrative of the popular movement, which rightly made heroes of individual martyrs but wrongly construed "Lithuania" as a collective martyr. Moreover, I am convinced that only by recovering the memory of everyday life under Soviet rule can one come to understand the pervasiveness of the social alienation that was part and parcel of Soviet modernity, and which remains a legacy in the region to this day.

I am not a demographer and I can only hope that experts in this and related fields will look kindly on my attempt to contextualize the social and cultural history of postwar Lithuania against the backdrop of mass population displacement. Scholars with greater competence in such matters have amply established its importance to the understanding of the history of East Central Europe. My purpose is merely to elaborate upon the long-term impact of displacement on social and cultural developments in Soviet Lithuania and after.

My interest in such matters is not purely academic. In the process of writing this book, I have come to a greater understanding my own family history.

I spent much of my early childhood living with my maternal grandmother on an old-fashioned homestead in the village, now extinct, of Šalnakundžiai (the name means "frostbite") in the Kupiškis district. I retain a vivid memory of the old house, built in the nineteenth century, and its massive wooden door, covered in ornaments, and the boulders erected on each side of the entrance. I remember the heavy, worn-out furniture along with the archaic household items and farm tools whose purpose I could hardly fathom.

This environment was sparse, lacking modern amenities and virtually impossible for my grandmother to manage on her own, but it was ideal for me as a small child: full of space, pastoral beauty, animals and constant adventure. When my grandmother was forced to move to the nearby city of Panevėžys in the 1970s during the last wave of rural melioration, it was a personal tragedy for us both. Almost all of the household effects, including the furniture, the great wooden door and the farm implements, were given to the local historical museum.

My mother had no time, conditions or even much interest in keeping such things in the family. Like the mainstream of her generation she was preoccupied with the difficulties of the present, not the past. She was born and raised on that very homestead, but she had left it willingly, looking to build her own life under difficult circumstances as an adult after the war. Though she always loved to work the land, and still keeps up a large city garden in her retirement, she saw the village as backward, and considered everything modern, even if it was Soviet, as an improvement.

My grandmother, a devout Catholic who hated the Soviets, also kept up with the times, to a degree. She escaped from her new surroundings through television and showed a clear preference for cheery, modernized versions of the songs she heard on the radio instead of the sad, archaic versions that folk revivalists during the late Soviet period sang and claimed were more authentic. At the same time, my grandmother would unfailingly break down and cry when she watched televised performances of *Kupiškėnų vestuvės*, an ethnographic ensemble performing a traditional folk wedding from her native district.

And there was no question of her adapting to life in the city. Her separation from the homestead was a trauma that I observed with curiosity but little understanding at the time. She was disoriented and at a loss for what to do during most of the day, and tried vainly to occupy herself with the care of the sole chicken and dog that she had battled furiously to bring with her into the new environment where she would spend her last days.

She never returned to the homestead to see what had become of it, even though it was just 50 kilometers away. She was a true autochthon, born of the earth. Once she had been uprooted, there was no going back. Fifty kilometres was the same as 500 or 5,000 – the numbers were meaningless except as a symbol of difference between one universe and another. "If I ever went back there," she often said, "I would just lie on the ground and cry until I die."

The neighborhood to which we had arrived in Panevėžys was populated with people like my grandmother, transplanted from their villages and made to live next to people they regarded as strangers. Some, I would find out later, had returned from the deportations. Our neighbors, to the best of my knowledge, were all Lithuanians – the Russians lived in a "soldier's city" somewhere on the outskirts of town. But our neighbors nonetheless spoke in a different dialect from my grandmother, and so for her they seemed foreign. Everyone still thought of their village of origin as their true home.

I had some awareness of the Holocaust thanks to the stories my grandmother told of Simute, the young wife of the rabbi of Kupiškis (Kupishok) and her beautiful infant son "Šlemkiukas" (the Lithuanian diminutive of Shlomo), with whom she, as a woman with small children of her own, shared a warm rapport. Or of the Jewish townsman forced to labour on her neighbour's field for a few weeks before he, his pregnant wife, Simute and Šlemkiukas were all killed. But these stories seemed distant, as if they happened in another land, in some other life.

It was only later, as an undergraduate at Vilnius University and especially during subsequent studies abroad that I discovered the rich history of the Jewish community of Ponevez, with its yeshivas, secular schools, synagogues and cultural centres, or of the Polish gymnasium and cathedral in the city. I apprehended none of this during my life there. Though I could not articulate it at the time, I had always felt a sense that something important was missing in that city, a palpable sense of emptiness.

Since then, after studying and working in England, Canada, and Belgium, among other places, and becoming a true migrant, I have come to understand the experience of my family and that of postwar Lithuanian society in the words of the British artist and writer John Berger: "emigration, forced or chosen, across national frontiers or from village to metropolis, is the quintessential experience of our time."[1]

While I would never choose to live in a village (not even in the Haute-Savoie, to which Berger retreated to learn peasant ways), I maintain a fondness for my attachment to the land, such as it is, and would like to convey this sense of origin to my daughter. And so it is to Elzė Mikaelė, and to the memory of my grandmother Ona Varslauskienė (Inčiūraitė), that I dedicate this book.

Acknowledgments

Many people helped me over the course of this project. I am grateful to Klaus Richter, Arūnas Streikus, and Theodore Weeks for kindly agreeing to read the manuscript and offering their thoughtful critiques. Dovilė Budrytė and Rasa Čepaitienė also read sections of this book and provided valuable remarks. Mindaugas Pocius was generous in sharing his insights and extensive research, and Valdemaras Klumbys graciously shared some interviews he recorded for his dissertation.

I also benefitted from conversations with Vytautas Rubavičius and Mikhail Iossel, while Jonas Ohman, director of the documentary film *Hitmen*, helped me to understand certain aspects of the postwar resistance. Very special thanks go to Tomas Balkelis, my friend and colleague since our early student days, and to my family for their assistance, support and patience. Research for this project was funded by a Global Grant of the European Social Fund.

Antanas Sutkus and Algirdas Tarvydas gave me permission to use their photographs, and were equally generous with their insights, good cheer and charisma. I am also grateful to Romualdas Rakauskas, Stanislovas Žvirgždas, Marija Drėmaitė and Rūta Mélyné for their responsiveness and collegiality. A special thanks to Milij Chwoles for his kind hospitality in Paris, for sharing his father Rafael's paintings and photographs, and for his family recollections of postwar Vilnius. Dr. Saulius Sužiedėlis kindly provided the image of his father's Vilnius Passport, and Raimondas Urbakavičius his photo of the legendary Neringa Café.

I am grateful to the Venclovas House Museum, the Tolerance Centre of the Vilna Gaon State Jewish Museum, the Vilnius County Archives, the Lithuanian Archives of Literature and Art, the Lithuanian Central State Archives, the Lithuanian Special Archives, the Lithuanian Theater, Music and Cinema Museum, the Archive of the Institute of Lithuanian Literature and Folklore, and the Martynas Mažvydas National Library of Lithuania for supporting my research and for permission to use photographs reproduced in this book. The personnel at each of these organizations were simply indispensable and I benefitted tremendously from their professionalism.

Most of all, I would like to thank all those who shared their time and memories of the postwar period with élan, generosity and patience: Algimantas

Apanavičius, Vitas Areška, Algimantas Baltakis, Vytautas Brėdikis, Vytautas Bubnys, Romualdas Granauskas, Ramūnas Katilius, Romualdas Lankauskas, Gytis Lukšas, Justinas Marcinkevičius†, Marcelijus Martinaitis†, Jonas Mikelinskas, Algimantas Nasvytis, Vytautas Nasvytis, Vincas Justas Paleckis, Algirdas Pocius, Bronius Raguotis, Romualdas Rakauskas, Vacys Reimeris, Kazys Saja, Rimtautas Šilinis, Mykolas Sluckis†, Aldona Šulskytė†, Antanas Sutkus, Irena Veisaitė, Tomas Venclova, Vytautė Žilinskaitė, Markas Zingeris, and Stanislovas Žvirgždas.

In this book have translated and reproduced passages from the poetry of Algimantas Baltakis, Justinas Marcinkevičius, Justas Paleckis and Petras Vaičiūnas. I am grateful to the authors or their heirs who have given me permission to do so, and would like to emphasize that my rough, literal translations are intended simply to convey the basic sense of the passages. In the case of Petras Vaičiūnas, I have made every effort but was unable to locate an heir who felt authorized to grant permission to translate his work.

Introduction
Misplaced memories

The decades following the end of World War II in East Central Europe have been all but lost in myth – popular historical narratives of the period do not stand up to scrutiny.[1] The old communist accounts of liberation and reconstruction were never fully convincing, and the fractious nationalist narratives of resistance to Soviet rule do little more than scratch the surface of events. Still, the story of universal national resistance proved its usefulness during the Velvet revolutions that toppled communist regimes in 1989, and it retains a strong position in popular memory throughout the region to this day.

But the end of the Cold War also ushered an era of methodological innovation and empirical discovery based on access to previously closed archives and the proliferation of published memoirs by people from all walks of life. Theories of *histoire croisée* and multiple modernities have helped to transcend the rigidly opposed narratives of East versus West; of communism versus nationalism. They help to contextualize the history of the lands subjected to successive Nazi and Stalinist occupations in a pan-European perspective, by underscoring how transnational processes of industrialization, urbanization and mass politics led to a range of outcomes across liberal and illiberal regimes during the twentieth century.[2]

This book seeks to examine the impact of these key twentieth-century developments on one of the more peripheral countries of the region – Lithuania. Because of its uncertain position among the more powerful nations and national narratives of Russia, Germany and Poland, Lithuania's history remains obscure to most in the West. But by the same token, the country's sheer exposure to the transnational currents of the twentieth century means that it provides an unusually clear example of how genocide, mass population displacement and Soviet-style modernization transformed what Timothy Snyder has so evocatively called the "bloodlands" of East Central Europe into the nation-states that they are today.[3]

In this context, Lithuania offers an improbably successful and paradoxically representative case study of twentieth-century modernization and nation-building in this historically fraught region. In 1918 it emerged as an independent state amid the geopolitical rubble of World War I, which gave 60 million people a state of their own and turned another 25 million people into national minorities. A predominantly agricultural people in the backwaters of the Russian Empire, the Lithuanians joined others in launching a process of intense nationalization. They institutionalized universal education in Lithuanian and promoted their language in the public sphere. They redistributed the large landholdings of the Polish gentry and encouraged the mass migration of Lithuanians from the farms to the cities, where the clash of national ambitions and the interests of the older and more established urban communities led to a steady rise of ethnic tensions and outbreaks of anti-Semitism in the years leading to World War II.[4]

On the eve of war in 1939, Lithuania had its third largest city Klaipėda taken by Germany. In October 1939 it regained its historical capital of Vilnius, held by Poland since October 1920, but only at the price of losing its independence to Soviet occupation in June 1940, just eight months after the outbreak of World War II. A year later, the Nazis invaded the Soviet Union and occupied Lithuania, but not before the Soviets had completed the first mass deportation of the population on 14–18 June 1941. The Nazis then set themselves to murdering the 200,000-strong community of Lithuanian Jews, a genocide in which many Lithuanians were active participants.[5]

All in all, the Holocaust, mass killings, and mass emigration drained the country of about one-fifth of its population, mostly from the cities. By the end of the war, the pre-war urban population (which comprised mostly Jews and Poles) had been cut in half, while the rural population (mostly ethnic Lithuanians) had been reduced by less than 10 percent. The postwar population exchanges greatly exacerbated the depletion of the cities by the repatriation of 170,000 Lithuanian Poles to Poland, including 88,000 from Vilnius alone, which recorded a population of just 110,000 in 1945.[6]

Postwar reconstruction under the Soviets dramatically reversed the wartime process of urban depopulation. Initially, the cities received a wave of officials, engineers, workers and soldiers from the USSR, but from the late 1940s onwards, they were increasingly filled by an influx of ethnic Lithuanians from the countryside, drawn by the opportunities afforded by reconstruction, and driven by the terror of the brutal anti-Soviet counter-insurgency that included mass deportations and forced collectivization as tools of the trade.

Accordingly, the urban population of Lithuania dipped to a pre-industrial low of between 10 and 15 percent of the total population in 1946, but it would rise to over 50 percent in less than twenty-five years – a rate of urbanization exceeding even that of the "Great Transformation" of the Soviet Union during the first five-year plans in the 1930s, widely considered to be among the fastest rates of urbanization ever seen by humankind.[7]

The rapid repopulation and reconstruction of cities by the ethnically Lithuanian population from the surrounding countryside would turn postwar Vilnius – like Moscow in the 1930s – into a "peasant metropolis," a city where the vast majority of the population had recently arrived from the village.[8] The processes of urbanization and Sovietization were fused, distorting the expected pattern of socialist modernization. Instead of turning peasants into workers, the industrial society of Soviet Lithuania assumed a rustic character: the urbanization of the nation amounted to the ruralization of the city.[9]

Recent studies of Stalinism have underscored how Sovietization involved much more than the imposition of external rule and institutions but extended to the generation of new configurations of collective identity, a process of profound internal transformation on an individual and collective level.[10] The simultaneous progression of urbanization and Sovietization gave postwar reconstruction and modernization in Lithuania a specific character.[11] The demographic and cultural appropriation of the cities – and of Vilnius in particular – were fashioned into the foundation of the modernizing ideology of the postwar Soviet regime, exhibiting a paradoxical continuity with the nationalizing agenda of the interwar government of independent Lithuania.

State patronage of the arts created a new urban Soviet Lithuanian intelligentsia that would lead this process of collective self-transformation through narratives which held a mirror to Lithuanian society – as the theory of Socialist Realism would have it – in the process of its revolutionary development.[12] However, the cultural elite also revived the intellectual traditions of the interwar period, and gained an exceptional level of cultural autonomy through de-Stalinization. At the peak of the "cultural renaissance" in the mid-1960s, they aspired to raise Lithuanian culture to the world level and were inspired with the spirit of urbanity and cosmopolitanism.

After the mid-1960s, however, disillusionment with Soviet modernization and internationalism led the intelligentsia to turn the forward-looking narrative of Socialist Realism on its head. Instead of looking towards the future, they turned towards the past as a source of inspiration and identity. Over time, a discourse of displacement, described in Chapter 7 as the "rustic turn," spread throughout Soviet Lithuanian culture as an emotional reaction to Soviet-style modernity, identified with deportation, collectivization, melioration, urbanization, and Russification. The rustic turn in culture established the foundations for the "return of memory" that was triggered by the publication of previously suppressed memoirs by Gulag survivors.

Today, the social transformation of the postwar period is deeply buried in collective memory. When the democratically elected Lithuanian parliament declared independence on March 11, 1990, it did not proclaim a new republic but quite deliberately reconstituted the interwar Lithuanian state. It affirmed that Lithuania's annexation by the Soviet Union in 1940 was illegal under international law, on the grounds that the Soviet regime was imposed through crimes against humanity, including mass deportations with genocidal intent, and opposed by a "universal, organized and armed resistance" that lasted until the early 1950s.

In this narrative, the active phase of postwar resistance was crushed by the overwhelming force of the totalitarian state, but it continued through the underground activities of the Catholic Church, political dissidence, and widespread expressions of social and cultural nonconformism. These currents later resurfaced as the popular movement against Soviet rule called *Sąjūdis*. The

Republic of Lithuania was thus, properly speaking, never Soviet. The historical hiatus from 1940 to 1990 was declared legally inoperative, politically illegitimate, socially perverse, and culturally inauthentic. The return to Europe marked a return to normality, and life picked up where it had left off some sixty years before.

From a political and ethical point of view, there is much to commend this narrative. It united the democratic opposition and the national communist elites in a common cause, and rallied the population to stand up to the use of force by Soviet troops. It helped to maintain a minimal level of social cohesion and stability through difficult years of economic transition. It continues to answer the basic human need for a vision of the future, and it was, for a time, not just basically factual, but explosively revelatory, speaking truth to the powers of the day that had a stake in masking the crimes of the past.

But for all that, this narrative of Lithuanian heroism and suffering in itself says next to nothing about the Holocaust, the almost total elimination of the extensive Jewish community that had lived in the region for hundreds of years. It says nothing of the hundreds of thousands of Poles who were compelled to leave Vilnius and other parts of the country during the postwar population transfers, or of the fates of other national minorities. Perhaps most importantly, it says nothing of the role of Lithuanians in the direction and management of the Soviet regime. The forgetting of sixty years of history may once have served a purpose, but it masks the cardinal social and cultural changes that made Lithuanian society what it is today.

Over the past ten to twenty years, Lithuanian scholars have begun to document and interpret these blank pages in the nation's historical self-representation. Some have analyzed the issues of collaboration, accommodation, and resistance to the Soviet regime, the nature and extent of Sovietization, and the continuities of the Soviet and post-Soviet eras.[13] More recently, a new generation of scholars have sought to identify the social groups and cultural processes that led to the emergence of the popular movement against Soviet rule in the late 1980s.[14] Another cluster of scholars have explored the Soviet period in Lithuania through the prism of the arts, notably architecture, town planning, art, and photography.[15]

This book seeks to contribute to each of these areas of inquiry, and perhaps even to synthesize some of the findings in a transnational perspective on Sovietization as a criminally rushed and traumatic variation of modernization that was otherwise common to all European nations in the nineteenth and twentieth centuries. More specifically, the story that follows retells the social and cultural history of Soviet Lithuania in light of its transformation from a rural to an urban nation and against the background of the experience of war, genocide, and mass population displacement.

Displacement and identity

The difficulty of coming to terms with history of World War II and its aftermath in Eastern Europe stems from the transformative effects that the displacement of war, occupation, resistance and repression had upon the complex, multi-layered societies in the region. The transformative processes of categorizing, separating, killing and moving people around had the effect of creating or consolidating collective subjectivities that recall "the war" from the singular perspective of the traumatic events that led to their emergence. The war affected different groups of people in such radically dissimilar ways that one feels compelled to speak of several different wars.

And yet, as Jan Gross convincingly argued in *Neighbours*, the tendency of mainstream historiography of World War II to treat the Holocaust of the Jews and the history of the other people in Nazi-occupied states as two separate stories is untenable.[16] Beyond the need to account for the agency of Lithuanians in the Holocaust or the postwar repatriation of the Poles, one also needs to explain what effect the sudden absence of Jews and Poles had on the subsequent development of Soviet Lithuanian society.[17]

In an earlier work, Gross had explained how "the immense population losses and shifts which occurred during the war and immediate postwar years had a profound impact on the process of consolidation and character of post-war regimes."[18] Czechoslovakia and Poland, for instance, were transformed from multi-ethnic states to homogenous societies after they lost their large minority populations of Jews and Germans. Millions of Czechs, Slovaks and Poles were resettled by the state (and the victorious Allies) to fill the empty space (mostly in the cities) left by the Holocaust and the postwar expulsion of Germans. The fabric of society was torn, as the ubiquity of state violence and the mass dislocation of communities destroyed civil society and left individuals almost completely dependent on the state for support.[19]

The sudden disappearance of Jews and Germans from the cities radically altered the labor force, property relations and the structure of the elites, generating unprecedented opportunities for upward social mobility. The ruralization of the local ethnic communities, which had taken place over centuries as Germans and Jews migrated eastward and developed the cities of East Central Europe, was dramatically reversed, particularly after World War II as Slovaks, Romanians, Bulgarians, Ukrainians, Belarusians, Lithuanians and other so-called "peasant nations" streamed into the cities, stimulating a mass process of individual and collective self-transformation.[20]

The traumatic effects of mass displacement on individual lives and collective identities have not always been recognized. Back in 1945, for example, Churchill, Roosevelt and Stalin could describe the uprooting of millions of families from their homes (i.e., the transfer of 10–15 million ethnic Germans from Poland and Czechoslovakia in 1945) as an "orderly and humane population transfer."[21] But having witnessed the resurgence of genocide in the former Yugoslavia, scholars have become more attuned to the intimate relationship between displacement and violence.[22]

Norman Naimark, among others, has shown how forced deportation seldom occurs without murderous violence because of the resistance that communities are prepared to exert in defence of their livelihood and collective identity:

> People do not leave their homes on their own. They hold on to their land and their culture, which are interconnected. They resist deportation orders; they cling to their domiciles and their possessions; they find every possible way to avoid abandoning the place where their families have roots and their ancestors are buried.[23]

Even where force is not used, migration has a profound effect on individual and collective identities. As the celebrated British novelist, critic, artist and poet James Berger put the matter: "Emigration, forced or chosen, across national frontiers or from village to metropolis, is the quintessential experience of our time."[24]

Several distinct but interrelated processes of displacement have had an immeasurable impact on the postwar development of Soviet Lithuania. Today, most Lithuanians still recall the deportation of some 150,000 of their compatriots to labor camps in Siberia and Kazakhstan – over 5 percent of the population – as the self-defining trauma of the twentieth century. But this deportation and exile *from* Lithuania are inseparable from another mass displacement *within* its postwar borders. This hidden exodus involved not 5 or 10 percent, but well over half of the entire population displaced from the countryside to the urban centres, including to the newly acquired capital of Vilnius after the war.

Against the backdrop of forced migration, civil war and collectivization in the countryside, the rapid urbanization of postwar Lithuania was a foundational social experience whose cultural legacy is poorly understood. The emergence in the late twentieth century of an independent Lithuania with Vilnius as its capital is now taken for granted, but it conceals a dramatic history that has been all but forgotten. For most Lithuanians, the memory of migration from the country to the city, the story of their "arrival" in the city and in particular in Vilnius, has long been obscured by the trauma of "departure," of their separation from the land and the destruction of the traditional way of life in the village.

The city and the country

Vilnius is famous as a border city, at the crossroads of nations and cultures, a city separating and joining East and West.[25] But another way in which Vilnius is a border city involves the border that separates the city from the country, the urban from the rural, and the rustic from the urbane. In this sense, of course, every city is a border city. The identity of a city depends on what it keeps outside as much as what it keeps inside. And the passage of people, things and ideas across this border is an important measure of change for a city, and for the country in which it is located.

In a pioneering work of cultural studies entitled *The City and the Country*, Raymond Williams states that the contrast of the urban and the rural is "one of the major forms in which we become conscious of a central part of our experience and of the crises of our society." Treating literature as a window on to social change, he looks to the works of English poets and writers to discern "structures of feeling," or traces of the lived experience of a community over the course of modern urbanization from the sixteenth to the twentieth century.[26]

This study takes a similar approach in seeking to trace the cultural impact urbanization had on Soviet Lithuanian society in light of its traumatically rapid pace – forty years compared to England's four hundred. This is a story that is more familiar to us in a number of separate narratives, like the Holocaust of the Jews, the postwar resettlement of the Poles, the emigration and deportation of the Lithuanian intelligentsia and urban bourgeoisie, along with the devastation of the countryside by collectivization, deportation and the war of resistance.

More recently, however, a few historians have begun to retell these stories and how they all came together to have a profound impact on the cities of East Central Europe and their subsequent development after the war. Karl Schlögel, for example, popularized the term "urbicide" to describe the fate of Vilnius, Lviv, Wrocław and other cities where the people, and thus the texture of urban life as it had developed over the course of generations, were completely destroyed.[27]

Beyond the sheer scale of urban depopulation, urbicide refers to the destruction of the cityscape; or when physical destruction was not total, to the destruction of the urban fabric, the intangible quality of complex urban communities that takes generations upon generations to build. The term implies a rupture not only to the continuity of the built environment, but also to cultural tradition, to experience and collective memory.

The constitutive force of mass displacement and its historical effect on the development of collective identities in postwar East Central Europe is dramatically illustrated by the fate of Vilnius. The city is known as *Vilne* by the Jews and *Wilno* by the Poles who have lived there for centuries and who identify with the city as their own. And in light of the thorough naturalization of this city over the past sixty years as the capital of Lithuania (Soviet and post-Soviet), it is by now quite difficult to convey the tragic significance that Lithuanians attached to the city during the interwar period when it was held by Poland (1920–39), when Kaunas was the so-called "provisional" capital of Lithuania.

The "Vilnius Question" arose upon the collapse of the Russian empire and the emergence of Poland and Lithuania as separate, independent states.[28] The Lithuanian claim on the city was based on history, in the sense that Vilnius was the historical capital of the Grand Duchy of Lithuania. For the Poles, *Wilno* was unquestionably "their" city. Along with the Jews, they constituted the largest ethnic group within the city. Józef Piłsudski, the Polish head of state, grew up in the Vilnius region, was educated in Vilnius, and his government put a high priority on regaining Poland's "eastern territories."

Intensive diplomatic negotiations were pursued, but the question was decided by force on October 9, 1920, when Polish divisions drove the Lithuanians out of the city. The dispute between Lithuania and Poland over the jurisdiction of Vilnius would stay on the agenda of European diplomacy for two decades; within Lithuania, it grew into a national obsession, "the same as Jerusalem for Jews, Transylvania for Hungarians and Kosovo for Serbs."[29] Having lost on the military front, Lithuanians mounted an intense ideological struggle from the provisional capital of Kaunas throughout the interwar period.[30]

The fact that Lithuania would ultimately regain Vilnius through Soviet intervention as a condition of the Molotov–Ribbentrop Pact turned out to be one of the great, bitter ironies of European history in the twentieth century. As the joke at the time went, Vilnius may have become Lithuania's, but Lithuania now belonged to Russia. Nonetheless, as the new capital of Soviet Lithuania, Vilnius became the focus of an intense reconstruction effort after the war and the social forge of a new collective identity. The possibility of starting a new life in the newly acquired capital was attractive to many Lithuanians, and the communist authorities exploited the situation by carefully aligning the process of urbanization with the cultivation of a Soviet consciousness and identity.

The transfer of the capital from Kaunas to Vilnius in 1940 had a profound effect on Lithuanian society. On the one hand, it reflected a continuity of purpose with the interwar period, insofar as some leading members of the postwar Lithuanian Communist government had been outspoken activists of the Vilnius Question during the interwar years. But on the other hand, it interrupted the short but significant social experience of urban development and social modernization that had occurred in Kaunas. In the postwar post-apocalyptic environment of Vilnius, almost completely depopulated of its Jewish and Polish populations, the new Lithuanian urban elites and the cultural intelligentsia were formed almost from scratch.

Generations and change

The memoirs and recollections of those Lithuanians who came of age after the conclusion of World War II provide a unique perspective on this period as one of profound transformation, both individual and collective. Transcending the limitations of the narratives of national resistance or communist liberation, their stories attest to continuities of Lithuanian social and cultural development in the twentieth century over and above the turmoil and trauma of war, genocide, occupation, and Soviet-style modernization. Today, their memoirs, letters, diaries and testimonies give expression to the emerging national subject that was shaped by the turmoil of the age. As such, their stories are critical to the recovery of the misplaced memory of Lithuanian cultural agency in the years after World War II.

The first postwar generation of Lithuanian intellectuals were born primarily to poor, rural households, where they witnessed the traumas of war, insurgency, mass deportations and collectivization as youths. Young enough to stand a chance at escaping active participation in the war and the anti-Soviet insurgency that followed, they became adults just as stability was imposed by the Soviets in the late 1940s. As such, they were the first generation to benefit from the upsurge of social mobility that accompanied the mass migration of peasants from the villages, destroyed by collectivization, to the newly reconstructed cities. Embarking upon their professional careers after Stalin's death, they largely escaped the terror and purges that had swept away earlier generations of the Soviet elites.

Prominently represented by contrasting figures such as Algirdas Brazauskas (1932–2010), the last leader of Lithuanian Communist Party, and Vytautas Landsbergis (b. 1932), the leader of *Sąjūdis*, key politicians from this generation gained international renown in the late 1980s, when they were at the peak of their careers and Lithuania was at the forefront of the national rebellions against Soviet rule.[31] Quite apart from these political figures, the postwar cohort of creative intellectuals known as the "Generation of 1930" – cultural icons such as the poet Justinas Marcinkevičius (1930–2012) and his peers Alfonsas Maldonis (1929–2007), and Algimantas Baltakis (b. 1930) – played a role in the cultural sphere that was no less important, but much less visible to the outside observer.

In Soviet society, where the freedom of speech was restricted and real politics were conducted behind closed doors, the cultural intelligentsia came to play an exceptionally important role. Especially in the non-Russian republics, where they took advantage of the relatively broad cultural autonomy that was a core if controversial and contradictory element of Soviet nationalities policy, the intelligentsia served as mediators between society and political power. Their works of literature and art, architecture, photography, film and performance constituted the only public sphere to speak of – constrained but real – in which various discourses of collective identity interacted and took shape.

Created by the Stalinist system of state patronage of the arts, the Soviet Lithuanian intelligentsia served as ideologues of modernization under Khrushchev – much like the *shestidesiatniki* in Soviet Russia – but later evolved into bards of national tradition who, as distinct from the Russian cultural elite as a corporation, gained prominence in the late 1980s as leaders of the popular movement against Soviet rule.[32] Earlier, select members of this generation had advanced swiftly in the post-Stalin years to occupy the commanding heights of politics, society and culture, where they remained until the last days of Soviet Lithuania. Sharing in the living memory of the interwar period of national independence, they would come to serve as a unique, living link between the pre-Soviet, Soviet and post-Soviet periods.

The recent publication of memoirs by leading members of this generation has put the question of Lithuanian agency during Soviet rule back on the table. The life stories of Brazauskas, who was the First Secretary of the Communist Party, or the former Chairman of the Supreme Soviet Lionginas Šepetys (b. 1927), among others, attest to the obvious but forgotten reality that Lithuanians, like the other national elites of the Soviet Union and communist Eastern Europe, played a significant role in the management of the regime.[33] Irrespective of how limited their authority may have been vis-à-vis the Kremlin, they claim to have been working for their nation's interest from within the system.

The memoirs of former Soviet officials are generally preoccupied with the political context, seeking to justify their involvement with the regime by

suggesting that the outer surface of their lives was false, a show of con-
formism to communist rule, while the inner reality of their being was nationalist. Only now, in the post-Soviet era, are they able to reveal the "hidden
transcripts" of their lives.[34] The memoirs of the cultural intelligentsia, on
the other hand, are less driven by the immediate political need to justify or
account for the past, and so they tend to shed a more intimate light on the processes of individual and social transformation that characterized the postwar
years.

Marcelijus Martinaitis (1936–2013), for example, recalls the "prayer" that
he and his fellow students would recite as an ironic joke after a drink: "I
thank Soviet power for providing me, the son (daughter) of a peasant with
little land, with education and enlightenment." He continues with a frank
meditation on the transformative effects of the system, which for all of its
faults and cruelty empowered him to rise above the lot to which he and his
peers – most of whom really were the sons and daughters of poor farmers –
were born.

> I could even put it like this: that horrible, repressive regime took me
> where I would not have gone myself. It could be put in an even stranger way,
> that it not only ruined but also triggered extremely strong vital forces that
> otherwise you might not have felt and which you might have suppressed.
> Sometimes horrid times remind you what a person is made of, and what
> he can unexpectedly make use of. I myself wonder how I got here, having
> transcended the fate to which I was born.[35]

In passages like these, Martinaitis breaks down the distinction between his
surface behavior and his hidden, "inner transcript," blurring the outer form
of Soviet ideology and the inner processes of subjective development. In the
political and cultural context of post-Soviet Lithuania, where the Soviet past is
generally seen as something to be forgotten, denied or driven away, his memoirs
are written with a lyrical voice evoking fear and dread of the destructive
power of the Soviet regime mixed with bewilderment and exhilaration at the
adventure of the individual subject swept away by history.

Methodology and argument

This tone of the traumatic sublime was not invented by Martinaitis in his
post-Soviet memoirs, but has served as a dominant register of Soviet Lithuanian
literature and culture since the mid-1960s. Works of Soviet Lithuanian poetry,
literature and art are now often rejected as "ideological" or "sub-literary,"[36] but
they were genuinely popular at the time, and played a key role in the development of discourses of cultural identity. Of course, any claim to the "authenticity" of such works is debatable and impossible to prove, especially in light of
the institutionalization of censorship. Suffice to say that this book aspires to
follow in the tradition of Vera Dunham's classic study of postwar Soviet

middle-brow fiction, and that one of its methodological assumptions is that works of Soviet Lithuanian culture need to be taken seriously in spite of the ideological constraints of the environment in which they were created.[37]

Stephen Greenblatt, another influential figure in the development of cultural studies, coined the term "New Historicism" in the 1980s to describe an approach to literary criticism that takes historical, social and psychological contexts into account, without reducing the meaning of text to its contextual background.[38] The approach pioneered by Greenblatt to take so-called "sub-literary" texts and non-literary texts side-by-side with "great works of literature" as documents of historical discourse is essential to any attempt to recover the story of individual and collective transformation that occurred in postwar Lithuania.

Indeed, a critical re-reading of key monuments of Soviet Lithuanian culture reveals a complex interaction of motifs that transcends any simple ideological narrative. For example, in an extremely popular cycle of three poems written in the 1960s entitled *1946*, Justinas Marcinkevičius depicts the struggle between the Soviets and the anti-Soviet resistance – a traumatic period recalled by every Lithuanian at the time as an intimate and recent personal and family experience.[39] One poem of the cycle, entitled "On Guard," captures the perspective of a boy caught up in the struggle between the rebel "forest brothers" and the Soviets during the early postwar years when the villages were a terrifying zone of dual authority, controlled by the Soviets during the day, and by the rebels at night:

> At night the forest thrusts into the hut
> Soaked and muddy, it starts to complain
> Oak and Birch dry their footcloths
> While young Ash slumbers on his gun.
> And the table gives food to the forest
> And the pot patiently boils an old chicken
> And I am squirming in an old rough sack
> Kicked out to guard – to guard the forest.
> Before dawn the city knocks at the hut
> And the dog – even he knows not to bark.
> And for the first time I hear how my father prays
> When he opens the door – a festering wound.
> I do not need to be told ... such are the times
> I grab bread and butter in the dark
> And once again, clothed in a sack
> I stand on guard. I guard the city.[40]

While the surface narrative of the cycle as a whole conforms to the teleology of Socialist Realism, in this particular poem the subject has not yet taken a side in the struggle. At this point, he is carried by the sweep of history that locked the town and country in a fatal embrace, a moment of transformation not unlike that recalled by Martinaitis in his post-Soviet memoirs. The poem speaks in the voice of an individual, and by the same token serves as the self-representation of a generation that made the passage from the country to the city under conditions of war followed by Soviet-style modernization.

The lyrical voice of Martinaitis' memoirs or the sixteen-year-old in this poem by Marcinkevičius – a poem memorized by generations of Lithuanians – is an example of what Raymond Williams called *structures of feeling*: the traces of lived experience, the affective elements of consciousness and relationships that can be discerned in memoirs, literature, and other forms of cultural discourse. Williams argued that each generation lives and creates a particular structure of feeling. And while some groups may express it more forcibly, the general commonality of experience allows for the creation of a "culture of a particular historical moment."[41]

In this way, the exodus from country to city of the postwar generations formed the essence of a narrative of social transformation and nation-building with the reconstruction of Vilnius as a national and socialist capital at its core. The postwar intelligentsia blended nationalist and communist discourse in popular works of culture, constructing a narrative of upward mobility with an undercurrent of the traumatic sublime as the paradigmatic life story of their generation.[42] Articulated in the discursive conventions of Socialist Realism, and disseminated through the monolithic institutions of Soviet culture, this was the key narrative of Soviet Lithuanian modernity propagated to the cultural mainstream.

In these narratives of experience, the memory of deportation and collectivization was suppressed but not destroyed. An abstract sense of trauma and deracination was latent in works of poetry, literature and other forms of Soviet culture such as the cinema, photography and art; a powerful and growing undercurrent that respected the surface conventions of Socialist Realism even while it undermined the ideology of progress and modernity by privileging the village and traditional agricultural communities as the source of authentic culture and identity.

The latter chapters of this book describe this cultural undercurrent as the "rustic turn," which grew into a "rustic revolution" with the triumph of the popular movement against Soviet rule. By the late 1980s, the rustic turn had deconstructed the postwar narrative of progress and modernization and transformed it into an accusation of ethnic and cultural genocide. The universal and traumatic experience of displacement was used to mobilize the population to reject Soviet rule, but it had the added effect of reinforcing an autochthonous sense of ethnic identity, blocking out the memory of the Holocaust and the experience of "other" groups living on the same territory.

Based on the published and unpublished memoirs of the postwar intelligentsia together with a series of first-hand interviews conducted by the author with its leading representatives, this book analyses the articulation of Soviet-Lithuanian identity against the social and historical backdrop of the experience of mass displacement.[43] It seeks to discern the structures of feeling latent in memoirs, diaries and works of literature, works of art, architecture, music, performance and other expressions of subjectivity that capture the essential significance of moments in the past to those who lived through them. In doing so, this book seeks to contribute to what might be described as a "second return" of memory, which would restore the agency, however limited and circumscribed under totalitarian rule, of the Soviet Lithuanian subject.

While the focus of this book is on cultural developments in Lithuania and the evolution of Lithuanian collective identity during the twentieth century, it begins by situating the Holocaust, the expulsion of the Polish population from Vilnius and the displacement of other ethnic groups as integral parts of Lithuanian history and identity. By recovering the memory of Lithuanian cultural agency and qualified self-expression during the Soviet period, this book seeks to loosen the grip of narrow perspectives on national identity. The intention is not to diminish the heroism or tragedy of any given historical actor or event, but rather to recover forgotten dimensions of experience as the basis for a more constructive and nuanced dialogue among the conflicting memories of this formative period in the history of East Central Europe.

Notes

1 Tony Judt made this point over twenty years ago and it remains essentially valid. "The Past is Another Country: Myth and Memory in Post-war Europe," *Daedalus* 21.4 (Fall 1992): 83–114.
2 Stephen Kotkin, "Modern Times: The Soviet Union and the Interwar Conjuncture," *Kritika: Explorations in Russian and Eurasian History* 2.1 (Winter 2001): 111–64. Michael Werner and Bénédicte Zimmermann, "Beyond Comparison: *Histoire Croisée* and the Challenge of Reflexivity," *History and Theory* 45 (February 2006): 30–50. Michael David-Fox, "Multiple Modernities vs. Neo-Traditionalism: On Recent Debates in Russian and Soviet History," *Jahrbücher für Geschichte Osteuropas* 54.4 (2006): 535–55.
3 Timothy Snyder, *Bloodlands: Europe between Hitler and Stalin* (New York: Basic Books, 2010).
4 Liudas Truska and Vygantas Vareikis. *The Preconditions for the Holocaust: Anti-Semitism in Lithuania: Second Half of the 19th century–June 1941* (Vilnius: Margi raštai, 2004), 332.
5 Alfonsas Eidintas, *Žydai, lietuviai ir holokaustas* (Vilnius: Vaga, 2002), 477.
6 Theodore Weeks, "Population Politics in Vilnius 1944–47: A Case Study of Socialist-Sponsored Ethnic Cleansing," *Post-Soviet Affairs* 23.1 (2007): 93.
7 From 1926 to 1939 (a period of thirteen years), the urban population of the Soviet Union grew by 119 percent, or from 13.3 to 25.3 percent of the total population (and from 17 to 34 percent in the RSFSR alone). From 1945 to 1959 (a period of fourteen years), the urban population of Soviet Lithuania increased by 173 percent, or from 15 to 38.1 percent of the total population (3.1 million in 1959). Moreover, the population counted in 1945 includes the 170,000 Lithuanian Poles who would leave a year later, most of whom lived in Vilnius and other cities, and so a low point approaching 10 percent may have been reached in 1946. See Table 2.2. Soviet figures for 1926–39 are taken from Charles Becker, S. Joshua Mendelsohn and Kseniya Benderskaya, *Russian Urbanization in the Soviet and Post-Soviet Eras* (London: International Institute for Environment and Development (IIED), 2012), 40.

8 David Hoffman, *Peasant Metropolis: Social Identities in Moscow, 1929–1941* (Ithaca, NY: Cornell University Press, 1994), 1–2.

9 Moshe Lewin, *The Soviet Century* (London: Verso, 2005).

10 For an overview of this literature, see Astrid Hedin, "Stalinism as Civilization: New Perspectives on Communist Regimes," *Political Studies Review* 2 (2004). Key works include Stephen Kotkin, *Magnetic Mountain: Stalinism as a Civilization* (Berkeley, CA: University of California Press, 1995); Jan T. Gross, *Revolution from Abroad: The Soviet Conquest of Western Ukraine and Western Belorusia* (Princeton, NJ: Princeton University Press, 1988); David Hoffmann, *Stalinist Values: The Cultural Norms of Soviet Modernity, 1917–1941* (Ithaca, NY: Cornell University Press, 2003).

11 For two studies of postwar Lithuania that highlight these demographic and cultural dimensions see Timofei Agarin, "Demographic and Cultural Policies of the Soviet Union in Lithuania from 1944 to 1956: A Post-Colonial Perspective," and Rudiger Ritter, "Prescribed Identity: The Role of History for the Legitimization of Soviet Rule in Lithuania," in *The Sovietization of the Baltic States, 1940–1956,* ed. Olaf Mertelsmann (Tartu: KLEIO Ajalookirjanduse Sihtasutus, 2003).

12 On the importance of Socialist Realism to Soviet culture see Katerina Clark, *The Soviet Novel: History as Ritual* (Chicago, IL: University of Chicago Press, 1981) and Andrei Sinyavsky, *On Socialist Realism* (New York: Pantheon Books, 1960).

13 See for example Kęstutis Girnius, "Pasipriešinimas, prisitaikymas, kolaboravimas," *Naujasis židinys-Aidai* 5 (1996): 268–79; Liudas Truska, *Lietuva 1938–1953 metais* (Kaunas: Šviesa, 1995); Nerija Putinaitė, *Nenutrūkusi styga. Prisitaikymas ir pasipriešinimas sovietų Lietuvoje* (Vilnius: Aidai, 2007); Arūnas Streikus, *Sovietų valdžios antibažnytinė politika Lietuvoje, 1945–1990* (Vilnius: LGGRTC, 2002).

14 See for example Valdemaras Klumbys, "Lietuvos kultūrinio elito elgsenos modeliai sovietmečiu" (Unpublished dissertation, Vilnius, 2009). Jūratė Kavaliauskaitė and Ainė Ramonaitė, eds, *Sąjūdžio ištakų beieškant: nepaklusniųjų tinklaveikos galia* (Vilnius: Baltos Lankos, 2011); Vilius Ivanauskas, "Intellectuals and Sovietization During Late Socialism: Shift from Indoctrination to National Processes: the Case of Writers in Soviet Lithuania" (Unpublished manuscript, 2011); Saulius Grybkauskas, Česlovas Laurinavičius, and G. Vaskela, *Sovietinė nomenklatūra ir pramonė Lietuvoje 1965–1985 metais* (Vilnius: Lietuvos istorijos instituto leidykla, 2011); Tomas Vaiseta, "Nuobodulio visuomenė: vėlyvojo sovietmečio Lietuva (1964–1984)" (Unpublished dissertation: Vilnius, 2012); Aurimas Šukys, *Alternative Activity of Intellectuals in Soviet Lithuania, 1956–1988* (Unpublished dissertation: Kaunas, 2012).

15 See for example Marija Drėmaitė, "Šiaurės modernizmo įtaka 'lietuviškajai architektūros mokyklai' 1959–69 m.," *Menotyra* 18.4 (2011): 308–28; "Naujas senasis Vilnius: senamiesčio griovimas ir atstatymas 1944–59 metais," in *Atrasti Vilnių: skiriama Vladui Drėmai,* ed. Giedrė Jankevičiūtė (Vilnius: Lietuvos dailės istorikų draugija, Vilniaus dailės akademijos leidykla, 2010), 183–201; Rasa Čepaitienė, "Tarybinės sostinės konstravimas J. Stalino epochoje: Minsko ir Vilniaus atvejai," in Alvydas Nikžentaitis, *Nuo Basanavičiaus, Vytauto Didžiojo iki Molotovo ir Ribbentropo: atmintis ir atminimo kultūrų transformacijos XX–XXI a.* (Vilnius: LII, 2011), 171–224; Margarita Matulytė, *Nihil Obstat: Lietuvos fotografija sovietmečiu* (Vilnius: Vilniaus Dailės akademijos leidykla, 2011).

16 Jan T. Gross, *Neighbors: The Destruction of the Jewish Community in Jedwabne, Poland* (New York: Penguin Books, 2001), 7–8.

17 On the subsequent history of Jews from Vilnius after the Holocaust, see Anna Lipphardt, *Vilne. Die Juden aus Vilnius nach dem Holocaust. Eine transnationale Beziehungsgeschichte* (Paderborn: Schöningh, 2010).

18 Jan Gross, "Social Consequences of War: Preliminaries to the Study of Imposition of Communist Regimes in East Central Europe," *East European Politics and Societies* 3.2 (Spring 1989): 203.

19 Gross, "Social Consequences," 204.

20 Istvan Deak, "How to Construct a Productive, Disciplined, Monoethnic Society: The Dilemma of East Central European Governments, 1914–56," in *Landscaping the Human Garden: Twentieth-Century Population Management in a Comparative Framework*, ed. Amir Weiner (Stanford, CA: Stanford University Press, 2003), 208.

21 *Foreign Relations of the United States, Diplomatic Papers: The Conference of Berlin (the Potsdam Conference), 1945* (Washington, DC: U.S. G.P.O, 1960), 1511.

22 The July 1995 Srebenica Massacre in Bosnia-Herzegovina in particular, as the largest mass murder committed in Europe since World War II, did much to bring a renewed attention to the relationship of displacement and violence. Bosnian Serb field commander General Ratko Mladic, since convicted of genocide, allegedly warned the Serbian political leadership:

> People are not little stones, or keys in someone's pocket, that can be moved from one place to another just like that … Therefore, we cannot precisely arrange for only Serbs to stay in one part of the country while removing others painlessly. I do not know how Mr. Krajisnik and Mr. Karadzic will explain that to the world. That is genocide.

In Edina Becirevic, "Bosnia's 'Accidental' Genocide," *TRI* 470 (5 October 2006).

23 Norman Naimark, *Fires of Hatred: Ethnic Cleansing in Twentieth-Century Europe* (Cambridge, MA: Harvard University Press, 2001), 4.

24 John Berger, *And Our Faces, My Heart, Brief as Photos* (New York: Vintage Books, 1984).

25 For cultural geographer's presentation of the city through the writings of Western travelers over the centuries, see Laimonas Briedis, *Vilnius: City of Strangers* (Budapest: CEU Press, 2009).

26 Raymond Williams, *The Country and the City* (London: Chatto and Windus, 1973), 2.

27 Karl Schlögel, "The Comeback of the European Cities," *International Review of Sociology/Revue Internationale De Sociologie* 16.2 (2006): 471–85. The term was perhaps first used after the destruction of the Stari Most in Mostar, Bosnia, when a group of Bosnian architects to introduce the term of "urbicide" to convey the effects of violence distinct from the killing of people through ethnic cleansing or genocide. For an in-depth study of the history of a single city after the destruction of World War II and the displacement that followed, see Gregor Thum, *Uprooted: How Breslau Became Wrocław During the Century of Expulsions* (Princeton, NJ: Princeton University Press, 2011).

28 On the Vilnius Question in diplomacy and international politics see Alfred E. Senn, *The Great Powers, Lithuania and the Vilna Question 1920–1928* (Leiden: E. J. Brill, 1967).

29 Tomas Venclova, *Vilnius, A Personal History* (Riverdale-on-Hudson, NY: Sheep Meadow Press, 2009), 73–74.

30 Dangiras Mačiulis, "Apie dvi propagandines kampanijas 20 a. Lietuvoje," *Inter-studia humanitatis* 9 (2009): 121.

31 Under Brazauskas' leadership, the Communist Party of Lithuania severed its ties with the CPSU in 1989, a move seen internationally to have confirmed the inevitability of the breakup of the USSR. But Brazauskas' blocking of an initiative to declare independence in October 1988 was seen as a failure of nerve among Lithuanian patriots and led to his replacement in March 1990 by Landsbergis as Chairman of the LSSR Supreme Council. Landsbergis was something of an exception to the Generation of 1930 insofar as he was born in Kaunas and came from an urban family of interwar intelligentsia.

32 By way of contrast, leading figures in the USSR and RSFSR Writers' Union turned these organizations into leading ideological opponents of *perestroika*. Speaking on behalf of this group, the Russian writer Yurii Bondarev assured the Nineteenth

Conference of the Communist Party of the Soviet Union that democracy "posed a mortal danger to the most gifted, creative people ever since the judges in democratic Athens sentenced Socrates to die." *Literaturnaia Rossiia* 27 (1988), 5–6, in Vera Tolz, "Cultural Bosses as Patrons and Clients: The Functioning of the Soviet Creative Unions in the Post-war Period," *Contemporary European History* 11.1 (2002): 87.

33 Algirdas Brazauskas, *Ir tuomet dirbome Lietuvai: faktai, atsiminimai, komentarai* (Vilnius: Knygiai, 2007); Lionginas Šepetys, *Neprarastoji karta* (Vilnius: Lietuvos rašytojų sąjungos leidykla, 2005); Lionginas Šepetys, *Ar galėjau?* (Vilnius: Lietuvos rašytojų sąjungos leidykla, 2011).

34 James C. Scott. *Domination and the Arts of Resistance: Hidden Transcripts* (New Haven, CT: Yale University Press, 1990).

35 Marcelijus Martinaitis, *Mes gyvenome: biografiniai užrašai* (Vilnius: Lietuvos rašytojų sąjungos leidykla, 2009), 30–31.

36 Literary critic Jūratė Sprindytė, for example, begins her analysis with the premise that the literature of the late Soviet period contained two types of prose narrative: "ideologically tainted" and "silent," in which silence refers to a stance of non-conformism vis-à-vis the ideological mainstream. "The Symbolic Capital of Ideologically Untainted Writers: Estonian, Latvian and Lithuanian Small Novels," in *Baltic Memory: Processes of Modernisation in Lithuanian, Latvian and Estonian Literature of the Soviet Period*, ed. Elena Baliutytė and Donata Mitaitė (Vilnius: Institute of Lithuanian Literature and Folklore, 2011), 83.

37 Vera S. Dunham, *In Stalin's Time: Middleclass Values in Soviet Fiction* (Cambridge: Cambridge University Press, 1976).

38 Stephen Greenblatt, introduction to "The Forms of Power and the Power of Forms in the Renaissance," *Genre* 15 (1982): 5.

39 In fact, the origins of the term "Generation of 1930" probably originated during the initial reception of *1946*; specifically, the poem "Šešiolikmečiai" (Sixteen-year-olds) where Marcinkevičius describes the dramatic experiences of those "born in the 1930s" in the postwar struggle between the "city" and the "village."

40 Justinas Marcinkevičius, "Sargyboje," in *Mediniai tiltai* (Vilnius: Vaga, 1966). Translated by the author with permission.

41 Raymond Williams, *Marxism and Literature* (Oxford: Oxford University Press, 1977).

42 On the relationship of the traumatic to the sublime and identity change see F.R. Ankersmit, "The Sublime Dissociation of the Past: Or How to Be(come) What One Is No Longer," *History and Theory* (October 2001): 295–323.

43 Records of the Writers' Union were consulted at Lietuvių literatūros ir meno archyvas (Archive of Lithuanian Literature and Art). The author conducted interviews with Algimantas Apanavičius, Vitas Areška, Algimantas Baltakis, Vytautas Brėdikis, Vytautas Jurgis Bubnys, Romualdas Granauskas, Ramūnas Katilius, Romualdas Lankauskas, Gytis Lukšas, Justinas Marcinkevičius†, Marcelijus Martinaitis†, Jonas Mikelinskas, Algimantas Nasvytis, Vincas Justas Paleckis, Algirdas Pocius, Romualdas Rakauskas, Vacys Reimeris, Kazys Saja, Rimtautas Šilinis, Mykolas Sluckis, Aldona Šulskytė, Antanas Sutkus, Algirdas Tarvydas, Irena Veisaitė, Tomas Venclova, Markas Zingeris, and Stanislovas Žvirgždas. Short biographies are provided in the Appendix.

1 Modernity and tradition between the wars

Modern Lithuanian nationalism was born in the second half of the nineteenth century with the celebration of the language and culture of the peasantry. By the beginning of the twentieth, it had evolved into a relatively small but fast-growing social and political movement that staked a claim to a Lithuanian presence in the cities as an essential precondition of modern nationhood. And as the sons and daughters of the more prosperous farmers began to migrate to the cities to study and find work, they formed the core of a small but ambitious urban elite, seeking to challenge the social, economic and political dominance of the more established communities.

The Lithuanianization of the cities accelerated dramatically upon the establishment of independence in 1918. Lithuanians streamed into Kaunas and other cities to work at government institutions, leading to an unprecedented degree of interaction between Lithuanians and Jews, communities that had lived next to each other in smaller towns and villages for centuries but with little direct interaction. In the countryside, land reform destroyed the dominance of the Polish aristocracy over the rural economy to establish the single-family, Lithuanian homestead as the social basis of what was remained an overwhelmingly rural society.

As the provisional capital, Kaunas became the focal point of a modernizing, nation-building project to articulate and project the essence of Lithuanian national identity. The desire to "catch up" with the advanced nations of Europe lay at the heart of a strong, modernist thrust seen in architecture, literature and the arts, but this competed with an equally strong, anti-modern impulse to assert Lithuanian distinctiveness, drawing from the folk customs of rural communities and the heritage of medieval statehood represented by the Lithuanian Grand Dukes.

After a military coup in 1926 installed the dictatorship of Antanas Smetona (1874–1944), Kaunas sought to emulate the centralized programmes of mass culture and politics pursued in Moscow, Berlin and Rome.[1] The popularization of national culture through folk art, concerts and mass festivals went hand-in-hand with a grass-roots cultural campaign asserting Lithuanian claims to Vilnius.[2]

The dream of returning to Vilnius was realized in October 1939 but swiftly turned into a nightmare as the country was subjected to successive Soviet

(June 1940) and Nazi (June 1941) occupations. The shock of war and occupation reinforced the nativist impulses of interwar Lithuanian culture, unleashing an outpouring of anti-Semitism and searing the agrarian myth of the homestead, the medieval heritage of the Grand Dukes, and an idealized vision of Vilnius into popular memory as key *loci* of native identity.

A peasant nation

Lithuania's predominantly agrarian society was still divided into clearly defined estates when industrialization and urbanization finally gathered speed in the late nineteenth century. The landowning aristocracy was mostly Polish, and the townspeople were mostly Polish and Jewish with some Russians, while Germans were predominant only in the coastal city of Klaipėda (*Memel*). The countryside was populated mostly by Lithuanians, and the very concept of being a Lithuanian had long become synonymous with the social status of the peasant.

At the close of the nineteenth century, the provinces of the Russian Empire that more or less corresponded to present-day Lithuania were populated by 2,676,000 people, of whom 58.3 percent were identified as Lithuanians, 14.6 percent as Russians, Belarusians and Ukrainians, 13.3 percent Jews, 10.3 percent Poles, with Germans, Latvians and Tatars making up most of the rest.[3] This territory included the *guberniia* or Russian province of Kaunas (Kovno), along with several districts of the Suwałki and Vilnius (Vil'na) provinces.[4]

Three quarters of the population were classified as peasants living in villages, cultivating small to medium-sized plots and earning their livelihood from agriculture. Of this population, 96 percent were ethnic Lithuanians.[5] Poles and Jews accounted for only one quarter of the overall population, but well over three quarters of those who lived in the cities, with Jews accounting for up to 80 percent of the population in many of the smaller towns.[6] Kaunas was the most "Lithuanian" of cities, with about 21.6 percent of its population classified as Lithuanian speakers in 1909. Lithuanian speakers comprised less than 10 percent of most other towns, and as little as 2 percent of the population of Vilnius.[7]

The typical Lithuanian village formed a clannish environment, a locally bounded network of ties among neighbors with relatively little interaction with the outside world.[8] As distinct from communal traditions of the typical Russian village, where parcels of land were redistributed among households according to current needs, Lithuanian land tenure was based on inherited right.[9] This led to a settlement pattern where several homesteads inhabited by closely related families formed the core of a settlement, with other homesteads distributed further away in the fields. On average, there were between two and four related families in a village, but in some large villages there could be up to eight such families established as separate households.[10]

Lithuanian society was thus characterized by a lack of mobility between town and country well into the late nineteenth century, which reflected the rigid categorization of ethnic groups into distinct social layers. To illustrate the persistence of these distinctions among the separate social groups and the quasi-feudal nature of their relations, historian Saulius Sužiedėlis cites the following vignette from a contemporary newspaper:

> ... a loaded wagon is flying with great speed toward the town in the hope of avoiding the guard and the required market levy. At this very moment, a war-like command reverberates: "Halt!" – in an instant, the wagon is stopped. The Lithuanian, caught in his reckless deed, scratches his head, then pleads that he has nothing with which to pay, that he has barely enough money for market. He steps down from the wagon, whip in hand, bargaining with the unyielding guard. Sometimes, he even refuses to obey; woe then to the impudent! A dozen Jews cluster around him, while the Lithuanian staves them off as best as he can with his riding crop – a little Jewish fellow, kneading the peasant constantly with his knees and mussing his hair, keeps crying: "Pay! Pay!" The Lithuanian ... seeks to lift his arms to beat off the unwelcome "guest", when a new rattling of arriving wagons and a dozen fists under his nose, or, on occasion, even a careful shove, applied from a careful distance, deflects his attention from his pestered head. Willy-nilly, he reaches into his breast pocket and pulls out a small bag ... Confused and unable to regain his composure, the peasant finally pays a few *groszy* with great difficulty ... There's nothing to be done; one must drive on. The peasant settles into his wagon, spurs on his horses, all the while shaking his head with dissatisfaction. However, once he arrives in the town square and glances at the white peasant overcoats ... a smile returns to his face. He greets his brothers happily and forgets about his ruffled hair.[11]

In this representation, the Lithuanians appear as peasants by definition, farming the land and bringing their goods to market, while the Jews occupy an equally stereotypical role as toll-collectors in service of the authorities. This condescending, Polish-language sketch, written from the perspective of the urbanite in Warsaw, was meant to entertain the reader with caricatures that were in all likelihood taken as self-evident at the time.

Indeed, for the vast majority of ethnic Lithuanians in the late nineteenth century, cities and towns figured as strange and foreign places, generally visited only for the purpose of trade or worship. Society in the larger cities was dominated by the Polish language and culture, while some dealings with official institutions were conducted in Russian. In the smaller towns, where Jews often formed a plurality or sometimes even a majority of the population, the Catholic church and the farmer's market were the only familiar spaces, encircled by buildings such as a synagogue and Jewish schools, shops and bathhouses.[12]

The ethnic division of society between the town and country was by no means unique to Lithuania. All along the East Central European strip running from Helsinki in the north to Sofia in the south, the cities were populated largely by people of nationalities different from those of the rural population. In the northern towns, Germans and Jews predominated, while Italians and Greeks predominated in the southern towns. Meanwhile Finns, Lithuanians, Ukrainians, Slovaks, Romanians, Bulgarians, and other nationalities living in the surrounding countryside were seen as "peasant" peoples. This ethnic stratification implied a close linking of the social and the national question, and a specific pattern of interaction between the city and the country.[13]

This pattern had evolved over several hundred years. Lithuania emerged as a medieval state in the thirteenth century with a simple social structure that consisted of the Grand Duke and his family, the nobles (*bajorai*) who served the duke as warriors, and a more numerous class of farmers (*laukininkai*). As the Grand Duchy slowly integrated into Western Europe through a dynastic union with the Kingdom of Poland in 1385, society became increasingly stratified, and relations between the estates became formalized. Lithuania still kept a separate set of institutions, but Polish and Lithuanian noble families had formed a common political identity, with the Lithuanian nobility having slowly assimilated to Polish culture.[14]

Meanwhile, as the rights of the Lithuanian *bajorai* increased to match privileges of the Polish *szlachta*, the rights of the *laukininkai* were circumscribed. Constant warfare throughout the fifteenth century made the monarch increasingly dependent on the nobility. To secure their services, the monarchs would provide them with *laukininkai* along with their plots of land as gifts. This created a new class of peasants who owned their land but had to pay the taxes and duties imposed by the nobles. Over time, rising grain prices in Western Europe created an incentive for the nobility to increase their control over agriculture, which culminated in the imposition of serfdom through the Wallach reform of 1557. Thus Lithuanian peasants became tied to the land and would remain so until the abolishment of serfdom in the Russian Empire in 1861.[15]

With the spread of printing and Renaissance humanism, Polish began to replace Latin as the language of literature, education and politics. For example, Jan Kochanowski (1530–84), the foremost poet of the Polish Renaissance, wrote his early works in Latin but switched to Polish in 1560. Lithuanian also gained ground with the printing of a Lutheran catechism in 1547 by Martynas Mažvydas (1510–63), but such publications would remain rare, and Lithuanian would not develop into a literary language until the late nineteenth century, despite the efforts of counterreformation activists like Mykalojus Daukša (1527–1613), who criticized the Lithuanian gentry for speaking Polish instead of Lithuanian.[16]

The linguistic stratification of Lithuanian society into Polish-speaking nobility and a Lithuanian-speaking peasantry was gradual but persistent. By the middle of the sixteenth century, Polish came to be used in the Grand Duke's court and it quickly spread through the nobility. The magnates and large landowners accepted Polish customs and language first, while the lesser gentry and townspeople continued to speak Lithuanian until the eighteenth century. The

Lithuanian gentry retained its identity as a distinct political entity, but over time came to express itself almost exclusively in Polish and to identify with Polish culture.[17] By the nineteenth century, Polish was firmly established as the language of the elite and urban classes throughout Lithuania.[18]

Modern identities in conflict

The reforms of the 1860s in the Russian Empire marked the emergence of the Lithuanian-speaking peasantry as a social and economic force, along with the creation of an intelligentsia that sought to modernize Lithuanian society.[19] The task of raising national consciousness and cultivating pride in the Lithuanian language and history was the focus of the first stage of the movement, associated with the publication of *Auszra* from 1883–86.[20] The next generation of nationalists, associated with the publication of *Varpas* from 1889 to 1905, focussed on the need to move to the city and to assert a Lithuanian cultural presence there. So long as the cities remained the nearly exclusive domain of Polish and Jewish communities, it was felt that Lithuanian culture would never rise to the status befitting a modern, European nation.[21]

Until this time, moving to the city inevitably meant speaking Polish and adopting Polish manners as a means of taking up a place in urban society. The intelligentsia frequently expressed widespread anxiety that Lithuanians who moved to the cities "disappeared like snow melts in the spring."[22] Accordingly, a focal point of social activism was to organize cultural soirées where Lithuanian was spoken. Lithuanian writers and publishers also sought to create a Lithuanian cultural presence through the media by publishing *Varpas* and other periodicals.

Bishop Motiejus Valančius, a key figure of Lithuanian nationalism, urged well-off peasants to take up commerce and crafts in the towns as early as in the 1860s.[23] This led to tensions with the Jewish tradesmen, which was sometimes exploited in the writings of Lithuanian nationalists, some of whom resorted to language that went beyond the traditional anti-Judaic prejudice of the peasants to include modern strategies of political anti-Semitism, imported from Poland and Germany. Vincas Kudirka's first article published in *Auszra* was a caricature entitled "Why Jews Don't Eat Pork." In another article in *Varpas*, he called Jews "our most terrible enemies ... the most vicious wolves dressed in sheep's clothing."[24]

When Lithuania emerged as an independent state in 1918, it was immediately drawn into a series of wars with its neighbors: the new Polish state, Soviet Russia, a roving army under the command of former Russian officer Pavel Bermondt-Avalov, and even some border skirmishes with the new Latvian state. To mobilize the population, the authorities promised to nationalize the land of the larger estates, owned by Poles, and make land grants to anybody who took up arms to fight for the Lithuanian cause. The call was successful, and the ranks of the Lithuanian army were bolstered by the rural Lithuanian population, as well as by Jewish and Belarusian volunteers.[25]

Lithuanian Jews, or Litvaks, had a strong sense of identification with Lithuania – *Lite* – as the land where they had lived for several centuries. For them, *Lite* embraced a larger geographic territory than it did for ethnic Lithuanians, and included the Russian provinces of Vilnius, Kaunas, Grodno, Suwałki and Vitebsk. Vilnius was the most important of several key centres of Jewish culture and commerce, and was known in Hebrew as the *Yerushalayim de Lita*, or the Jerusalem of Lithuania.

The Litvaks were generally supportive of Lithuanian statehood, and they hoped to secure broad rights of communal autonomy in exchange for this support. Strong anti-Semitism in Poland and the pogroms carried out in Vilnius by Polish soldiers in 1919–20 reinforced their sympathy for the Lithuanian cause, and some even fought with Lithuanian guerrillas in combat against the Poles for the Vilnius district. When Polish General Lucjan Żeligowski occupied Vilnius in October 1920, the Kaunas detachment mobilized to fight back included more Jews than Lithuanians.[26]

For its part, the new Lithuanian state needed the support of the Jewish community, the largest minority in the country, to help it secure international recognition at the League of Nations, and so Lithuania readily granted the Jewish community cultural autonomy and independent control over education. This created relatively positive conditions for Jews at that period compared to the situation in neighboring Poland and the Soviet Union. After visiting Kaunas in the 1920s, the Zionist leader Hayim Bialik said: "if Vilnius is known as the *Yerushalayim de Lita*, then all Lithuania should be known as *Eretz – Yisrael de Galuta* (the land of Israel in exile)."[27] The situation in Lithuania also compared favorably at the time to the condition of Jews in Polish-occupied Vilnius.[28] Financial support for Jewish autonomy was cancelled in 1924, when conservative parties took control of the *Seimas*, and the *kahal* councils lost the right to collect taxes by themselves. Nonetheless, the Jewish community retained control over education and exercised defacto autonomy until the war.

The Lithuanian Poles, on the other hand, were seen as potentially sympathetic to a hostile neighboring power. Moreover, they owned 26 percent of the land, even while they constituted only 3 percent of the population before the reforms. In 1922 Polish landowners were implicitly targeted by the reform that nationalized the land of any estate above the limit of 80 hectares. While the reform legislation was technically blind to the ethnicity of the landowner, the fact is that 80 hectares was roughly the upper limit of what Lithuanian landholders held, and the lower limit of the estates held by the Polish gentry. Over the next few years, until 1926, three-quarters of the estates held by Poles were transferred to the peasantry, with only minimal compensation provided.[29]

The land reform changed the social structure of Lithuania's rural society dramatically.[30] It broke up what remained of the old manorial system and created an entirely new class of independent, mostly Lithuanian farmers who came to form the social base of the country. For the first time since the middle ages, the majority of the rural population now owned the land it cultivated, while hired hands constituted only 15 percent of the population engaged in agricultural production. In the late 1920s, the ruling conservatives amended the reform act to increase the maximum size of a holding up to 360 acres.[31] But by this point the critical nationalist goal had been achieved, and the conservative, Catholic Lithuanian farmer was established as the dominant social class of the nation.[32]

Meanwhile, Lithuanians streamed into the provisional but rapidly developing capital city of Kaunas to take up jobs in government, creating new urban communities, even while the majority of the population continued to work the land.[33] In the cities, ethnic Lithuanians came to interact with the established Jewish communities, which led to a degree of friction. The new Lithuanian arrivals were irritated by the prevalence of shop signs in Yiddish and Russian, and in the spring of 1923, a number of Jewish shops had their windows broken and signs painted over, mostly by Lithuanian students. Leaders of nationalist organizations condemned the violence, arguing that the beleaguered state still required the support of its minorities. And while the government issued an order against the spoilage of non-Lithuanian signs in 1924, it also limited the use of such signs to inner yards and walls that were not visible from the street, a restriction that the Jewish community felt was unreasonable.[34]

Most Jews were accustomed to speaking Russian with people from other communities, but they adapted to a new situation where Lithuanian was the official language. In 1929, an editorial published in *Lietuvos aidas* noted with satisfaction that just "a few years ago it was difficult to find a Jew who could speak fine Lithuanian and was acquainted with Lithuanian literature, but now we can see among the Jews young philologists who easily compete with young Lithuanian linguists."[35] In 1937, Jewish organizations in Kaunas passed a resolution condemning the use of Russian in public places, noting the irritation it caused for Lithuanians.[36]

To advance their economic interests the Lithuanians organized themselves into a "League of Lithuanian Merchants" (*Lietuvių verslininkų sąjunga*) in 1930. This organization was opposed to the presence of "aliens" in Lithuania, including Poles and Germans, but its members generally saw Jewish economic influence in the towns as the key obstacle to the modernization of Lithuanian society. They set 85 percent Lithuanian participation in the economy as a goal to be achieved by natural evolution. Their efforts seemed to have had an effect, for if in 1923 there were about seven Jewish shops for every Lithuanian shop, the proportion between the two was roughly equal by 1936.[37]

By the late 1920s and early 1930s, a new generation of Lithuanians had formed in the nationalist environment, and yet were unable to find employment in the saturated government sector. Faced with strong competition from the Jewish community in the free professions and commerce, they were vulnerable to anti-Semitism and recruitment by organizations like the Lithuanian Home Guard Union, Young Lithuania or the Iron Wolf, which were inspired by the civil guard, fascist or similar right-wing models in Germany, Finland and Italy.[38]

By the late 1930s, anti-Semitism had become widespread. In 1936, Jewish leaders complained that popular hysteria over "ritual murders" had reached unprecedented levels. In 1938–39 the Lithuanian State Security Department recorded almost daily incidents of property damage and distribution of anti-Semitic leaflets, calling for the re-Lithuanianization of the cities and the expropriation of Jewish property.[39]

Nationalizing the masses

Soviet Lithuanian historiography portrayed the interwar government of independent Lithuania as "fascist," but although a military coup in 1926 disbanded the *Seimas* and installed Antanas Smetona as a dictator, the regime differed markedly from the dictatorships of Berlin or Rome. Smetona belonged to the older generation of nationalist intellectuals who had made common cause with the Jews and other national minorities in the fight for independence from the Russian empire. For them, anti-Semitism was quite alien as an ideology and they spoke out against it, if only for practical reasons. As distinct from Poland or most other countries in the region, the Lithuanian authorities never passed anti-Semitic laws, and took some measures to restrain its growth.

Nonetheless, the government pursued an explicitly nationalist policy and sought to promote the advancement of Lithuanian language and culture in public life in a manner similar to that of other nationalizing states between the wars. In the 1930s, it sought to emulate the policy of corporatism pioneered by Mussolini's Italy and advanced most dramatically in Soviet Russia and Nazi Germany, seeking to organize and control the various cultural organizations and movements into professional unions. Notably, the establishment of such unions was not forced and was actually encouraged by the writers and artists themselves, since they saw it as a means of accessing steady funding from the state.[40]

Before independence, the Lithuanian intelligentsia was scattered throughout the four corners of the Russian Empire as a result of the displacement caused by the Great War, with the largest concentrations to be found in Riga, St. Petersburg and Voronezh, replete with Lithuanian schools, theatres, publications and cultural activities. In that context, it was relatively easy for them to cultivate a sense of difference from their surroundings due to their distinct language, customs and history, and this bound them together and provided a clear sense of identity. But upon their return to the newly proclaimed Lithuanian state, the chaos of competing interests among Lithuanians themselves undermined this sense of unity.[41]

The diffusion of nationalist goals after the achievement of independence typically complicated the definition of cultural policy, an issue that seems self-evident during the pre-state phase of nationalist movements.[42] In Lithuania, the intelligentsia was surprised to discover that independence had made it quite difficult to agree on the content of the national idea. Ignas Šeinius, a writer and diplomat at the time, wrote:

> The Lithuanian spirit is indeed not so easy to grasp. You can virtually touch the Lithuanian character of many educated Lithuanians, and even more so the farmers, with your bare hand. But when you want to describe the Lithuanian "we", a great fog appears to blur everything. We can easily grasp and feel the "we" of the English, French, Germans, Swedes, or Russians. Why not Lithuanians?[43]

The initial steps in the area of cultural policy were focussed on practical measures such as the introduction of compulsory education in the Lithuanian language and the establishment of Lithuanian schools, which met with great success. Lithuanian language courses were introduced almost immediately into primary and high schools, cutting illiteracy among the rural population from about 32 percent in 1918 to negligible levels by the late 1930s.

Kaunas University was founded in 1922, and was soon followed by colleges for agriculture, veterinary practice, a music conservatory and an art institute. Foreign specialists were recruited to teach at these institutions, and celebrated Lithuanian writers like Maironis, Vaižgantas, Vincas Krėvė, Balys Sruoga and Vincas Mykolaitis-Putinas devoted a great deal of their time to teaching literature.[44]

The early years of independence also saw a proliferation of cultural movements. Over 2,000 periodicals were published (mostly short lived) representing a range of social and political perspectives from communist to liberal and clerical. In the absence of state funding, writers and artists clustered into informal groups for mutual support and to promote shared aesthetic and ideological programmes. Each was represented by a signal publication: *Keturi vėjai* (Four Winds) for the avant-garde, *Trečias frontas* (Third Front) for the socialists and *Naujoji Romuva* (New Sanctuary) for the Catholics.[45]

The intellectuals were driven by the felt need to adapt traditional Lithuanian culture to the methods and impulses of modern art. Ignas Šeinius and Jurgis Savickis, two Lithuanian writers who served as diplomats abroad, wrote of the challenge of overcoming the "peasant viewpoint" and engaging modern civilization. Vincas Mykolaitis-Putinas highlighted the urgency and chaos of this enterprise: "We arrived late, and life forced us to move ahead in leaps and bounds. We couldn't decide on a single style and develop it properly."[46]

A number of young Lithuanians travelled to Paris, Berlin and Rome to work and study, returning to Kaunas armed with the latest intellectual trends. Kazys Binkis, for example, came back in 1921 from a two-year stay in Berlin and Leipzig to give lectures at Kaunas University, where he founded the Four Winds movement. Preaching the creed of modernism in a popular collection of poetry called *100 Springs*, he called on writers to leave their village sentimentalism behind: "Take the sheepskin / Off your soul / And let it out to the wind."[47]

The modernist thrust was also clearly visible in the architecture and planning of Kaunas as a capital city of the interwar republic. With the establishment of a national university and the construction of several new buildings, Kaunas took on the appearance of a modern city. Given the general lack of funds and the reluctance to overinvest in the provisional capital's representational buildings (the expectation was that Vilnius would be restored as the true capital), the number and scale of new construction projects were relatively limited, but they nonetheless served to express a national vision that was clearly modern in its horizons.[48]

Lithuania also began to receive visiting artists like Marc Chagall, who stopped with his art exhibition and readings in Kaunas in 1922 on his way from Moscow to Berlin. The event was attended by Lithuanian and Jewish cultural elites, but the reaction of Lithuanians to Chagall's art was much more reserved. The artistic life of the Jewish community of Kaunas was more receptive to trends coming from Moscow, Berlin, Munich and Paris, and Jewish artists were criticized for their "spiritual anarchy" and "uncritical adoption of every novelty."[49]

A renewed emphasis on the native sources of Lithuanian culture became pronounced in the late 1920s and into the 1930s. Young nationalist thinkers like Juozas Keliuotis (1902–83) and Antanas Maceina (1908–87) writing in the pages of *Naujoji Romuva*, *Lietuvos Aidas* and other nationalist journals became preoccupied with the influence of foreigners and the need to develop native Lithuanian culture in support of the nation-state.

The nativist campaign was driven by young students and was often expressed as conflict of generations, pitting the first generations of Lithuanians who moved from the villages and received higher education in Lithuanian against the older generations of more cosmopolitan urban dwellers who were educated in Polish or Russian universities and less likely to embrace a narrowly construed ethnic identity.[50] For the Lithuanian nativists, the contemporary West was seen as pervaded by philistinism, having departed from its roots in the Christian tradition. As such, the modernization program advanced by *Romuva* was open to foreign influence only insofar as it was necessary to adopt the civilizational achievements of the West.

For the cultural mainstream and in public works, the tension between nativism and cosmopolitanism was generally resolved in the attempt to recast traditional Lithuanian culture in a way that would reinforce Lithuania's image as a modern nation with an ancient and distinct pedigree.[51] Folk culture became the "business card" of the nation in terms of its representation abroad, and memory politics based on the cult of medieval dukes and the glorification of the Middle Ages became the mainstay of national discourse.

The exhibition of Lithuanian folk art at various international exhibitions was another important aspect of Lithuanian cultural self-representation. Neo-traditionalist styles dominated among painters, and the new buildings typically had modernist exterior façades while interiors were given over to representations of traditional culture. The Officer's House in Kaunas, for example, boasts a modernist exterior together with an officer's club decorated in the style of a medieval banquet hall.[52]

Efforts to assert Lithuania's unique past wavered between the choice of emphasizing the agrarian traditions of the peasantry or Lithuania's medieval legacy of statehood. The ethno-cultural heritage of the peasantry served the purpose of distinguishing Lithuanians from other ethnic groups, but for many newly urbanized Lithuanians who had just left their "moss-covered huts," the ethnic heritage of the villages they had just left were reminders of their poverty, something to be overcome, and not a treasure to be valued.[53]

Meanwhile, the history of the Grand Duchy of Lithuania was valuable to the newly established republic as a legacy of statehood, proof that Lithuania was a "historical" nation. In 1930, the Smetona regime launched a major campaign to commemorate the 500th anniversary of the death of the medieval Grand Duke Vytautas the Great (1392–1430), the Lithuanian ruler who personally commanded the forces of the Grand Duchy in the victorious Battle of Grunwald in 1410.

The anniversary provided an excellent opportunity to mobilize popular culture in support of the state. Monuments to Vytautas were built and his portraits were exhibited across the country, followed by a wave of festivities, and his name given to thousands of newly born boys. While some argued at the time that the epoch of the grand dukes was too distant to be of any practical use to meet the challenges of contemporary government,[54] the cult of Vytautas served the eminently practical purpose of demonstrating Lithuania's historical legacy of statehood to the international audience, and of cultivating a political culture of devotion among Lithuanians even as it provided them with popular entertainments.[55]

The Vilnius campaign

The cult of Vytautas was part and parcel of a broader political-cultural campaign to retake the city of Vilnius and to claim its cultural heritage for the building of a modern Lithuanian identity. After the severance of relations between Lithuania and Poland, the Vilnius Question grew into a national obsession, and a campaign to retake the city was launched in tandem with the cult of Vytautas and the glorification of Lithuania's medieval past. Political speeches of the time, like this one by President Smetona, unfailingly ended with a call "never to forget" about Vilnius:

> The absence of Vilnius is felt to the very depths of our consciousness both in our cities and villages. Young and old, all carry an image of Lithuania in their hearts with the capital of Gediminas, and no one will ever be able to erase that image ... Can we ever forget and keep silent about Vilnius? Can we ever forget the oath given by our volunteer soldiers in 1919, given in the spring, to their homeland? We cannot, and do not, have the right to

do so. That oath binds us; our ancient leaders are buried in Vilnius, as are those who inspired our rebirth.[56]

Very few Lithuanians considered Kaunas to be the real capital of Lithuania. It was seen as a city without a history, while Vilnius was, according to the symbolist poet Motiejus Gustaitis, the "Jerusalem of our souls."[57] Nationalist writers like Vytautas Alantas understood the urban modernity of Kaunas in negative terms, as a consequence of the absence of any pre-existing Lithuanian culture in that city, and the separation of the Kaunas republic from the heart of Lithuanian history and identity in Vilnius:

> It was easy for modernity to root itself in Lithuania because we, having lost Vilnius, did not have any point of resistance in order to defend ourselves from foreign influences. Kaunas, the face of modern architecture in Lithuania, was an empty field from an architectural point of view, void of any traditions, a place where anyone could build what they wanted in any manner they chose.[58]

But in reality, the vast majority of Lithuanians had never been to Vilnius and had very little by way of cultural representations to give them any idea of what it was like. In Lithuanian folklore, for example, Vilnius is encountered less frequently than Riga or Tilsit, and when it does appear, it is portrayed as a foreign place, seen only from the perspective of the outsider looking at the

Figure 1.1 Lithograph of Gediminas Mountain. Early twentieth century
Vilnius County Archives. VAA. F. 9, ap.-, b. 18, l. 29. Permission granted by archive.

"green gates" to the city, beyond which the Lithuanian language could not be heard.[59] Similarly, the city was rarely represented in nineteenth-century Lithuanian paintings, and when it was depicted, it was generally as a pastoral landscape, with very little prominence given to architectural or urban features.[60]

Activists compensated for this by promoting the cult of Vilnius through the use of innovative techniques of mass politics and culture. They began by founding in 1925 the Union for the Liberation of Vilnius, a mass organization administered by the state similar to those founded across Europe during the interwar period.[61] At its peak in 1938 the Union had become the most powerful civic organization in the country with 30,000 active members and 600,000 supporters.

October 9, the day of the Polish takeover of Vilnius, was declared a day of national mourning, on which all business would close and public transportation would stop. Lithuanian passports were stamped "Valid for entry to all countries except Poland." Political posters showed the Polish eagle tearing the heart out of Lithuania. A poem written by poet and playwright Petras Vaičiūnas, one of the most passionate advocates of the Vilnius Question, entitled "Hey World, We Will Not Relent Without Vilnius!" became a second national anthem.[62]

Other poets like Bernardas Brazdžionis contributed to a heroic, epic tradition of literary representations of the city, as with his 1939 award-winning collection of poems entitled "Vilnius, the City of Dukes," which glorifies the medieval history of the city and its role as the seat of the Lithuanian state. "Oh, Vilnius," the poet exclaims, "you have always consoled the Lithuanian heart ... Live and grow and lead the nation to the glory of our fathers, that it may reign free on this earth forever!"[63]

The campaign relied on innovative forms of mass communication and reproduction to disseminate some key popular images of the city that resonated in the minds of rural Lithuanians. The most important was the image of the medieval castle of Gediminas on the mountain – a key icon of the city. Of all the architectural features of Vilnius, the castle was one clearly visible remnant of the medieval state that attested to the original Lithuanian identity of the town. With the spread of photography in the early twentieth century, the castle mound became the favored representation of the city.[64]

Postal stamps and postcards were issued featuring the famous Vilnius icon, and schoolchildren were taught songs and games about the Castle of Gediminas and the legendary Iron Wolf of Vilnius.[65] A multitude of "castles" sprung up like mushrooms throughout the Lithuanian countryside. An entire generation of children who entered school during the interwar years memorized for the rest of their lives the lines full of longing to travel "to Vilnius, to Vilnius, to our beloved land, there at the Gediminas mound, to be among our brothers."

Symbolic "Vilnius Passports" issued by the Vilnius Liberation Union were treasured by every schoolchild. Children competed to collect the greatest number of stamps with images of the city to place in the passports, and revenues from the sale of stamps were directed towards the campaign to liberate the city. Pedagogical materials about Vilnius were distributed to schools and teachers were encouraged to insinuate the Vilnius Question into all school subjects. History lessons focussed on the suffering of Lithuanians and the treachery of the Poles. Religion classes told of the Gate of Dawn and other Vilnius churches. During art lessons, students were assigned the task of drawing the Castle of Gediminas or to make a papier-mâché sculpture of it.[66]

Local sections of the Liberation Union were instructed to install large models of the Castle Tower wherever possible. Such images became a common sight, prompting Jurgis Savickis to note how the Vilnius city castle tower had become the "favorite monument of the Lithuanian farmer and the local committee, the invariable, patriotic choice for rural festivities of all kinds."[67] This image united ordinary peasants and professional artists, city-dwellers and residents of distant rural areas, and was spread through the Union's journal *Our Vilnius* (1928–38). The image of Vilnius, once seen by the peasant

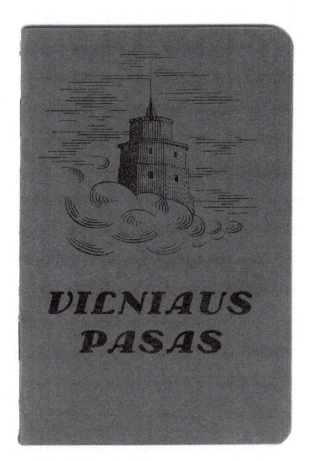

Figure 1.2 Vilnius Passport. Kaunas, 1936
Courtesy of Saulius Sužiedėlis.

masses as a distant, foreign town, was made into something familiar and close, something that was an indispensable and recognizable part of every household in the land, a symbol of belonging to the nation.

The shock of the real

When the Nazis invaded Poland in September 1939, Vilnius and the Vilnius region were spared thanks to the secret terms of the Molotov–Ribbentrop Pact, which left the city in the Soviet sphere of influence.[68] Soviet tanks reached the city on September 18 with hardly a shot fired. The city was initially incorporated into the Byelorussian SSR, but on October 10 was transferred to Lithuania under the terms of a Lithuania–USSR agreement that allowed for the establishment of Soviet military bases at strategic points in the country.

The distance between the myth of Vilnius and the actual, living city meant that when Vilnius was suddenly transferred to Lithuania by the Soviets in 1939, the Lithuanian authorities were poorly prepared to deal with it. Having arrived to the city, Lithuanian officers were astonished to find that nobody spoke Lithuanian and they had to converse with the population in French and German.[69] When the local Polish population initiated a large-scale pogrom a few days after the transfer, the newly arrived Lithuanian police were unable to control the violence, as they could understand neither Polish nor Yiddish and were unfamiliar with the streets.[70]

During the brief period of Lithuanian rule in Vilnius before the arrival of Soviet tanks in June 1940, there were frictions among different ethnic groups, including Poles and Lithuanians. Most of the Polish residents of Vilnius considered the Lithuanians to be occupiers, and cherished hopes that Germany would quickly lose the war and that Vilnius would be returned to Poland. There were shortages of bread, long line-ups and high inflation. Radical Polish groups frequently provoked riots, and a pogrom erupted on October 31, 1939, damaging property and seriously wounding twenty-two Jews, after rumours had spread that Jewish shopkeepers were hoarding food.[71]

Meanwhile, the Lithuanians implemented an intense campaign to Lithuanianize the city and the surrounding region. The streets were renamed and Poles were dismissed from the local government, the university and other positions. Nationalist corporations and student organizations moved in to conduct "national work," seeking to spread Lithuanian identity to those parts of the country where it was damaged by the propaganda of the occupiers. They were soon joined by other nationalist and some extremist organizations, occasionally mounting attacks in the cafes and streets of Vilnius.[72]

The smaller towns and villages in the Vilnius region that was transferred to Lithuania were also targeted for assimilation. Jeronimas Cicėnas, a member of the community of Lithuanian cultural activists who actually lived in Vilnius during the interwar period, emphasized the need to focus national consciousness-raising activities in those areas where the Lithuanian peasantry had been Polonized. "The duty of the Lithuanian writer is to go to the Vilnius region and to assume the role of cultural educator. Ukmergė, Pilviškiai and Balbieriškis can wait. Writers should now go to Trakai, Eišiškės, Riešė, Švenčionėliai and other locations" – i.e., to those areas where Polish was the dominant language.[73]

In general, the return of Vilnius to Lithuania led to a cultural shock. After twenty years of isolation, Vilnius was run-down and shabby compared to Kaunas, in spite of its much more developed tradition of urbanity. Balys Sruoga commented on the irony of how the Lithuanian "peasants" from Kaunas were descending on Vilnius, "no longer from the village but from the city."[74] But after years of dreaming about the return of Vilnius, the city's diminished grandeur failed to meet their expectations.

Efforts to familiarize the educated public with the historical cityscape of the city were quickly initiated. In 1940, extensive studies on the art and architecture of Vilnius were published, as well as a 300-page guide to the capital and its surroundings.[75] However, for all the enthusiasm they expressed over Vilnius while it remained under Polish control, many Lithuanian intellectuals were reluctant to move to the city when it was annexed to Lithuania. The university faculty was compelled to relocate to Vilnius, and a number of notable literary celebrities like Vincas Mykolaitis-Putinas and Petras Vaičiūnas moved to Vilnius with enthusiasm, but many others did not. This reluctance prompted local Vilnius activists like Cicėnas to complain bitterly."Let's be honest," he wrote in his memoirs in the 1950s:

> in the autumn of 1939 most Lithuanians looked at the newly opened gates of Vilnius as if they were the gates to hell. My fellow writers, supplied with travel money and per diems, simply forgot about the expectations they had built up over two decades, and now measured the meaning of Vilnius by, pardon me, the comfort of bedrooms, baths and bathrooms.[76]

Some writers made an attempt to introduce an urban dimension to Lithuanian literature by planning a journal named after a suburb of Vilnius called Šeškinė, but these efforts failed.[77]

Even the government was not in a hurry to move to Vilnius. The mutual assistance treaty by which Vilnius was transferred to Lithuania included a clause allowing Soviet troops to be stationed on its territory. Smetona and his advisors feared that if the government would relocate to Vilnius, it would be too easily captured by Soviet forces, and be compelled to give up sovereignty altogether.[78] In the end, the long-desired Lithuanianization of Vilnius would be accomplished not by the government of independent Lithuania, but by the Soviets in the postwar period, under the leadership of some of the most ardent supporters of the Vilnius Question from between the wars.

Notes

1 On mass politics and culture, see George L. Mosse, *The Nationalization of the Masses: Political Symbolism and Mass Movements in Germany from the Napoleonic Wars through the Third Reich* (New York: New American Library, 1977). On the commonalities of the modernizing projects pursued by liberal and illiberal states during the interwar period in Europe, see Stephen Kotkin, "Modern Times: The Soviet Union and the Interwar Conjuncture," *Kritika: Explorations in Russian and Eurasian History* 2.1 (Winter 2001): 111–64.

2 Dangiras Mačiulis, "Apie dvi propagandines kampanijas 20 a. Lietuvoje," *Inter-studia humanitatis* 9 (2009): 119–38.

3 All-Russian Census of 1897. In Piotr Eberhart, *Ethnic Groups and Population Changes in Twentieth-Century Central-Eastern Europe: History, Data, and Analysis* (Armonk, NY: M. E. Sharpe, 2003), 27.

4 These were Mariampol, Władysławów, part of Sejny, Kalwaria, Wyłkowyszki, Vil'na, Svencjany, Troki. The Lithuanian districts of the Suwałki were historically part of the Polish Kingdom and thus had a distinct social structure compared to the Kaunas and Vilnius provinces. Serfdom was abolished in 1810 rather than 1861, and the rules governing the settlement of Jews were somewhat different. Located on the western bank of the Nemunas, that is, on the far side of the river from the rest of Lithuania, Lithuanians refer to this area as the *Užnemunė* district.

5 Leonas Mulevičius, "Agrarinis klausimas Lietuvoje 1905 metų revoliucijos išvakarėse" (The agrarian question in Lithuania before the 1905 Revolution) *Lietuvos istorijos metraštis, 1975 metai* (1976): 5–21; Liudas Truska, "Emigracija iš Lietuvos 1868–1914" (Emigration from Lithuania, 1868–1914), *LTSR Akademijos darbai* A.1.10 (1961): 71–85.

6 With the exception of the Užnemunė district, Jews were generally forbidden to own land or settle in the villages. A.S. Stražas, "From Auszra to the Great War: The Emergence of the Lithuanian Nation," *Lituanus* 42.4 (Winter 1996): 34–73.

7 Saulius Sužiedėlis, *Historical Dictionary of Lithuania* (Lanham, MD: Scarecrow Press, 2011).

8 Kazys Šešelgis, *Lietuvos urbanistikos istorijos bruožai: nuo seniausių laikų iki 1918 m.* (Vilnius: Mokslo ir enciklopedijų leidykla, 1996), 145.

9 Christine Worobec, *Peasant Russia: Family and Community in the Post-Emancipation Period* (Princeton, NJ: Princeton University Press, 1991), 20. Antanas Tyla, "Lietuvos valstiečių istorijos bruožai, 1795–1861," *Lietuvių atgimimo istorijos studijos* 4 (1993): 25–88.

10 Pranė Dundulienė, *Senieji lietuvių šeimos papročiai* (Vilnius: Mokslo ir enciklopedijų leidybos institutas, 2002), 130–32.

11 *Gazeta Warszawska*, 206 (August 8, 1857). In Saulius Sužiedėlis "The Historical Sources for Antisemitism in Lithuania and Jewish-Lithuanian Relations during the 1930s," in *The Vanished World of Lithuanian Jews*, ed. Alvydas Nikžentaitis, Stefan Schreiner and Darius Staliūnas (Amsterdam: Rodopi, 2004), 119.

12 Jurgita Šiaučiūnaitė-Verbickienė and Larisa Lempertienė, *Jewish Space in Central and Eastern Europe: Day-to-day History* (Newcastle: Cambridge Scholars Publishing, 2007); Klaus Richter, "Anti-Semitism, Economic Emancipation, and the Lithuanian Cooperative Movement before World War I," *Quest. Issues in Contemporary Jewish History* 3 (July 2012): 193.

13 Göran Therborn, "Eastern Drama. Capitals of Eastern Europe, 1830s–2006: An Introductory Overview," *International Review of Sociology* 16.2 (July 2006): 209–42.

14 S.C. Rowell, *Lithuania Ascending: A Pagan Empire within East-Central Europe, 1295–1345* (Cambridge: Cambridge University Press, 1994).

15 Zigmantas Kiaupa, Jūratė Kiaupienė, and Albinas Kuncevičius, *The History of Lithuania before 1795* (Vilnius: Lithuanian Institute of History, 2000).

16 Jurgis Lebedys, *Mikalojus Daukša* (Vilnius: Valstybinė grožinės literatūros leidykla, 1963), 9–26.
17 Daniel Stone, *The Polish–Lithuanian State, 1386–1795* (Seattle, WA: University of Washington Press), 2001.
18 Saulius Sužiedėlis, "Language and Social Class in Southwestern Lithuania before 1864," *Lituanus* 27.3 (Fall 1981): 35–58. Theodore Weeks, "Russification and the Lithuanians, 1863–1905," *Slavic Review* 60.1 (Spring 2001): 96–114.
19 A.S. Stražas, "Lithuania 1863–93: Tsarist Russification and the Beginnings of the Modern Lithuanian National Movement," *Lituanus* 42.3 (Fall 1996): 36–77.
20 *Auszra* (The Dawn) was the first Lithuanian-language newspaper dedicated to literature and politics. It was succeeded by *Varpas* (The Bell) as the most influential nationalist periodical. Because the Russian authorities imposed a press ban after the uprising of 1863 against Lithuanian publications in the Latin script, *Auszra* and *Varpas* were both published in East Prussia and smuggled into Lithuania.
21 Tomas Balkelis, *The Making of Modern Lithuania* (London: Routledge, 2009), 36. A.S. Stražas, "From *Auszra* to the Great War: The Emergence of the Lithuanian Nation," *Lituanus* 42.4 (Winter 1996): 34–73.
22 Juozas Tumas-Vaižgantas, "Lietuviai miestuose" 10 *Tėvynės sargas* (1899). Tumas-Vaižgantas (1869–1933) was a prominent Lithuanian writer, social activist and Roman Catholic priest.
23 Motiejus Valančius (1801–75) was the Catholic Bishop of Samogitia. He was an educator, a pioneering writer of Lithuanian prose, and the initiator of the temperance movement.
24 In Saulius Sužiedėlis, "The Historical Sources," 122. Vincas Kudirka (1858–99) was a doctor, writer, translator, one of the initiators of the Lithuanian national revival, and the author of the current Lithuanian national anthem.
25 A. Eidintas, Vytautas Žalys, and Edvardas Tuskenis, *Lithuania in European Politics: The Years of the First Republic, 1918–1940* (New York: St. Martin's Press, 1988), 37.
26 Dov Levin, *Fighting Back: Lithuanian Jewry's Armed Resistance to the Nazis, 1941–1945* (New York: Holmes & Meier, 1985), 8. Truska and Vareikis, "Preconditions for the Holocaust," 21.
27 Norman Berdischevsky, "The Baltic Revival and Zionism," *Lituanus* 38.1 (1992): 76.
28 Lithuanian Zionist leader Jokūbas Vygodskis (Jacob Wygodzki) wrote that during the inter-war period "the Kaunas Lithuania" was heaven to the Jews in comparison to "the Vilnius Lithuania," in Ezra Mendelsohn, *Zionism in Poland: The Formative Years, 1915–1926* (New Haven, CT: Yale University Press, 1981), 121.
29 By 1930, landowners with over 100 hectares owned just 6 percent of agricultural land on 1602 farms. Peasants with smallholdings of 10–20 hectares owned 30 percent of the land (92,808 farms) while peasants with medium sized farms of 30–100 hectares owned 27.5 percent of the land (27,073 farms). There were 131,700 smallholdings of less than 10 hectares, and 154,000 agricultural labourers. Gediminas Vaskela, "The Land Reform of 1919–40: Lithuania and the Countries of East and Central Europe," *Lithuanian Historical Studies*, 1 (1996): 116–32; Eidintas *et al.*, *Lithuania in European Politics*, 45–49.
30 While the reforms were implemented most thoroughly under Lithuanian independence the process was actually launched by the Stolypin Reforms under the Russian Empire. See Klaus Richter, *Antisemitismus in Litauen Christen, Juden und die "Emanzipation" der Bauern (1889–1914)*. Unpublished Ph.D. Thesis, Technical University of Berlin, 2011.
31 Pranas Pauliukonis, "Mykolas Krupavičius and Lithuanian Land Reform." *Lituanus* 16.4 (Winter 1970): 12–38.
32 Gediminas Vaskela, "The Land Reform of 1919–40: Lithuania and the Countries of East and Central Europe," *Lithuanian Historical Studies*, 1 (1996): 116–32; Eidintas et al., *Lithuania in European politics*, 45–49.

33 Up until 1939, 75 percent of the labor force was still employed in agriculture, with only 6 percent in industry, 3.5 percent in commerce and communications, and 3 percent in the civil service and the professions. Saulius Sužiedelis, *Historical Dictionary of Lithuania* (Lanham, MD: Scarecrow Press, 2011).
34 Truska and Vareikis, "Preconditions for the Holocaust," 26.
35 In Sužiedėlis, "The Historical Sources," 126.
36 In Sužiedėlis, "The Historical Sources," 126.
37 In Sužiedėlis, "The Historical Sources," 127.
38 Tomas Balkelis, "Turning Citizens into Soldiers: Baltic Paramilitary Movements after the Great War," in *War in Peace: Paramilitary Violence after the Great War, 1917–1923*, ed. Robert Gerwarth and John Horn (Oxford: Oxford University Press, 2012), 126–45.
39 Truska and Vareikis, "Preconditions for the Holocaust," 36.
40 Dangiras Mačiulis, *Valstybės kultūros politika Lietuvoje 1927–1940 metais* (Vilnius: Lietuvos istorijos institutas, 2005).
41 See Balkelis, *The Making of Modern Lithuania*, 104–17. Pranas Čepėnas, *Naujųjų laikų Lietuvos istorija* (Chicago, IL: Kazio Griniaus fondas, 1977).
42 Rogers Brubaker, *Nationalism Reframed: Nationhood and the National Question in the New Europe* (Cambridge: Cambridge University Press, 1996).
43 Ignas Šeinius, "Lietuviškos dvasios beieškant" *Vairas* 12 (December 1932): 302.
44 Vytautas Kubilius, *Lithuanian Literature* (Vilnius: Vaga, 1997), 172.
45 Kubilius, *Lithuanian Literature*, 173–74.
46 In Kubilius, *Lithuanian Literature*, 176.
47 Kazys Binkis, *100 pavasarių* (Kaunas: Niola, 1923). In Kubilius, *Lithuanian Literature*, 201.
48 Vaidas Petrulis, "Erdvinės lietuvių tautinio stiliaus politikos projekcijos 1918–39 metais," in *Meno istorija ir kritika 4. Menas ir tapatumas* (Kaunas: Vytauto Didžiojo universiteto leidykla, 2008), 31.
49 Jolita Mulevičiūtė, *Modernizmo link. Dailės gyvenimas Lietuvos Respublikoje 1918–1940* (Kaunas: Nacionalinis M. K. Čiurlionio dailės muziejus, 2001), 91–92.
50 See for example the article by Juozas Keliuotis, "Senieji ir jaunieji," *Naujoji Romuva* 147 (1933): 860.
51 The combination of modernist and neotraditionalist elements illustrates Stephen Kotkin's point that "the idea of an antithesis between modernism and traditionalism is a trope of modernism that modernism in practice contradicts." "The Interwar Conjuncture," 120, ft. 24.
52 Stephen A. Mansbach, "Modernist Architecture and Nationalist Aspiration in the Baltic: Two Case Studies," *Journal of the Society of Architectural Historians* 65.1 (March 2006): 99.
53 Balys Sruoga, "Vilniaus ir Kauno visuomeninė sanveika," *Vairas* 4 (1940): 347.
54 Juozas Keliuotis, "Politikos etika," *Naujoji Romuva* 12 (1931): 273. Vytautas Kavolis makes a similar argument in *Žmogus istorijoje* (Vilnius: Vaga, 1994), 267.
55 Dangiras Mačiulis, "Vytauto Didžiojo metų (1930) kampanijos prasmė," *Lituanistica* 2.46 (2001): 54–75.
56 Antanas Smetona, *Rinktiniai raštai* [Collected Works], ed. Alfonsas Eidintas (Kaunas: Menta, 1990), 424.
57 Motiejus Gustaitis was a Roman Catholic priest and an important literary critic and author. Contrasting Kaunas to Vilnius, he wrote: "In one city only the faceless, cold walls of the modern buildings rising among pitiful slums were seen, and in the other one the play of the baroque forms and the grandeur of classicism." In "Vilnius," *Baras* 4 (1925): 5.
58 Vytautas Alantas, "Tautinės kultūros problemos," *Vairas* 1 (1940): 159.
59 Tomas Venclova, "Vilnius: The City as Object of Nostalgia," *Eurozine* (July 27, 2010), www.eurozine.com/articles/2010-07-27-venclova-en.html.

60 Laima Laučkaitė, "Vilniaus sostapilis kaip miesto ikona XX amžiaus pradžioje" *Naujasis Židinys* 7 (2009): 225.
61 Gregory J. Kasza, *The Conscription Society: Administered Mass Organizations* (New Haven, CT: Yale University Press, 1995).
62 This poem was included in a collection *Amžiais dės galvą už Vilnių lietuvis* (the Lithuanian will forever lay down his head for Vilnius) published in 1928.
63 Bernardas Brazdžionis, *Kunigaikščių miestas* (Kaunas: Sakalas, 1939).
64 Laima Laučkaitė, "Vilniaus sostapilis kaip miesto ikona XX amžiaus pradžioje," *Naujasis Židinys* 7 (2009): 225.
65 Legend holds that Duke Gediminas dreamed of an iron wolf, an ominous sign that prompted the medieval ruler to found the castle and city of Vilnius.
66 Interviews with Jonas Mikelinskas, Justinas Marcinkevičius, Algimantas and Vytautas Nasvytis, Algimantas Baltakis and others convey the strong emotional importance that this campaign had to them as youths during their school years. Dangiras Mačiulis, "Vilniaus vaizdinys Vilnių vaduojančioje Lietuvoje," *Acta litteraria comparative* 4 (2009): 92.
67 In Mačiulis, "Vilniaus vaizdinys," 92.
68 In Polish tradition this area was called *Wileńszczyzna*. While it was historically associated with Lithuania, the population was heavily polonized and generally aligned itself with Poland. The fact that it was populated mostly by Polish speakers was the main reason why the Western Powers did not support Lithuanian claims to the area.
69 Timothy Snyder, "Memory of Sovereignty and Sovereignty over Memory: Poland, Lithuania and Ukraine, 1939–99," in *Memory and Power in Post-War Europe: Studies in the Presence of the Past*, ed. Jan-Werner Müller (Cambridge: Cambridge University Press, 2002), 48.
70 Alfred Senn, *The Great Powers, Lithuania and the Vilna Question 1920–1928* (Leiden: E. J. Brill, 1967), 42.
71 Regina Žepkaitė, *Vilniaus istorijos atkarpa, 1939–1940* (Vilnius: Mokslas, 1990), 66–68. Stanislawa Lewandowska, *Życie codzienne Wilna w latach II wojny światowej* (Warsaw: Neriton, 1997), 34.
72 Žepkaitė, *Vilniaus istorijos atkarpa*, 115.
73 Jeronimas Cicėnas, *Vilnius tarp audrų* (Chicago, IL: Terra, 1953), 264.
74 Balys Sruoga, "Vilniaus ir Kauno visuomeninė sanveika," *Vairas* 4 (1940): 246.
75 Jūratė Markevičienė, "Senamiesčio įvaizdžiai Vilniaus kultūros paveldo saugoje XX a.: nuo kraštovaizdžio iki praeities skeveldrų," in *Kultūrologija* 10 (2003): 247.
76 Jeronimas Cicėnas, "Balys Sruoga Vilniuje," in *Susitikimai su Kaziu Boruta* (Vilnius: Rašytojų sąjungos leidykla, 2005), 126.
77 Cicėnas, *Vilnius tarp audrų*.
78 Aleksandras Merkelis, *Antanas Smetona: jo visuomeninė, kultūrinė ir politinė veikla* (New York: Amerikos lietuvių tautinė sąjunga, 1964), 567–68. Alfonsas Eidintas, *Antanas Smetona ir jo aplinka* (Vilnius: Mokslo ir enciklopedijų leidybos centras, 2012), 372.

2 War, the city and the country

The first two waves of modernization in Lithuania of the late nineteenth and early twentieth centuries were driven by the increase of physical and social mobility as peasants moved to the city, bringing social and ethnic groups that were historically separate into contact and interaction with one another. The third wave of Stalinist modernization in the wake of World War II was triggered by genocide, mass killing and displacement, which depopulated the cities and led to a massive rush of urbanization.

The destruction and reconstruction of Vilnius is only the most dramatic and important example of how massive displacement transformed the relationship between town and country throughout Lithuania and the region as a whole. To put the question in the starkest of terms, the people who lived in the cities before the war were killed or driven far away, while the people who had lived in the surrounding countryside moved into the empty buildings they left behind.

The cities were destroyed first through the flight of the elites beginning in 1940 and the Soviet deportations of June 1941, the Holocaust of the Jews that began almost immediately thereafter, and the forced repatriation of the Poles after the war. Then came the destruction of the countryside in what Lithuanians call the "war after the war," when the Soviets suppressed the widespread insurgency through mass deportations of the rural population.

The net result was the elimination of the centuries-old urban communities of Poles, Jews and Germans and the destruction of traditional Lithuanian rural communities. The subsequent migration of the rural population to the cities created a "mass" of individuals who had been severed from their communal ties in the village, and had precious little by way of a pre-existing urban society and culture into which they could integrate.

Murder of the city

The Nazi invasion of Poland in September 1939 drove a wave of refugees into Lithuania, particularly to the city and region of Vilnius, which had just recently been transferred from Polish to Lithuanian jurisdiction under the terms of the Molotov–Ribbentrop Pact. As the Lithuanian authorities struggled to cope with this influx of people, on top of the already difficult task of absorbing the new territory, they nonetheless pressed forward with the broader policy of Lithuanianization.

One measure was to deny citizenship to the large number of Poles who had settled in the Vilnius area between 1920 and 1939 – i.e., during the period defined by Lithuania as an illegal occupation of the region. The authorities classified these settlers as *ateiviai*, or "newcomers," and the Lithuanian Red Cross estimated that there were about 150,000 people in this category, of whom 83,000 lived in the city of Vilnius. They were obliged to register as "war refugees," but unlike those who arrived after the Nazi invasion, they were not granted official assistance. Their rights to travel or purchase property were curtailed, and many were dismissed from jobs they held in government or state-owned companies like the railroads and postal service. By February 1940, there were some 27,000 officially registered refugees in Vilnius, including 12,000 Poles and Byelorussians, 11,000 Jews and 3,700 Lithuanians. The real numbers were probably over 30,000, since those who could do without state assistance avoided registration, for fear that the Soviets could gain access to the list.[1]

Such fears were not unfounded. The Soviets would occupy Lithuania just a few months later (14 June 1940) and immediately begin to compile a list of "anti-Soviet, socially dangerous and criminal elements." A decision to resettle "socially harmful elements" from the Soviet western borderlands was taken in May 1941, and about 19,000 people were deported on June 14–18.[2]

The vague and seemingly arbitrary criteria by which the Soviets targeted individuals and the fact that they deported "socially harmful" individuals along with their entire families have been interpreted as evidence of state terrorism and even genocidal intent.[3] However, the targets for deportation do not seem to have been selected on the basis of ethnicity, as the deportee population was roughly representative of the population as a whole (70 percent of those deported were Lithuanian, 17.7 percent Polish, 9.2 percent Jewish and 2 percent Russian).[4] However, the Soviets clearly targeted the elites, the educated and professional classes – dealing a severe blow to the subsequent development of a modern urban society in postwar Lithuania.

The destruction of the city continued one week later, on June 21, 1941, with the Nazi invasion. This time, the targets were defined explicitly in terms of their ethnic and religious identity. Over the course of a few months, 196,000 Lithuanian Jews would be killed, some 90–95 percent of the Jewish population before the war.[5] They were killed regardless of their place of residence in the cities, the smaller towns or the countryside, but since Jews made up such a significant part of the urban population, the Holocaust in Lithuania effectively marked the end of a distinct urban civilization that had developed over several hundred years.

An estimated 42,000 people evacuated to the Soviet Union on the eve of the Nazi invasion, including about 4,000–6,000 Jews. German planes targeted the departing refugees, and there are numerous reports of their harassment and even shootings by the local Lithuanian population. Before the arrival of

German forces, pogroms broke out in forty localities. In Vilnius, the killing began with the kidnappings of Jewish men and a series of massacres along the streets designated for the future Jewish ghetto. About 21,000 Jews had already been arrested and killed in a suburb of Vilnius called Paneriai (Ponary), a wooded area six kilometers from the city center, before the ghetto was created.[6]

Aldona Liobytė, one of the relatively few Lithuanian natives of Vilnius, left the following account of the removal of Jews to the ghetto:

> One night I heard shooting. In those days, shots at night were nothing new, but in the quiet of night I heard a woman's scream that gave new meaning to the expression "hair raising." In the morning one could find bits and pieces of hastily bundled-up things left behind on the streets: here a woman's shoe, here a child's toy, there a scarf. There were covered corpses which, most likely, were either not transported in time or intentionally left to frighten people. That was the night the Jews were moved to the ghetto. ...
>
> One afternoon I encountered a column of people being taken to Lukiškės prison. They still were carrying things in small bundles although we already knew that Lukiškės was a stop from where there is only one route – to Paneriai. The crowd was walking apathetically, with only an occassional glance in our direction, forcing us to lower our eyes. How could we help? Soldiers were butting those at the end of the column with rifles – it looked as if this crowd was being taken to their daily work. And suddenly, while crossing the street, right on Lukiškės square, an old lady fell down, and an officer started to kick her. "What is he doing? Why is he beating her?" screamed little girl on her fathers arms. "Stop it!" The young, brown-haired man turned his face towards us. Sadly, he was a compatriot, wearing the uniform of an officer from interwar Lithuania.[7]

By the time the German forces retreated in 1944, over 60,000 Jews had been removed from the city, brutally murdered and buried at Paneriai. Virtually the entire prewar population of Vilnius Jews had been exterminated.

Across Lithuania, the Nazis also killed about 45,000 ethnic Lithuanians, sent 36,500 forced laborers to the Reich, and repatriated 40,000 Germans from Klaipėda (Memel). When the Soviets returned in 1944, some 140,000 people from the Klaipėda region fled to Germany, and another 120,000 Lithuanians from across the country sought refuge in the West.[8] As with the first occupation of 1941, the Soviets began the second occupation in 1944 by arresting and deporting "suspect" populations of all nationalities, including some 2,000 Poles living in Vilnius. By the time the Red Army reoccupied Vilnius in July of 1944, NKVD figures put the population of the city at just 106,500, including 84,900 Poles and 7,958 Lithuanians.[9]

The retreat into dreamworld

After the Soviet deportations of June 14–18, many Lithuanians greeted the arrival of German forces, believing that they would restore Lithuanian independence. This proved to be an illusion, and the Provisional Government of Lithuania, proclaimed on June 23, was stripped of power by early August and the country put under the authority of the *Reichskommissariat Ostland*. High-ranking Germans made the policy decisions but local government was staffed by Lithuanians.

In this context, many Lithuanian individuals and some institutions were involved in cooperation and collaboration with the German forces, such as a volunteer police force that was used to assist with the massacre of Jews, or the Lithuanian Security Police that operated in Vilnius.[10] But in other cases Lithuanians resisted German plans, obstructing efforts to conscript Lithuanians as forced laborers or to raise troops to create a Lithuanian Waffen-SS unit. As the occupation became increasingly harsh on the Lithuanian population in 1943, a number of active resistance groups were created.[11]

In the cultural sphere, the Nazis launched a broad propaganda campaign through a number of mass-circulation newspapers. The newspapers typically devoted about a page to Lithuanian cultural affairs, posting advertisements of plays, concerts, cultural articles, publishing poems and excerpts of novels and stories.[12] This provided steady employment for many Lithuanian writers, some of whom continued to write for the official press right to the end of the war.[13]

Playing to nationalist sentiment, the Vilnius Question was exploited to the fullest degree in this media. "Vilnius is drowning in national flags," declared the front pages of *Naujoji Lietuva* in June 1941, praising the palpable "improvements" to the cityscape during the weeks when the Jewish population was being rounded up and shut into the ghetto:

> Vilnius is rapidly changing: the city squares, streets and palaces are cleaner and better ordered. Residential areas are improving as well ... Lithuanians are dominant in the central streets, one can see them stepping out of lively cafes ... Vilnius is not only becoming but has already become a Lithuanian center.[14]

Similarly, an unsigned article entitled "Vilnius begins a new life" proclaims:

> Vilnius is becoming completely Lithuanian. Grandfather Gediminas mountain can once again hear the speech of his children, and he feels the tremendous efforts of his grandchildren to return to Vilnius all that has been stolen from it, hidden and destroyed for centuries, to adjust to the rhythm of the Lithuanian spirit.[15]

The Nazis exploited popular anti-Semitism, saturating the media with the ideology of national socialism.[16] The provocative association of the Jewish Lithuanians with the Bolshevik regime was obsessively emphasized in countless articles with titles like: "Life without Jews," "Wolves in Lambs Clothing," "Out with the National Enemy," along with select anti-Semitic citations from the writings of the forefathers of the nationalist movement from the beginning of the century like Vincas Kudirka.[17] The Nazi newspapers also propagated the myth that Jewish Lithuanians were somehow responsible for the deportations of June 1941:

> After Stalin's "sun" shone on the Lithuanian land, the Jews stood toge-ther against the interests of the Lithuanian nation... On the red horse of Communism, they began to trample the Lithuanian nation, to suppress the Lithuanian element of the cities, to push Lithuanians out of offices and enterprises, to Russify and to Judaize them! ... Thousands of grey-haired women are now gazing with tears in their eyes along the road by which their sons, betrayed by Jews, were transported away. Thousands of orphans and unhappy deportees are screaming: "Eliminate the Jews!"[18]

Newspaper articles often represented the departure of the Soviets in terms of the changing cityscape:

> The "invincible" army, unable to defend Jewish interests, has left Lithuania. At the very same moment, Jews disappeared from public life ... Loitering in the streets, the gods of yesterday are spreading gossip that without their help, Lithuanians will be unable to organize commerce and the work of offices will be disrupted. Fortunately, they were painfully wrong. In the offices with-out Jews the mood is completely different. Employees are jolly and peaceful in accomplishing their daily work ... And through the window curtains, through the gaps in the fences, Jews are staring at the street life of the free Vilnius. They are staring and shedding crocodile tears, unable to understand how the Lithuanian "peasants and slaves" are able to build their life.[19]

And as the following article by Pulgis Andriušis about Kaunas makes clear, the motif of the Lithuanianization was not restricted to Vilnius:

> But now that we no longer have these filth-makers in the old town, we once again will be able to walk along the dreamy streets and romantic river banks. And the youth will be able to dream peacefully under chestnut trees, watch the coming and going of ships ... And in the heat of the summer we will rest in the silvery sand of the riverbank without fear that Jewish haulers will throw their trash upon us. Without fear that our rest may be disturbed by the stench from the neglected courtyards. Let's return honor to the old town![20]

Aside from such pieces about the cities, considerable attention was also devoted to the portrayal of the "new life" in the countryside, praising the "free Lithua-nian farmer" who, "having overthrown the Bolshevik yoke, sharpens his scythe in the early morning and gleefully goes out to cut the hay."[21] Poems about nature, about the landscape and the sacred, ancient origins of the Lithuanian language complemented ethnic pastoral motifs, along with articles exploring folk culture, such as Lithuanian dance, textiles, ornaments, sculptures, and so on.

In the early years of the war, Lithuanian cultural representations played an important role in this process, adding strong accents on the idyllic utopia of city and country, where the romantic, mysterious streets of the old town of Vilnius and the homestead in the countryside were praised as the foundation of a traditional, agrarian society. Intentionally or not, the themes and motifs used by Lithuanian writers conformed to the image of a pastoral utopia promoted by the Nazis, featuring pictures of men in straw hats harvesting hay, blond lads and ladies in national dress in flower gardens before their wooden houses, and so on.

In a book-length study of Lithuanian culture under the Nazi occupation, the renowned Lithuanian historian and literary critic Vytautas Kubilius summarizes the images and clichés features of this pastoral aesthetic as follows:

> Here, life was flowing along its usual path without changing even a bit – taking the cattle to pasture in the spring, having sprayed them with holy water; the daily sharpening of scythes in the morning, white-shirted men cutting the meadow, women weaving linen cloths; a white haired elder gathering honey; a young farmhand taking the horses out to ride; bread baked on leaves of cat-tails and maple; children bringing a share of the slaughter to their neighbours; village youths gathering at night, their songs echoing in the misty twilight edges of the fields; the May Litany chanted at the shrine to the Blessed Virgin in the pantry, decorated with blossoming flowers.[22]

The retreat of the Lithuanian cultural imagination to the idyllic countryside bears a striking resemblance to the *retour à la terre* movement in Vichy France, where the humiliation of defeat and occupation is said have to driven the French imagination into the timeless sphere of myth.[23] According to Philippe Burrin, the *retour à la terre* movement in Vichy represented a persistent but vain effort to "to reconstruct a national spirit in which the memory of a mythical past would erase the perception of a present that could lead a person to try, to think, to act. It was a formidable aspiration to escape from time itself."[24] The peasant and the landscape (*paysan* and *paysage*) were presented as symbols of *la France profonde*, as guarantees for the permanence of the nation through the vicissitudes of history.[25]

In Lithuania under German rule, the return to the soil was at once a return to Vilnius – in each case a return to the realm of dreams and myth. Vanda Zaborskaitė, a Lithuanian student at Vilnius University during the Nazi occupation, recalls that the cultural efforts of Lithuanians at the time were directed first and foremost to returning Vilnius to its native, Lithuanian culture, understood in purely ethnic terms, to "strengthening the weakened Lithuanian basis of the city."[26] Even as Lithuania's sovereignty was trampled, the city was seen as evidence of the lasting guarantee of statehood, *la Lituanie profonde*, a living sign of the romanticized historical-mythological past.

The words of sculptor Gediminas Jokūbonis about the place of Vilnius in his consciousness may well be representative of attitudes at the time:

> The teacher told us a lot about Vilnius. We were mesmerized by its return. We lived it and only it. The war, which started far in the West, did not seem so meaningful ... To see Vilnius was so wonderful and fantastic that upon return home I lived only these impressions. They overshadowed everything—the real world became distant, although at that time Europe was in flames, the Germans were marching in France and in our country fatal events were brewing.[27]

This pastoral bliss appeared to insulate wartime Lithuanian culture from the horror of the Holocaust, from the scenes in Vilnius described by poet and writer Abraham Sutzkever, among others: frightened and hounded people chased along the winding streets, others desperately looking for hiding places, horror and madness all around.[28] Lithuanian literature had nothing like Czeslaw Milosz's elegiac and accusatory poem "Biedny chrzescijanin patrzy na ghetto" (A Poor Christian Looks at the Ghetto), or the clandestine publication in 1944 of poems by Jan Kott, Miecyslaw Jastrun, Czesław Miłosz, Michal Borwicz and others on the extermination of the Jews in Poland.[29]

In reality, many Lithuanians risked their lives to help their Jewish compatriots. Over 800 Lithuanians have been honored with the title of Righteous among the Nations by the Yad Vashem directorate, like Vilnius librarian Ona Šimaitė, who became a messenger to the Vilnius ghetto.[30] But for the consumption of the masses, Lithuanian popular culture under Nazi occupation offered refuge in a dreamworld where their Jewish compatriots were represented either as the right hand of the Bolshevik oppressors or disappeared entirely against a background of pastoral bliss.

After the Apocalypse

Along with the Jews, the Poles were the largest ethnic group living in Vilnius. A census taken in 1931 by the Polish authorities was the last to be made before the outbreak of war. It put the population of Vilnius at 195,071, of which 66 percent were Poles, 28 percent Jews, almost 4 percent Russians, and less than one present Lithuanians (see Table 2.1).[31] However, in 1945–46, 170,000 ethnic Poles were "repatriated" to Poland in the context of the postwar population exchanges negotiated among the victorious Allies.[32]

The word "repatriation" is a misnomer since the vast majority of these people could trace several generations of ancestry to Vilnius and the surrounding region. There is a longstanding debate over the extent to which the displacement was forced or voluntary and the fairness of the compensation for property left behind. Clearly, many felt they would be better off in communist Poland than the Soviet Union, and a number of Lithuanians and Jews also used the program to escape.

Table 2.1 Population of Vilnius by ethnic group, 1939–1989

Nationality	1931	1940	1944	1959	1970	1979	1989
Jews	54,596	58,263	1,160	16,354	16,491	10,723	9,109
Poles	128,628	87,855	81,966	47,226	68,261	85,562	108,239
Lithuanians	1,579	51,111	6,897	79,363	159,156	225,137	318,500
Russians	7,372	4,090	7,363	69,416	91,004	105,618	116,618
Belarusians	1,737	5,348	1,261	14,686	24,170	30,623	30,282
Ukrainians			419	6,575	9,379	10,889	13,294
Others	1,159	3,062	269	2,458	3,683	72,73	7,678
Total	195,071	209,729	99,335	236,078	372,100	475,825	576,747

Source: Adapted from Victor H. Winston, "Observations on the Population of Vilnius: The Grim Years and the 1942 Census," *Eurasian Geography and Economics* 47 (2006): 180, 196; Theodore Weeks, "Population Politics in Vilnius 1944–1947: A Case Study of Socialist Sponsored Ethnic Cleansing," *Post-Soviet Affairs* 23.1 (2007): 80.

But as Theodore Weeks argues, the number of Poles who departed from Vilnius was disproportionately higher than those living in other areas, which suggests that the Lithuanian communist authorities were pursuing a policy of de-Polonization with respect to the capital city. In any case, by September 1946, a total of 88,808 Poles were evacuated from the city of Vilnius, along with another 71,775 from the suburban areas around Vilnius.[33]

In summary, of the roughly 750,000 people who were killed or displaced to points outside of the country during this period, most came from the cities. The "class enemies" targeted by the initial Soviet deportations of June 1941 belonged mostly to the professional and educated classes of all ethnic groups. The hundreds of thousands of Germans, Jews and Poles who were killed or made to leave Lithuania were also mostly urban dwellers.

Many people living in rural areas were killed or went abroad as well, but the losses to the urban population were higher in absolute and especially in relative terms. From 1939 to 1945, the urban population was cut in half – a loss of 320,000 souls – while the rural population dropped by 215,000 people, a loss of some ten percent (see Tables 2.2 and 2.3). As a result, the mass killing and displacement of World War II, together with the transfer of the Poles right after the war, had the combined effect of creating a human vacuum in the cities that would be filled largely by ethnic Lithuanians living in the surrounding country-side. The need for workers was especially urgent, and the authorities tried to fill the gap by mobilizing peasants to migrate from the surrounding countryside.

Newspapers were filled by exhortations calling on Lithuanians to step up to the task of rebuilding the new Lithuanian capital, and enthusiastic exclamations about thousands of people flowing into the cities. The Soviet authorities planned to mobilize 20,000 workers to Vilnius from other parts of the country from March to August 1945, and the total need was estimated at more than 30,000. However, the mobilization of the population behind the reconstruction effort was stymied by the initial reluctance of the rural population to move to the unfamiliar cities damaged by war and prolonged anti-Soviet insurgency in the

Table 2.2 Rural and urban population of Lithuania, 1939–1989

Year	Population	Urban pop.	Urban %	Rural pop.	Rural %
1939	3037.1	695.5	22.9	2341.6	77.1
1941	2958.4	684.2	23.1	2274.2	76.9
1945	2500.0	375.0	15.0	2125.0	85.0
1959	2690.4	1024.9	38.1	1665.5	61.9
1970	3128.2	1571.7	50.2	1556.5	49.8
1979	3419.6	2105.9	61.6	1313.7	38.4
1989	3689.8	2509.3	68.0	1180.5	32.0

Source: Adapted from S. Vaitekūnas, *Lietuvos gyventojai: per du tūkstanmečius* (Vilnius: Mokslo ir enciklopedijų leidybos institutas, 2006).

Table 2.3 Population of main Lithuanian cities, 1939–1989

City	1939	1945	1959	1970	1979	1989
Vilnius	209.4	110.0	236.1	371.7	497.5	582.4
Kaunas	154.1	80.0	219.3	306.2	379.8	422.6
Klaipėda	47.2	3.6	90.5	140.6	179.4	204.0
Siauliai	31.6	19.0	59.7	92.8	122.8	145.0
Panevezys	26.7	12.0	41.1	73.5	105.2	126.5

Source: Adapted from S. Vaitekūnas, *Lietuvos gyventojai: per du tūkstanmečius* (Vilnius: Mokslo ir enciklopedijų leidybos institutas, 2006).

country. For example, only 832 people were mobilized to Vilnius from March to May of 1945, and only 1,782 by April 1946. And even then, half of these people ran away shortly after arriving, presumably back to their villages.[34]

Moreover, the Old Town of Vilnius was severely damaged. The Polish ethnographer Marija Znamierowska-Pruffer, who lived in the city between the wars, compared it to the ancient Roman town of Herculaneum, destroyed along with Pompeii by the eruption of Mount Vesuvius:

> You walk along the street and it seems that it is completely fine, untouched, but in fact you see only the external building walls, as if these were run-down theatre decorations made of cardboard or plywood. Behind them lay only ruins and piles of rubble. The yards radiate emptiness, death, horror.[35]

The "foreign" character of Vilnius also posed an obstacle for Lithuanians thinking of moving there after the war. The capital city presented an unfamiliar way of life in which Polish and Russian were the main languages of communication. Farmers were reluctant to give up their plots of land, which provided sustenance and relative security during these uncertain times. Moreover, the anti-Soviet insurgents threatened to murder the families of anyone who complied with the Soviet labor mobilization orders; and rumours that the Western Allies would not allow the Baltic States to remain within the Soviet Union stoked fears of another war.[36] The general tendency was to wait and see. Only about a half of those few who were persuaded to move to Vilnius in 1945–46 stayed longer than a few weeks. During the initial postwar years, the authorities and heads of large factories in Vilnius were more successful in attracting workers from Russia, Belarus and Ukraine.[37]

Destruction of the countryside

It would take the destruction of the traditional rural environment through collectivization and deportations before Lithuanians from the country would start moving to the cities after 1949. Along with the extensive violence of the anti-Soviet insurgency and its suppression, these two events resulted in the "murder" of the countryside – the physical and moral devastation of the population and the destruction of centuries-old traditions of village life.

As the Germans retreated before the Soviet advance, tens of thousands of Lithuanians took to the forests to launch a guerrilla war of independence, a fight that would continue until the early 1950s. During the first Soviet occupation of 1940–41, any potential resistance was destroyed through pre-emptive deportations and subsequent police action. With the Soviet reoccupation of 1944, the cities were quickly brought under control, and the center of resistance shifted to the countryside.

People joined the resistance from all walks of life, and for many different reasons. Most were driven to defend Lithuania's statehood and fight against the foreign occupation. Some joined in defiance of orders to mobilize to work in the cities.[38] Some also feared being drafted into the Soviet army or felt they would be targeted by Soviet repressions, including those who had collaborated with the Nazis, a category estimated to comprise about one in twenty members of the resistance.[39] Judging from Soviet police statistics of those killed in the fighting, the majority were young men from rural areas aged 16 to 21.[40]

Dismissed by Soviet propaganda as "bandits" and "renegades," the insurgents were more like an underground national army, with an estimated 35,000 Lithuanians taking part over the course of the conflict. For a brief time at the outset, the resistance was led by officers in uniform with soldiers subject to a disciplined chain of command and fighting open battles. But the "war after the war" quickly transformed into the struggle of irregular partisans against an occupying power that was systematically extending its authority from the cities to the countryside.

Like partisans everywhere, the strength of the Lithuanian "forest brothers" lay not in their numbers or equipment, but in their privileged relationship to the land, what Carl Schmitt described as the "telluric" or "terrestrial" essence of the partisan.[41] Their intimacy with the terrain gave them superior speed, agility and the advantage of surprise, allowing them to tie down, but not defeat, a much larger and better-organized force. They hid in underground bunkers deep in the forests and would also hide in plain sight among ordinary villagers, who gave them shelter, food and supplies.

As a result, the frontlines of this battle lay not between two separate territories, but between the city, controlled by the Soviets, and the country, controlled by the partisans. From 1945 until about 1947, the villages of Lithuania were liminal zones of mixed and incomplete authority. During the day, Soviet militias and civilian authorities would come from the city looking for "bandits," collecting taxes, and spreading communist ideology. And at night, members of the resistance would emerge from the forest: punishing "collaborators," collecting supplies, and preaching resistance. The insurgency was ultimately defeated not by the mere killing of combatants, but by the violent and irrevocable transformation of the traditional, agrarian society that sustained them.[42]

This division between the country and the city was bitterly articulated by the partisans themselves, who associated the city not only with the Soviet regime but also with the treachery of the more educated Lithuanian classes:

> Where are those who earlier injected a love for the homeland into us, who raised our courage, who preached the pleasure to die for the homeland? In fact, it has always been the village that fought for the homeland. ... When somebody threatened the homeland, the village would step forth with its pure, simple, and tough Lithuanian heart to fight. The village knows that enemies need to be fought, and so it fights ... [43]

It was only through the printed word that the guerrillas could publicize the goals and meaning of their struggle, and the shortage of talented journalists posed a great problem in this respect. According to Nijolė Gaškaitė, a Soviet dissident and chronicler of the postwar resistance, several intellectuals joined the resistance immediately after the war, but it was only after a year or two that "the intellectuals and other urban residents proved to be the layer of society that adjusted most quickly to the occupational regime."[44]

Indeed, although the "war after the war" was fought against a foreign occupation, a considerable degree of the violence occurred among Lithuanians themselves. Since the "forest brothers" would not be drawn into a direct and open battle, the Soviets resorted to what Stathis Kalyvas calls "selective violence," that is, the elimination of targeted individuals based on information gained from denunciations and the collaboration of the local populace. These tactics compelled the tightly knit village communities to turn out the insurgents themselves.[45]

The Soviets appointed villagers to local administrative positions, and organized them into militias to fight against the insurgents, as well as into special killing squads (*istrebiteli* in Russian or *stribai* in Lithuanian) to infiltrate the resistance and to kill its activists. The motivation of individuals who participated in such actions was mixed, but almost never ideological.[46] While their training and skills were inferior to those of regular Soviet troops, they had an advantage in terms of their knowledge of the local terrain, and their participation gave the conflict the colour of a civil war. The terror of violence was never far away as the bodies, sometimes mutilated, of killed partisans were routinely laid for all to see on the street in front of the police headquarters, market squares, schools and churches.

Perhaps most importantly, populist land redistribution from wealthy to poor peasants initiated during the first Soviet occupation in 1940–41 and resumed in 1944 devastated the economy and intensified the polarization of rural society. For these traditional, rural communities, where families had occupied the same soil for several generations and communal ties were extremely close, the splitting of families and communities left deep psychological wounds quite apart from any physical distress caused by the fighting.

This dimension of the "war after the war" in Lithuania reflects what Kalyvas describes as the "intimacy" of violence typical of civil wars throughout history. The issue remains extremely sensitive in Lithuania because of the way in which Soviet propaganda over-emphasized the fratricidal aspect to efface the reality that the conflict was caused in the first instance by foreign occupation. Aleksandras Shtromas, a noted Lithuanian émigré political scientist, expresses the matter in a balanced way by describing the conflict as a civil war not only because a few Lithuanians sided with the Soviets for ideological reasons, but due to the inevitable clash of political perspectives between those Lithuanians who sought to resist the Soviets at all costs, and those who decided to preserve what they could in the face of an unavoidable fate.[47]

Collectivization and counterinsurgency

As it happens, the Stalinist practice of collectivization enforced by mass deportations provided the basis for a effective counterinsurgency strategy, not to mention social modernization. Lynne Viola describes Stalin's First Five-Year Plan (1928–32) as an attempt to "catapult an agrarian nation into modernity, an attempt to industrialize the country at lightning speed," and the uprooting of some 2 million peasants in 1930–31 (called *spetspereselentsy* or special settlers, sent to the high north to build colonization villages) marked the birth of the Gulag system. Stalin himself said that industrialization would be based on a "tribute" from the peasantry, and this tribute was exacted through a purge of the countryside known as *dekulakization*: the removal of "undesirable" elements and the decapitation of traditional structures of authority designed to break down social cohesion in the village.[48]

During these initial postwar years, however, the Lithuanian communist authorities proceeded cautiously, for fear of provoking an even greater number of people to take to the forest. Already in 1940, during the first Soviet occupation, the Lithuanian communist government had argued that collectivization would be counterproductive. As a result, the Soviets limited themselves to redistributing land from rich farmers to poor, without destroying the institution of private property as such. The goal at that time was to reduce the size of landholdings to a maximum of 30 hectares, confiscating land above this limit and giving it to poor farmers and agricultural laborers "in perpetual tenure."[49]

After the war, the menace of real collectivization made the peasants suspicious, but the government again proceeded slowly, and continued to polarize the countryside through populist redistributions of property. The ultimate goal of

Soviet policy was to prepare for collectivization, and this implied an end to the single-family homestead created by the land reforms of the Lithuanian Republic and which served as the social foundation of interwar Lithuanian society.

In 1946, homesteads comprised 90 percent of peasant farms, and those who were awarded land grants from the Soviets sought to organize them into homesteads. In light of the core social significance of the homestead system, local communists resisted the drive to resettle peasants into villages, which was a prelude to the collectivization of their farmland. Reports from inspectors sent from Moscow complained: "all decisions of the republican and local party and Soviet agencies aim to consolidate the homestead system."[50]

But in the end, directives from Moscow decided the matter, and the final stage in the destruction of the countryside was launched in May 1947, with preparations for mass collectivization throughout the Baltic States. The Soviets sent large reinforcements of troops and militia, and launched a full-scale offensive to proceed with collectivization and root out the insurgents. The first operation was launched in March 1948, and resulted in the forced deportation of almost 40,000 individuals from the Lithuanian countryside. A second operation was launched in the spring of 1949, and deported over 30,000 farmers. Statiev notes that the if the scope of the deportations was initially focussed on known insurgents and their families, these major sweeps in the late 1940s targeted so-called *kulak* farmers irrespective of whether or not they were involved in the resistance.

By this point the tide of the battle against the resistance fighters had turned decisively. The deportations were implemented by a surge of Soviet troops, aided by a growing number of local collaborators. Collectivization, which stood at just 4 percent at the beginning of 1949, went up to 60 percent by the end of the year. Soviet power had finally extended from the major cities to the regional centers and finally, by the end of 1949, to the village localities, which until then had been largely controlled by the partisans, especially at night.

Records of the resistance at this time reveal a desperate effort to continue the battle and a no less desperate belief that the partisans might somehow succeed in triggering a new war involving the Western powers against the Soviet Union. "I am convinced that the conflict will take place," one partisan recorded in his diary in June 1948, "but I don't expect it this year. If the others heard me say this, they would call me a heretic: all of them, like the population at large, are counting the days until the new war begins."[51]

On February 16, 1949, eight leaders of the Lithuanian partisan movement gathered at a secret location deep in the forest to put their names to a document entitled the *Declaration of the Council of the Movement of the Struggle for Freedom of Lithuania*. Claiming to represent the highest political and military authority in the land, they recorded their determination to fight for freedom, end foreign occupation, and organize democratic elections. Fifty years later, on February 16, 1999, this document was enacted into law by the Lithuanian Parliament, and cited as proof that a "universal, organized, armed resistance" was active in Lithuania from 1944–53.[52]

Such mainstream Lithuanian chronicles of the resistance typically mark its conclusion with the capture of the last heroic insurgents who survived in the remote forests until the late 1950s. However, this periodization reflects the ideological bias typical of what Kalyvas calls "urban" analyses of partisan wars that are actually fought out in the countryside. Focused on the dramatic, political and leadership-oriented aspects of war, such analyses tend to neglect the social roots and effects of the conflict.[53] From a social perspective, the survival of a few partisans into the early 1950s was of little practical consequence, and the real tipping point against insurgency came in 1949, when collectivization was essentially accomplished, and the telluric link between partisans and the land was broken.

Indeed, from this point onwards, as the resistance movement lost momentum, the partisans resorted increasingly to retribution, and even terror, against the Lithuanian members of the rural population whom they identified as collaborators.[54] If a date for the end of the insurgency must be set, it could well be 16 February 1949, which was marked not only by the signing of the aforementioned declaration, but by a shift of tactics from open resistance to sabotage and the targeted killing of local government officials and collective farm organizers.[55] With the subsequent degeneration of the resistance, the Soviet conquest of the countryside was complete. The solidarity and cohesion of the tradition-bound agrarian society was broken, leading to the massive movement of villagers to the city.

Exodus to the city

After collectivization, the land provided neither sustenance nor protection from the political turmoil, repressions, crime, chaos and destitution that the villagers had come to associate with the cities during World War II. If the labor mobilization campaigns of 1945–46 failed to motivate the peasantry to migrate to the cities, they left in droves after 1948–49. With the borders to the West sealed, there was no alternative route of escape from rural desolation. Meanwhile, the cities had become much more attractive as destinations. Crime fell to its prewar levels, and a currency reform in 1947 put an end to the rationing of food.[56] Postwar reconstruction and Soviet-style modernization offered jobs and education for a rural population seeking to escape from collectivization, endemic violence and the poverty of the countryside.

In quantitative terms, the exodus of Lithuanians from the country to the city far exceeds any estimate of the numbers of those deported to the Gulag or exiled to the West. By one count, over 700,000 Lithuanians packed up and left their homesteads and small villages between 1951 and 1976 to resettle in towns and cities.[57] This parting, however, was nothing short of traumatic, and for many it most frequently resembled a rapid evacuation. Marcelijus Martinaitis (1936–2013), the son of a small landholder, vividly remembers his parents telling him, the only adult son who would have helped them to work the land: "there is nothing for you here [in the village], not even enough food, no future. Disappear from here, run."[58]

Alfonsas Maldonis recalls his last parting hours from his village in a similar light:

The nights were restless. I had just returned from a neighbour's place on the last night before I left the village. I climbed up the Žverynė hill and looked around. Fires were burning everywhere – the first harvest of the *kolkhoz* farms had been set alight. I gazed for hours at the northern lights, tinged with red, and listened to the sporadic machine gun fire. This is how I parted from my native home.[59]

These recollections capture the experience of many migrants, especially the younger ones who, as Tomas Venclova puts it, filled the cities with their "gloomy memories of the postwar resistance."[60]

The overall level of urbanization in Lithuania shot up from an all-time low of 15 percent in 1945 (down from the 23 percent before the outbreak of hostilities) to reach 50 percent in 1970 and a peak of 68.1 percent in 1989. From 1949 to 1965, urbanization affected the lives of some 105,000–115,000 individuals per year (Table 2.3). Vilnius and other Lithuanian cities also saw a large influx of Russian speakers from the Soviet Union including bureaucrats, factory administrators, workers and military personnel.

However, the internal migration of ethnic Lithuanians from the country was much higher, and so the cities were not extensively Russified as they were in Estonia and Latvia.[61] Paradoxically, Lithuania's relatively low level of urbanization before World War II meant that the need for labor could be met by the "surplus" of ethnic Lithuanians living in the surrounding country, reducing the need for immigrant workers.[62] Moreover, the percentage of Lithuanian migrants as a proportion of the total number of the migrants to the capital city increased steadily, rising from 60 percent between 1952 and 1957 to 70 percent between 1963 and 1965.[63]

Soviet urbanization processes were on the whole more rapid than in the West, reflecting the brutality of forced modernization, particularly under Stalin. Russia, for example, went from 13 percent urbanization just before World War I to about 70 percent in 1989.[64] In Lithuania, the same transformation occurred in just half the time. As subsequent chapters will show, these extraordinary demographic shifts and displacements would have dramatic and traumatic effects on the societies and cultures of the peoples affected.

Notes

1 Tomas Balkelis, "War, Ethnic Conflict and the Refugee Crisis in Lithuania, 1939–40," *Contemporary European History* 16.6 (2007): 464.
2 Eugenijus Grunskis, *Lietuvos gyventojų trėmimai, 1940–1941 ir 1945–1953 metais* (Vilnius: Lietuvos istorijos institutas, 1996), 23.
3 Norman Naimark, *Stalin's Genocides* (Princeton, NJ: Princeton University Press, 2010).
4 Tomas Balkelis, "Lithuanian Children in the Gulag: Deportations, Ethnicity and Identity Memoirs of Children Deportees, 1941–52," *Lituanus* 51.3 (Fall 2005); Birutė Burauskaitė, ed., *Lietuvos gyventojų genocidas*, vol. 1 (Vilnius: Represijų Lietuvoje tyrimo centras, 1992), 782–84.
5 Victor H. Winston, "Observations on the Population of Vilnius: The Grim Years and the 1942 Census," *Eurasian Geography and Economics* 47.2 (2006): 183. The Roma population of Lithuania, estimated at about 1000, was also destroyed. Vytautas Toleikis, "Lietuvos čigonai nacių okupacijos metais," in Christoph Dieckmann, Vytautas

Toleikis and Rimantas Zizas, eds, *Totalitarinių režimų nusikaltimai Lietuvoje: karo belaisvių ir civilių gyventojų žudynės Lietuvoje* (Vilnius: Margi raštai, 2005): 55–72.

6 Christoph Dieckmann and Saulius Sužiedėlis, *The Persecution and Mass Murder of Lithuanian Jews during Summer and Fall of 1941: Sources and Analysis* (Vilnius: Margi raštai, 2006).

7 R.Z. Saukienė, ed. *Šmaikščioji rezistentė Aldona Liobytė: publicistika, laiškai, atsiminimai* (Vilnius: Lietuvos rašytojų sąjungos leidykla, 1995), 81–82.

8 Tomas Balkelis, Violeta Davoliūtė, "A Study on How the Memory of Crimes Committed by Totalitarian Regimes is dealt with in Lithuania," *KKTC* (1 October 2009).

9 Theodore Weeks, "A Multi-ethnic City in Transition: Vilnius' Stormy Decade, 1939–49," *Eurasian Geography and Economics* 47.2 (2006): 165.

10 For the definitive treatment of the Nazi occupation of Lithuania, which is fair in its treatment of the occupied nation and yet proves beyond any doubt the deep involvement of many Lithuanians in the Holocaust, see Christoph Dieckmann, *Deutsche Besatzungspolitik in Litauen 1941–1944* (Göttingen: Wallstein, 2011).

11 Indeed, Lithuania was one of very few countries under German occupation (along with Poland, Greece and Czechoslovakia) to successfully resist German attempts to raise a Waffen-SS unit from among its citizens. In retaliation, the German authorities closed Vilnius and Kaunas universities and sent 46 Lithuanian intellectuals to the Stutthof concentration camp for promoting anti-German sentiment. For more on this, see for example Arūnas Bubnys, *Nazi Resistance Movement in Lithuania 1941–1944.* Vilnius: Vaga, 2003.

12 The analysis in the following paragraphs is based on a survey of the content of two major newspapers allowed under the Nazi occupation: *Į laisvę* [Towards Freedom] published in Kaunas, along with *Naujoji Lietuva* [New Lithuania], published in Vilnius.

13 Some of the writers who published their works were Juozas Žlabys-Žengė, Bernardas Brazdžionis, Henrikas Nagys, Faustas Kirša, Kazys Bradūnas, Mykolaitis-Putinas, Antanas Miškinis and others. Their fates varied after the war. Most, like Brazdžionis, Nagys, Kirša, Bradūnas and many others escaped to the West, while others were sent to the Gulag, returned, forced to make public denunciations of their previous activities, and then continued to work in the Soviet press, like Miškinis. Yet others, like Žlabys-Žengė, a member of the editorial board of *Į laisvę*, returned after deportation and stayed out of public life.

14 "Vilnius toks mielas," *Naujoji Lietuva* 1 (June 29, 1941).

15 "Vilnius jau atgijo," *Į laisvę* 17 (July 12, 1941): 6.

16 The ideology of national socialism was throughly introduced to readers in long series of articles written by the Lithuanian philosopher Juozas Girnius.

> It would be only half a problem if the Jews were a culturally fruitless nation. Unfortunately, the eternal Jew is also an eternal enemy and a vicious destroyer of every true culture. He spares no means to ruin the eternally hated Arian populace. He tries to penetrate parasitically into the body of Arian cultures and, having masked himself with various innocent names, starts polluting the blood of the nation that gave him shelter, to destroy the basis of its economic life, desecrate its moral ideals; in other words, to drag it it down to his own base level.
>
> Juozas Girnius, "Idėjiniai nacionalsocializmo pagrindai" *Į laisvę* 63 (September 4, 1941): 3.

17 See for example the text attributed to Kudirka in "Nuo amžių lietuviui teko kovoti su žydais" [Lithuanians have had to fight the Jews through the ages], *Naujoji Lietuva* 13 (July 12, 1941): 4. The question of whether Kudirka was an anti-Semite or whether certain of his writings have been cited out of context to create this impression is hotly debated in Lithuania today.

18 Vytautas Labūnaitis, "Mūsų tautos priešai," *Naujoji lietuva* 16 (12 July 1941): 4. In fact, nearly 9.2 percent of those Lithuanian citizens who were deported in 1941 were Lithuanian Jews – about 2000 – roughly their share of the overall population at the time.

19 Vytautas K. Labūnaitis, "Gyvenimas be žydų," *Naujoji Lietuva* 10 (July 9, 1941): 2.

20 Pulgis Andriušis, "Grąžinkim garbę senamiesčiui!" *Į laisvę* 47 (August 16, 1941): 5. Pulgis Andriušis was the pen name of Fulgencijus Andrusevičius (1907–70), a well-known Lithuanian interwar journalist and writer. In 1944 he fled to Germany and later to Australia where he took active part in a cultural life of Australian Lithuanian community.

21 "Klaikioji ir kylančioji Lietuva" *Į laisvę* 17 (July 12, 1941): 4.

22 Vytautas Kubilius, *Neparklupdyta mūza: Lietuvių literatūra vokietmečiu* (Vilnius: Lietuvių literatūros ir tautosakos institutas, 2001), 135.

23 Three days after signing an armistice with Nazi Germany, Maréchal Pétain outlined the ideological basis for his regime in a radio speech to the populace: "The land," he said, "does not tell lies. It remains your salvation. The land is the nation. A field that goes fallow is a part of France that dies. A plot that is newly seeded is a part of France that is reborn." P. Pétain, *Actes et Ecrits* (Paris: Flammarion, 1974), 479.

24 Philippe Burrin, "Vichy," in Pierre Nora, ed. *Les Lieux de mémoire vol. 3* (Paris: Gallimard, 1992), 335–36.

25 See Pierre Bitoun, *L'Equivoque Vichyssoise* (Paris: INRA, 1986), for a discussion of the blend of modernism and nativism in the ideology of Vichy France.

26 Vanda Zaborskaitė, "Kultūra kaip gyvybės forma mirties kontekste" in *Vilniaus kultūrinis gyvenimas, 1939–1945*, ed. Alma Lapinskienė (Vilnius: Lietuvių literatūros ir tautosakas institutas, 1999), 15.

27 Gediminas Jokūbonis, *Kai žaidė angelai: atsiminimai* (Vilnius: Vilniaus dailės akad. leidykla, 2009), 30.

28 Abraham Sutzkever, *Vilner Geto, 1941–1944* (Paris: Aroysgegebn durkh dem Farband fun di Vilner in Frankraykh, 1946). See also Yitzhak Arad, *Ghetto in Flames: The Struggle and Destruction of the Jews in Vilna in the Holocaust* (Jerusalem: Yad Vashem, Martyrs' and Heroes' Remembrance Authority, 1980). See also Herman Kruk and Benjamin Harshav, *The Last Days of the Jerusalem of Lithuania: Chronicles from the Vilna Ghetto and the Camps, 1939–1944* (New Haven, CT: YIVO Institute for Jewish Research, 2002).

29 John Neubauer, "1945," in Marcel Cornis-Pope and John Neubauer, *History of the Literary Cultures of East-Central Europe: Junctures and Disjunctures in the 19th and 20th Centuries* (Amsterdam: Benjamins, 2004), 152–53. Czeslaw Milosz grew up in Vilnius but moved to Warsaw and joined the resistance when the Nazis invaded.

30 http://db.yadvashem.org/righteous/search.html?language=en. Last accessed on 8 May 2013. Šimaitė moved from Kaunas to Vilnius in 1940. Not a writer herself, she socialized with left-leaning Lithuanian writers like Salomeja Nėris, Kazys Jakubėnas, Kazys Boruta and others. Her heroic activity in the Vilnius Ghetto was approved and supported by the rector of Vilnius University, Mykolas Biržiška (1882–1962), and other university staff.

31 In 1939, the Lithuanian authorities completed their own census, which showed a much higher number of Lithuanians, and a lower number of Poles. While this difference reflects the arrival of many officials from Kaunas, it is also probably the result of Polish and Lithuanian officials counting people who self-ascribe their ethnicity as "local" or *tutejszy* and language as the local vernacular or *gwara tutejsza*, as Poles or Lithuanians, respectively. See Victor H. Winston, "Observations on the Population of Vilnius: The Grim Years and the 1942 Census," *Eurasian Geography and Economics* 47.2 (2006): 179.

32 Ironically, the Poles from Vilnius were mostly resettled within Poland to the new territories transferred from Germany, to towns like Gdansk and Wroclaw. Krystyna Kersten describes the same process of urbicide in these towns in the western territories of postwar Poland in "Forced Migration and the Transformation of Polish Society in the Postwar Period," in Phillip Ther and Anna Siljak, ed. *Redrawing Nations: Ethnic Cleansing in East-Central Europe, 1944–1948* (Oxford: Rowman and Littlefield, 2001), 75–86.

33 Theodore Weeks, "Population Politics in Vilnius 1944–47: A Case Study of Socialist-Sponsored Ethnic Cleansing," *Post-Soviet Affairs* 23.1 (2007): 76–95. See also Krzysztof Buchowski, "Resettlement of the Polish Population from Ethnic Lithuania in 1945–47," *Dzieje Najnowsze* 1 (2005): 69–78.

34 Vitalija Stravinskienė, *Tarp gimtinės ir Tėvynės: Lietuvos SSR gyventojų repatriacija į Lenkiją (1944–1947, 1955–1959 m.)* (Vilnius: Lietuvos istorijos institutas, 2011), 187, 191.

35 In *Vilniaus kultūrinis gyvenimas, 1939–1945*, ed. Alma Lapinskienė, 162. Vilnius: Lietuvių literatūros ir tautosakas institutas, 1999.

36 Liudas Truska, "Ilgas kelias į Vilnių," *Kultūros barai* 5 (2010): 58–65, 62.

37 Nonetheless, the number of ethnic Lithuanians in Vilnius rose from about 10,000, as counted by the Soviet passports first issued in 1945 to 41,500 in 1951. Stravinskienė, *Tarp gimtinės ir Tėvynės*, 103, 195.

38 Truska, "Ilgas kelias Į Vilnių," 58–65.

39 This very loose, informal estimate was suggested in personal communications with Mindaugas Pocius and Arūnas Bubnys.

40 Nijolė Gaškaitė, Dalia Kuodytė, Algis Kašėta and Bonifacas Ulevičius, *Lietuvos partizanai: 1944 – 1953 m.* (Kaunas: Lietuvos Politinių kalinių ir tremtinių sąjunga, 1996), 355–56.

41 Carl Schmitt, *Theory of the Partisan: A Commentary on the Concept of the Political* (Berlin: Duncker & Humboldt, 1963), 49.

42 Alexander Statiev analyzes the Soviet use of collectivization and agrarian policy as a means of pacifying a rebellious rural population in Chapter 5 of *The Soviet Counterinsurgency in the Western Borderlands* (Cambridge: Cambridge University Press, 2010), 139–63.

43 *Liongino Baliukevičiaus – partizano Dzūko dienoraštis*, entry on November 10, 1948 (Vilnius: LGGRTC, 2006), 57.

44 Nijolė Gaškaitė, *Pasipriešinimo istorija: 1944–1953 metai* (Vilnius: Aidai, 1997), 98–99.

45 On the theory of selective violence and the devastating effect it has on the social fabric of the target communities, see Stathis N. Kalyvas, *The Logic of Violence in Civil War* (Cambridge: Cambridge University Press, 2006), 173.

46 Swedish documentary filmmaker Jonas Ohman interviewed several people recruited to these squads during the making of his documentary *The Hitmen* (2008) and concluded that given the extreme risks involved, virtually all were coerced through threats or blackmail by the Soviet security police, with greed or a desire for revenge as important but secondary motivations (personal communication, June 21, 2011). More broadly, in a comparative study of denunciation in the Soviet Union and Nazi Germany, Sheila Fitzpatrick and Robert Gellately encountered comparatively few cases where denunciations seemed to be motivated by genuine ideological fervor. See, *Accusatory Practices: Denunciation in Modern European History, 1789–1989* (Chicago, IL: University of Chicago Press, 1997), 10.

47 Aleksandras Shtromas, "Official Soviet Ideology and the Lithuanian People," in Rimvydas Šilbajoris, ed. *Mind against the Wall: Essays on Lithuanian Culture Under Soviet Occupation* (Chicago, IL: Institute of Lithuanian Studies Press, 1983), 62. The notion that the postwar partisan struggle had at least some elements of a civil conflict is hotly contested in Lithuania today. After citing Shtromas' argument in a public seminar, this author made headlines in the Lithuanian press and was accused in social media as being a Soviet collaborator. This extreme sensitivity arises from the fact that during Soviet times the authorities did indeed exploit the motif of "brother against brother" to distort the nature of the postwar struggle, casting it as a "class struggle" and effacing the reality of foreign occupation.

48 Lynne Viola, *The Unknown Gulag: The Lost World of Stalin's Special Settlements* (Oxford: Oxford University Press, 2007), 6–9.

49 The government also gave loans for the purchase of horses, cows, equipment, and cancelled debts owed to the former government. The popularity of these limited but confiscatory land reforms, and the potential for divisive social policies to divide rural society, is attested by the fact that the majority of peasants filed requests for land, filing a total of 261,172 applications for allotments, relative to a total of 354,854 farms existing in Lithuania prior to the reforms. Moreover, many requested that more be confiscated from their neighbors than the law allowed. Alexander Statiev, *The Soviet Counterinsurgency in the Western Borderlands* (Cambridge: Cambridge University Press, 2010), 136.

50 According to Statiev, between 1944 and 1948 96,330 Lithuanians were awarded land seized from: 3,926 farmers suspected of passive collaboration with the Germans, 19,505 farmers who owned land above the limit, 16,143 farms that were confiscated from the families of guerrillas, and 6,975 from Lithuanians who fled with the German retreat. In total, 96,330 farmer families gained and 39,574 lost land through the reform. Of the total amount of land confiscated in 1944–47, 58 percent was given to individual farmers, while the rest was retained for collective and state farms. Statiev, *The Soviet Counterinsurgency*, 146.

51 *Liongino Baliukevičiaus – partizano Dzūko dienoraštis*, entry on November 10, 1948 (Vilnius: LGGRTC, 2006), 27.

52 Seimas of the Republic of Lithuania, *Law on the February 16, 1949 Declaration by the Council of the Movement of the Struggle for Freedom of Lithuania*, Law No. VIII-1021, January 12, 1999, Vilnius.

53 Stathis N. Kalyvas, "The Urban Bias in Research on Civil Wars," *Security Studies* 13.3 (2004): 160–90.

54 Mindaugas Pocius, *Kita mėnulio pusė: Lietuvos partizanų kova su kolaboravimu 1944–1953 metais* (Vilnius: LII leidykla, 2009), 195.

55 Stanley Vardys, "The Partisan Movement in Post-war Lithuania," *Lituanus* 15.1 (1969).

56 Liudas Truska, "Ilgas kelias į Vilnių," *Kultūros Barai* 5 (2010): 58–65.

57 V. Rupas and S. Vaitekūnas, *Lietuvos kaimo gyventojai ir gyvenvietės* (Vilnius: Mintis, 1980), 99.

58 Marcelijus Martinaitis, Interview by author. Audio recording. Vilnius, November 12, 2008. Most contemporaries interviewed for this book recall the option of moving to the cities as a means of escaping the violence of the countryside and material hardships resulting from collectivization.

59 Donata Mitaitė, "Kelios Alfonso Maldonio archyvo pasiūlytos temos," *Lituanistica* 55.3–4 (2009): 144–52.

60 Tomas Venclova, *Vilnius, A Personal History* (Riverdale-on-Hudson, NY: Sheep Meadow Press, 2009), 154.

61 The lower level of Russification in Lithuania as compared to Estonia and Latvia is sometimes mistakenly attributed to a slower rate of urbanization during the Soviet period. See for example Peter V. Elsuwege, *From Soviet Republics to EU Member States: A Legal and Political Assessment of the Baltic States' Accession to the EU* (Leiden: Martinus Nijhoff Publishers, 2008), 39. In fact, while Estonia and Latvia were only marginally more urbanized by the close of the Soviet period, Lithuania had begun from a much lower level after the war, and its rate of urbanization throughout the Soviet period was significantly higher.

62 The net migration to Lithuania from other parts of the USSR between 1959 and 1979 was only 115,200 persons, or 16.8 percent of the overall population increase. Augustine Idzelis, "Industrialization and Population Change in the Baltics," *Lituanus* 30.2 (1984).

63 Liudas Truska, "Ilgas kelias į Vilnių," *Kultūros barai* 5 (2010): 58–65.

64 Piotr Eberhart, *Ethnic Groups and Population Changes in Twentieth-Century Central-Eastern Europe: History, Data, and Analysis* (Armonk, NY: M. E. Sharpe, 2003), 27.

3 Reconstruction and nation-building

We have returned to Vilnius, ruined and bleak,
Not to live in agony but to burn as an everlasting fire.
Lithuanian girls will make wreaths for Vilnius,
While their brothers brighten the city with the spirit of work.
Our longing for Vilnius and determination to liberate it,
The joy of victory sounds like an anthem.
These we carry as a sacred offering to Vilnius,
So that its name shall thunder through the land.
We have returned to Vilnius having trampled the fascists,
We are in bloom with heroic deeds, strong after the battle,
So that Vilnius should shine at Lithuania like the sun,
So that it should be as one with the heartbeat of Lithuania!
Where eyes are now crying for the light of a fire,
Where spirits are heavy from the rubble of the ruins,
Here, once again in Vilnius, a golden-domed castle will rise,
And once again the walls will speak legends to the centuries.[1]

On August 30, 1944, slightly over one month after the defeat of the Nazi forces in Vilnius by the Third Belorussian Front commanded by General Chernya-khovsky, Petras Vaičiūnas wrote a letter to his fellow Lithuanian writer Vincas Mykolaitis-Putinas.[2] "Dear Vincas," he wrote,

> Although Vilnius has become a horrible place after the tornado of war, you must still come here as soon as possible. The earlier you arrive, the easier it will be to find yourself a new apartment and in general to set yourself up ... Our Muscovite colleagues are very concerned about your fate, and look forward to shaking your hand as soon as possible. You will get a certificate either from the University or from the Writers' Union which will make your trip to Vilnius easier.[3]

In this manner Vaičiūnas, the author of the famous interwar Vilnius liberation slogan "We will not relent without Vilnius," passed a key message from the Soviet authorities to the esteemed Lithuanian writer who was then taking shelter from the war in the countryside at the homestead of his wife's parents. Soon thereafter, Vaičiūnas was again writing poetry about Vilnius, such as the lines above published on the front page of *Tiesa* in 1946, only now for the Soviet regime.[4] Vaičiūnas assured Mykolaitis-Putinas that he too was needed by the new order and that he would be given a dignified position in the new capital.

Mykolaitis-Putinas held immense authority among Lithuanian writers as well as the educated public, and was considered by many to be a real moral guide. A former member of the Catholic clergy, a famous poet, professor of literature and author of the extremely popular psychological-intellectual novel *In the Shadow of the Altars* (1933), he was also highly respected among left-leaning intellectuals – including the "Muscovites," i.e., the pro-Soviet Lithuanian intellectuals who were evacuated to Russia when the Nazis invaded and spent most of the war in Moscow, preparing for their return to the Lithuanian SSR.[5]

Many of the most prominent Lithuanian writers like Vincas Krėvė, Bernardas Brazdžionis, Alfonsas Nyka-Niliūnas, along with the majority of the interwar political and cultural elites, fled the Soviet advance to displaced persons camps in Germany and ended up being dispersed across Europe, North and South America, and even Australia. In this context, it was clear that the decision by a figure of such moral and intellectual standing as Mykolaitis-Putinas not to emigrate would provide a much-needed boost to the legitimacy of the Soviet regime in Lithuania. It was thought that a demonstration of allegiance from the brightest talents would dissuade many from further acts of sabotage or resistance.

Vaičiūnas, a mediator of sorts between Putinas and the "Muscovites," was by no means a communist or even a leftist but like many members of the interwar intelligentsia he had developed rather close friendships with leftists who supported the common cause of Vilnius.[6] Putinas was in something of the same position. A strong Lithuanian patriot and enthusiast of the Vilnius question, he was one of the first writers to move to the city after it was returned to Lithuania in 1939, taking up a position at the newly reformed Vilnius University. After the war, this network of Vilnius activists served as a bridge between the pro-Soviet Lithuanian *literati* and members of the interwar cultural elite.

Justas Paleckis (1899–1980) was another such Vilnius activist, a personal friend of Vaičiūnas and one of key "Muscovites." A journalist and director of the national news agency ELTA between the wars, Paleckis was not a fanatical communist, but more of a romantic socialist and well-known activist for the Populist party. He and Vaičiūnas' family retained close ties: Paleckis took care of him until his death and later supported his wife, the theatre actress Teofilija Vaičiūnienė. He began to promote the cause of independent Lithuania during World War I as part of the patriotic émigré community in Riga, and he very quickly developed a reputation as an ardent supporter of the Vilnius cause, to the point that he even named his first-born son "Vilnius Vytautas." Many

Lithuanian children were (and continue to be) named Vytautas, after the Lithuanian Grand Duke who was made into a cult figure during the interwar period, but to name one's child "Vilnius" marked an exceptional degree of enthusiasm for the cause.[7] After Vilnius was returned to Lithuania by the Soviets, Paleckis was the first to congratulate Vaičiūnas, saying: "Our common dream has come true. Get ready, we will go to Vilnius soon."[8] Chosen to serve as the first Soviet Lithuanian head of state in 1940, he emerged in the postwar era as an important ideologist of continuity between the interwar republic and Soviet Lithuania.

Right after the war, Paleckis relentlessly toured the Lithuanian provinces, urging the cultural elite, among others, to move to Vilnius. The composer and orchestra conductor Mykolas Karka recalls how, sometime around 1944–45, Paleckis approached him after the conclusion of a meeting in Panevėžys with a plea: "We have been fighting for Vilnius for so many years and now, when the capital lacks experts of every kind, nobody seems to be in a rush to go. Why aren't you moving to Vilnius?"[9] Paleckis delivered the same message in Kaunas, where he was trying to convince teachers of the Music Conservatory to move their institution to the new capital. "The stones of war-ravished Vilnius are cold. They must be warmed up immediately," he implored, "revived by Lithuanian music and song."[10]

Paleckis' fervour was perhaps given additional fuel by circumstances that were both political and personal. Just weeks before the city was named the capital of Soviet Lithuania in 1944, his son Vilnius, who served as a pilot in the Red Army, died in a plane crash near Moscow. At about the same time, according to the recollections of Paleckis' other son Justas Vincas, Antanas Sniečkus, the First Secretary of the Lithuanian Communist Party, voiced doubts whether Vilnius should indeed be made the capital. The son of a Lithuanian farmer, Sniečkus had the pragmatic instincts of a cautious and thrifty peasant, and little patience for urban romantics like Paleckis.[11] Sniečkus felt that for practical reasons, the capital should remain in Kaunas, while Vilnius, with its ancient university and architectural heritage, could be a cultural capital.[12]

Kaunas was relatively unscathed by the war, he is said to have argued, and its central location made communication with all parts of Lithuania much easier, especially in light of persistent fuel shortages. Paleckis vehemently rejected this idea, as it would destine Vilnius to the fate of a provincial city as it had been under Poland. Most importantly, he asserted, a provincial Vilnius would not go through the degree of transformation necessary to make it into a properly Lithuanian city. The two leaders could not come to terms and at one point, while debating the question on the road from Minsk to Vilnius, their argument became so bitter that Sniečkus told the driver to stop, and got out to sit in a different car. In the end, the matter was decided by Stalin, who told Sniečkus that Vilnius would have to be the capital.[13]

To be sure, the decision to make Vilnius into the new Soviet Lithuanian capital was not based on the whim of any one individual, but was driven by a number of political, social and economic factors. The destruction and displacement of the urban population during the war, the devastation of the rural communities, and the subsequent exodus of peasants to the cities meant that Sovietization would proceed hand in hand with reconstruction and urbanization.

Village youths caught up in the "war after the war" faced a clear choice of retreating to the forests to fight with the partisans, or migrating to the city to study or work for the Soviets. While the anti-Soviet insurgents vilified and sometimes punished those who chose the latter as "collaborators," migration to the city and accommodation to the regime were nonetheless chosen by the vast majority as a way of satisfying individual and collective aspirations.

The opportunity to make a fresh start in the newly acquired capital of Vilnius was attractive to many, at least once the reconstruction of the city got underway, and this circumstance was exploited by the Soviets to alleviate popular hostility towards the regime. And as the activism of Vaičiūnas and Paleckis demonstrate, the political Sovietization of the population was closely related to a cultural campaign that incorporated many elements of the activities of the interwar nationalists of making Vilnius into the Lithuanian capital.

As Mark Mazower has argued, the historiography of postwar reconstruction in Europe has long focussed too narrowly on the construction of the two opposing blocs of the Cold War, and not enough on how the postwar Soviet-bloc regimes were coping with the social dislocation caused by the war, and the legacy of the social issues inherited from the interwar period, and most importantly the postwar implementation of the solutions to those problems as developed by the interwar regimes.[14] In postwar Lithuania, several factors contributed to the focus on the reconstruction of Vilnius as a central platform of the ideology of the new regime: the pragmatic need to get the new capital city to function, the desire of the communist leadership to rally the populace around a universally acceptable goal, and the continuity of public sentiment with the Vilnius Question from the interwar period.

The dilemmas of reconstruction: clearing the rubble

The ideological thrust of postwar Sovietization was not only "national in form and socialist in content," but surprisingly national in its content as well. Indeed, the continuity of the communist cult of Vilnius with the key ideological drivers of the interwar nationalist regime was one of the initial signs of the inherent strength of a nativist national communism that would become increasingly apparent towards the end of the Soviet era. Architecture and public rituals meant to mobilize the masses were deployed as key elements of the capital's reconstruction. These were top-down processes initiated by the communist authorities, but the effort was geared to enlist popular support.

The regime's postwar focus on the reconstruction of Vilnius was prefigured by the manner in which Stalinist ideology had already established a key role for Moscow in propagating the values of the regime. In the 1930s, Moscow was cast as a showcase for new forms of social life as authorities invested huge sums into the city's reconstruction. As Katerina Clark notes,

> in Party rhetoric the rebuilding of the Soviet city came to stand for the moral and political transformation of the entire society into a communist one. Architectural schemes and tropes became dominant sources for political rhetoric throughout this most formative period in the history of socialist realism.[15]

The new plans for Moscow reflected much of the standard thinking on how to modernize European cities after World War I. With the arrival of the motorcar, streets needed to be widened. There was increasing awareness of pollution and the need to establish green belts, to clean up the river system and make room for housing. But as Clark emphasizes, the pan-European concern with public health and general efficiency was in the case of Moscow subordinate to the construction of the capital as a "template for the Soviet cultural order."[16]

The state aimed at Sovietizing urban space as it replaced a pre-revolutionary spatial order with new Soviet standards. According to the 1935 General Plan for the Reconstruction of Moscow, the "dirty, dark and crooked" streets of the old Moscow would be straightened out and widened. Large boulevards cut through old neighbourhoods and large squares were created. The "barbaric character of Russian capitalism" was blamed for the chaotic, haphazard layout of cities, and remnants of the petty bourgeois order like small shops, market stalls and enterprises, as well as historical structures like towers, walls and city gates, were all destroyed.[17]

The reconfiguration of urban space in Moscow was closely linked to the requirements of conducting mass festivals, suggesting that the creation of new spaces for Soviet-style celebrations was an explicit goal of reconstruction. In cities throughout the Soviet Union, the main avenue leading to the central square was often widened to allow masses of demonstrators to enter the square. Older buildings were destroyed, no matter what their value, if necessary to make way for the processions. In Moscow, for example, the Iberian chapel was destroyed for this purpose.[18]

A similarly iconoclastic plan for Vilnius was prepared during the first Soviet occupation of Lithuania in 1940–41. Written in Russian, it adheres closely to the key motifs of the Moscow plan of 1935, articulating the standard Stalinist vision of transformation and development of a well-built socialist city. Its principal aim was to rid Vilnius of its old-town core, with its irrational, narrow, serpentine streets, including the old Jewish quarter. The layout of the city described as "semi-feudal," and the "chaotic, haphazard arrangement" of buildings was blamed on "bourgeois Poland." The principles of socialist city planning were said to militate against any thought of preserving the old town.[19]

The emphasis was placed on the widening of streets, the expansion of squares, i.e., the creation of vast public spaces where the symbols of socialist civilization would serve to engender a Soviet mentality in Lithuanians. Similarly, an article published in *Vilniaus balsas* called "The Story of the New Vilnius" laid down a militantly modernist line towards the medieval history of the city that was so dear to Lithuanian collective memory:

> romantic tales about Vilnius, as a town of ancient dukes and kings may have something attractive about them, but they are no longer relevant ... We must leave these legends and fairy tales, even though they are beautiful, to the sentimentalists of the past.[20]

But when the Soviets returned after defeating the German forces in 1944, the Stalinist visions of the 1940–41 report were by and large abandoned as impractical. While the reconstruction of Moscow emphasized a conscious and militant eradication of its architectural heritage as a centre of Orthodox religion, such ideological factors were greatly attenuated when it came to the actual reconstruction of Vilnius. With the counterinsurgency raging in the countryside, an economy in ruins and an exhausted population, there was little energy and few resources to implement such grand designs.

Vilnius was badly damaged by the war, with about 40 percent of residential buildings damaged, but it was not razed to the ground like Minsk or Warsaw. According to the official account commissioned by the War Commissariat in 1944, out of 525 buildings in the historically significant Old Town, only 11 were completely destroyed, 45 were severely damaged, and 125 needed capital renovation. The remaining 344 buildings were either not damaged or needed simple renovation.[21]

The challenge of reconstruction was thus inextricably intertwined with the question of restoration, and the political choices involved in what to restore and what to write off as mere rubble to be cleared. Indeed, "rubble" took on the status of a metaphorical category and the symbol of the dark past, of the barbarity of German fascists, of the bygone fragment of history. Consequently, the act of clearing the rubble was no less symbolic and significant in psychological terms, coming to signify the building of a new life, a new future, a new community. And what precisely could be labelled "rubble"? Inevitably, the decisions taken in this context addressed more than the simple dilemma of preserving the past or building the future, and implied the preservation or erasure of one or another period of the long history of Vilnius associated with Lithuanian, Jewish or Polish collective memory.

Historians have offered a number of competing motivations for the choices that were made. For example, some have argued that Polish engineers on the above-mentioned Soviet commission in charge of evaluating the soundness of buildings were inclined to slate Russian Tsarist-era buildings for destruction, while preserving the Baroque and Renaissance buildings associated with the

Polish era of Vilnius, a goal that was actively discussed in Polish-controlled Vilnius between the wars, but not acted upon at that time.[22]

Theodore Weeks suggests that the Soviet and Lithuanian approaches to reconstruction were in implicit agreement on the point that the bourgeois (read Polish) heritage of the city could be dispensed with to make way for the city's Soviet Lithuanian future.[23] Arūnas Streikus argues instead that the Soviets were careful not to offend the national sentiments of the neighbouring People's Republic, and were focussed on eliminating the city's Catholic heritage, noting the closure or conversion of many of the city's churches to profane uses.[24] Given the overlapping of religious and ethnic identities in the city, these competing explanations are not mutually exclusive.

In general, the widespread perception of Vilnius being "in ruins" fuelled the sentiment that the best way to rebuild the city was to destroy the old and to start afresh. Researchers have noted that more damage was done to the architectural heritage of the Old Town in the postwar period than during the war itself.[25] From a technical point of view there was a general consensus that the overall living quality and sanitary conditions of many Old Town quarters were extremely poor, and that many buildings should be torn down in order to reduce the density of settlement and to establish green areas. The lack of qualified engineers was cited as another reason to favour the destruction rather than reconstruction of many old-town buildings.[26]

Certainly, this was the attitude that prevailed when it came to making decisions about the city's Jewish monuments. They were not targeted for destruction as such, but little effort was made to preserve them. The Great Synagogue, for example, was severely damaged but structurally intact. It was designated as a historical monument, but severely damaged in 1947, and not included in the 1955 General Plan for reconstruction. Similarly, the old Jewish Quarter was the site of the most radical clearing in the city. And while the arguments that the ruined quarter posed a risk to public health and safety were probably valid, it is equally true that a proposal to establish a museum to the Ghetto was rejected. The local Jewish community made efforts to preserve the Great Synagogue, including the sending of an official letter to Justas Paleckis and other high Soviet Lithuanian officials, but these failed to save the building from destruction.[27]

Artist Rafael Chwoles, a member of the Young Vilna group between the wars, was one of the first people to photograph, sketch and portray in paintings the ruined Vilnius ghetto, the streets and buildings that he, a native of Vilnius, knew so well. Most of the buildings he immortalized were subsequently destroyed (see Figures 3.1 and 3.2). The construction of sporting facilities in the place of the old Jewish cemetery (relocated to a less central location) also testifies to the priorities of the authorities, not to mention the absence of a strong Jewish constituency. Similarly, the old Tartar cemetery near Lukiškės prison was removed, and the surrounding streets lost their historical names of Mohammed street, Mosque street and Mosque lane, and were renamed Apple, Pear and Plum streets.[28]

Figure 3.1 Rafael Chwoles, *Grande Synagogue. Ruines.* Oil on canvas. Vilnius, 1945

The new, Soviet face of the city was to be created by a new team of architects "parachuted" into the capital from the Soviet Union. However, none of the radical plans designed at the time to reshape the city in a socialist mould, like the Palace of Soviets designed for Tauras Hill, were ever implemented.[29] Owing to the lack of resources and a practical approach to building legitimacy for the regime, new buildings served everyday purposes: a new train station, cinema, and the Pedagogical Institute. Other prestige projects reflected a catering to new classes of privileged Lithuanians, such as a luxurious block of flats for intellectuals called the Academician's House, which boasted flats of 120 square meters each with separate rooms for servants.[30]

The city was provided with its share of monuments to communist leaders, with Lenin on the former Lukiškės square, Stalin near the train station, and the remains of General Cherniakhovsky buried in a monument off the main street. But these monuments never overwhelmed the cityscape, and the main street even kept the name of the city's medieval founder Gediminas until 1952, when it was belatedly renamed after Stalin. Many streets were renamed after communist heroes, but even more had Polish names replaced with Lithuanian ones.[31]

The complex and contradictory array of factors influencing the direction of the city's reconstruction is evident in the experience of Vladislovas Mikučianis, an ethnic Lithuanian born and raised in Leningrad, who was appointed the city's chief architect in 1945.[32] Like Paleckis, Mikučianis spent the first

Figure 3.2 Rafael Chwoles, *Grande Synagogue. Ruines.* Photo. Vilnius, 1945

months after his arrival in Lithuania trying to convince and cajole experts to move from Kaunas to Vilnius – not for ideological but rather practical reasons. He recalls the desperate efforts he made together with Jonas Kumpis (1895–1960), the Head of the Architectural Board:

> We went and bowed down before them, trying to convince them to move to Vilnius. But our invitations were not answered. They had excellent apartments in Kaunas and some even had private houses. We could not match this in Vilnius. And many probably did not believe that Soviet power was there to stay. They felt the war was still not over.[33]

The lack of qualified staff forced him to work on the basis of the detailed city plan developed in 1943–44 by Vytautas Landsbergis-Žemkalnis, the chief architect of Vilnius under the Nazi occupation. As a result, Mikučianis writes, the main principles guiding the city's reconstruction were essentially conservative, aiming at preserving the rich silhouette of the Old Town and the natural setting of the city in the surrounding hills and forests. This set Vilnius apart from nearby Soviet capitals like Minsk and Kyiv, where the plans drawn up before World War II and the principles of socialist reconstruction were implemented far more consistently.[34]

Historians are divided as to why the architectural heritage of the Vilnius Old Town was relatively unscathed by postwar reconstruction. Rasa Antanavičiūtė claims that the local authorities did everything possible to curry the favour of the new Soviet authorities, but they simply did not have the resources to carry out the more radical visions for the city's reconstruction. On the other hand, in her comparative study of the postwar reconstruction of Vilnius, Riga, Lviv and Kyiv, Ūla Tornau expresses the more convincing view that Lithuanian officials exercised a restraining influence on Soviet plans to transform the Old Town of Vilnius.[35]

Steeped in the cult of Vilnius and the notion that the buildings and architecture of the city embodied the history of the nation, they were unlikely to adopt any radical plans for the reconstruction of the city without implicit resistance at the very least. Notably, the Soviet Lithuanian authorities followed the same path established during the interwar period of neglecting the architectural and cultural heritage of the great manors, which were seen as the embodiment of Polish culture and having nothing to do with the past of the Lithuanian nation.

The poetics of reconstruction

Indeed, the focus in public discourse on the restoration of key monuments to a narrowly construed Lithuanian ethnic identity makes it clear that the preservation of much of the Old Town of Vilnius cannot be explained by accident or the lack of resources alone. The restoration of the Castle of Gediminas would not begin until the late 1940s, but was identified as a national priority already in 1945.[36] Not surprisingly, the poetry of Petras Vaičiūnas, like "We Have Returned to Vilnius" reproduced above, was used prominently on the front page of *Tiesa* to proclaim the task of rebuilding Vilnius, with the poetic allusions divided equally between the pagan Lithuanian past, the "sun" of Stalin and the "golden domes" of the future city.[37]

Vaičiūnas, Paleckis and other "Vilnius activists" managed to build upon the interwar cult of Vilnius by integrating select dimensions of the city's Lithuanian past into a broader Soviet narrative. News articles published in *Tiesa* also put an emphasis on the restoration of historical monuments as an integral part of the process of socialist reconstruction:

> Today, the pathos of reconstruction has reached the oldest stones of Lithuanian history. Scaffolding covers the Castle of Gediminas, and a road up the castle mound has been constructed: a true symbol of the

newly reconstructed Soviet Lithuania. We are standing on the scaffold built around Gediminas castle. In front of us is beautiful Vilnius. In the soft rustling of tree leaves, which resembles the sound of breathing, we hear the chopping of axes and the heaving of saws. Lithuania is rebuilding itself, reconstructing itself; it is becoming younger. Instead of the battles that recently took place, a new life is in blossom. Many challenges are still ahead but we will have a younger, more beautiful Vilnius than ever before.[38]

By linking the medieval past of Lithuania to its Soviet future, and by enveloping the tower of Gediminas with the canonical imagery of "Moscow covered in scaffolds," the passage endows the key symbol of Lithuanian nationalism with an aura of Soviet legitimacy.

For the sake of preserving the aura of *socialist* legitimacy for what might otherwise have been criticized as a nationalist undertaking, the physical restoration of the "oldest stones of Lithuanian history" was given a modern, forward-looking orientation through the repeated emphasis on youth. The bifocal vision of the past and the future echoes the nation-building ideology of the interwar period, only recast in the language of postwar Stalinism.

Figure 3.3 J. Kalnaitis (pseudonym of Judelis Kacenbergas), *Žilojo Vilniaus jaunystė* (The youth of grey-haired Vilnius). Undated photo
Illustration No. 79 in *Vilnius*. Vilnius: Valstybinė politinės ir mokslinės literatūros leidykla, 1960.

Cleansed of the reactionary past through its association with youth, the tower in turn offers a physically elevated, and thus ideologically privileged, vantage point from which to view the "younger and more beautiful" Vilnius, and the entire country that is also "becoming younger" through the process of reconstruction.

In 1949, Paleckis contributed a poem entitled "Vilnius" to *Pergalė* (*Victory*), the official literary journal of the Soviet Lithuanian Writers' Union.[39] By signing with the pen-name "Palemonas," he invokes the Roman origins of the Gediminas dynasty, a myth created in the sixteenth century by Lithuanian nobles seeking to present an ancient pedigree on par with that of the Poles, with whom they had just joined in a dynastic alliance. Stalinist imagery aside, the Vilnius of Paleckis in 1949 shares the epic, state-centred perspective as the Vilnius of the interwar period, with its focus on the medieval legacy of Lithuanian statehood before the union with Poland and subsequent Polonization of the Lithuanian nobility.[40]

The imagery taps into the Lithuanian interpretation of the city as the symbol of national historical continuity. The ancient origins of Lithuania in Vilnius are glorified, with references to key mythical sites, such as the sacred fires on Cathedral Square, and the tower of Gediminas. Situated high on the hill at the centre of Vilnius, the tower symbolically links the city with higher Soviet ideals but also serves as a concrete physical reminder of Lithuania's heroic past. The "Polish period" of Vilnius is portrayed as an age of feudalism, during which Lithuania suffered but swore that it would one day regain Vilnius. With the arrival of Stalin, the peasants and workers became the new masters of the city, and are busy reclaiming the houses of Vilnius from the rich.

An earlier volume of *Pergalė* included another representation of Vilnius by poet Vladas Grybas. The opening line of his poem, "You have been created for the joy of Lithuanians," again echoes Brazdžionis in its assertion of the relationship between the city and Lithuanian national identity.[41] The concrete reality of Vilnius appears first and foremost as rubble left after the battle, and introduces a motif of historical trauma, of catastrophe, and the joy of reconstructing a new life.

The poem contains very few actual topographical markers, and everything is presented in highly mythologized terms, like the "sacred shrines of our forefathers" or construction campaigns that were common at the time, like "broadening the streets" and "planting trees."[42] The recent traumatic history of World War II and the mass displacement of the postwar period are glossed over in a fused vision of the pagan ethnic past and the utopian Soviet future. The theme of Vilnius as the ancient cradle of Lithuanian identity was blended seamlessly into the communist narrative of reconstruction and the creation of new identities.

The performance of reconstruction

Just as socialist models of architecture fell far short of the ideal and had to reach compromises with social expectations and the built environment, so too the performance of socialist reconstruction through parades and festivals in postwar Lithuania contained a strong element of staged nationalism and continuity with practices of mass identity politics developed during the inter-war period. The authorities organized song and sports festivals closely pat-terned on the tradition of mass festivals that flourished during the interwar period throughout Europe, including the Soviet Union.

The first such festival was timed to celebrate the first anniversary of the liberation of Vilnius on July 13, 1945. It featured an outdoor concert in an improvised stadium against the slopes of Gediminas mountain, with crowds applauding choirs that sang a mix of folk Lithuanian and Soviet-Russian songs.[43] The choice of the setting was important and imparted a visual message with a clear appeal to Lithuanian national sentiment. Indeed, the festival marked a formal continuation of the song and dance festivals that were such an important part of the interwar practice of mass, nationalist politics of all the Baltic States.[44]

The festival held on the next anniversary was said to involve 12,000 youths and was widely transmitted through newspapers and documentary newsreels, showing images of crowds of people dressed in national costumes and trans-fixed in a moment of singing. The message of a mass cultural revival was reinforced and every conceivable opportunity to weld Soviet and Lithuanian narratives in the mind of the public was seized:

> An unforgettable image was created by the giant choir and the giant sta-dium. It was a real celebration of national culture. Never in the history of Lithuania has Lithuanian art, Lithuanian song, and Lithuanian music received so much attention from the masses; never before did it achieve such a massive scope. Art is becoming a mass phenomenon. Soviet order is leaving the doors of the sanctuary of art wide open for the working people.[45]

The story and the images served to demonstrate not only the power of Vilnius as the new cultural centre, but also insisted on it as the model for the future. Indeed, the implied contrast between the desperate conditions of the insurgents in the countryside and the opportunities of those who came to the city and gave their support to the new regime was an illustration of the political choice to be made by young Lithuanians: to continue to risk one's life by participating in the increasingly futile resistance, to remain in the trap of war, conflict and destruction, or to come to an accommodation with the Soviet regime and grasp the opportunity of a new start in the city of Lithuanian dreams.

> Twelve thousand Soviet youths came today to the ancient city of Gediminas – Vilnius – from the four corners of Lithuania. Many thousands more who could not travel accompanied them in their thoughts and deeds, as they climbed up the mountain of Gediminas. Through song they announced to all fraternal Soviet nations and to the entire world that Soviet Lithua-nia has forever shaken off the German threat, that it has regained its holy

city of Vilnius, its seashore with Klaipėda, that it has confidently begun to create a new culture – national in form and socialist in content.[46]

The key formula of Soviet nationalities policy – national in form and socialist in content – created an opening to pursue the same nationalizing project of the interwar regime with similar, though better resourced and more elaborately articulated, techniques of mass politics. Lithuanians walking the streets of Vilnius brought not only their peasant customs and manners, but also their dreams and visions of the city, which had been shaped by the nationalist elites during the interwar period and disseminated to every village in the country. Given the historical memory of Lithuanians about the political and cultural hegemony of the Poles, it was a relatively straightforward matter to identify the "Polish" period of Lithuanian history as "bourgeois" and to assert the traditional identity of the Lithuanian peasantry as the "toiling class" of history.

Notes

1 Petras Vaičiūnas, "Mes grįžom į Vilnių" *Tiesa* 162 (13 July 1946): 1. Translated by the author. Other contributors to this special issue of *Tiesa* dedicated to the second anniversary of the liberation of Vilnius included well-known leftists from the interwar period such as Antanas Venclova, Salomėja Nėris, and Liudas Gira.
2 The Soviets marked the victory of the Third Belorussian Front in the "Vilnius Offensive" (part of Operation Bagration) on July 13, 1944. The Polish Home Army mounted a simultaneous offensive against the Nazis called Operation Ostra Brama and cooperated with the Red Army to liberate Vilnius, until July 16 when the Soviets arrested and interned the Poles involved.
3 Petras Vaičiūnas' letter to Vincas Mykolaitis-Putinas, Vilnius, August 30, 1944 in Petras Vaičiūnas, *Laisvės keliais* (Vilnius: Vaga, 1991), 492–93.
4 "Mes grįžom į Vilnių," *Tiesa* 162 (13 July 1946): 1.
5 The "Muscovites" included intellectuals such as Kostas Korsakas, Petras Cvirka, Antanas Venclova, Salomėja Nėris, Justas Paleckis, Eduardas Mieželaitis and others. For a thorough analysis of the life of the leftist interwar cultural elites see Mindaugas Tamošaitis, *Didysis apakimas* (Vilnius: Gimtasis žodis, 2010).
6 Vaičiūnas was a member of the editorial board of the first issues of the Soviet literary journal *Pergalė* together with the group of leftist intellectuals. It is certainly not a coincidence that an early issue of the almanac opens with the long hymn to Vilnius, "Our eternal city" written by Antanas Venclova: "Oh, Vilnius, our noble city! You are our dream and honour! Never stop shining to us in struggle, creation and work! Honour to those who fought for your freedom and future!" Antanas Venclova, "Amžinasis mūsų miestas: giesmė apie Vilnių," *Pergalė* 2 (1944): 3–6.
7 Vilnius Vytautas Paleckis was born in 1925. His younger brother Justas Vincas Paleckis claims to know of only two other cases where somebody was named after Vilnius. Vincas Justas Paleckis, Interview by author. Audio recording. Vilnius, April 4, 2012.
8 Teofilija Vaičiūnienė, "Širdies šilumos užteko" in *Taurios širdies žmogus* (Vilnius: Vaga, 1987), 244. Paleckis was a family friend; he supported Vaičiūnas' wife after the death of the writer.
9 Mykolas Karka (1892–1984) was a famous pedagogue, conductor, musician and composer and a passionate Lithuanian cultural activist. Like many other Lithuanians he retreated to Saint Petersburg during World War I and was actively involved in

Lithuanian cultural activities there. In 1924 he organized the first song festival in the city of Panevėžys. Paleckis' connection to Lithuanian cultural activists like Karka came from the Lithuanian cultural activist networks that grew in strength during World War I in exile in such urban centres as St. Petersburg, Riga and Voronezh. Mykolas Karka "Kuriame naują Lietuvą" in Alfonsas Bieliauskas, J. Jakaitienė, Justas V. Paleckis, and M. Tamošiūnas, *Taurios širdies žmogus: atsiminimai apie Justą Paleckį* (Vilnius: Vaga, 1987), 162–63.

10 Paleckis' words are recalled by Teofilija Vaičiūnienė in Alfonsas Bieliauskas, J. Jakaitienė, Justas V. Paleckis, and M. Tamošiūnas, *Taurios širdies žmogus: atsiminimai apie Justą Paleckį* (Vilnius: Vaga, 1987), 345. The same phrase is citedin the memoirs of Jonas Mackonis, *Boružės odisėjos* (Vilnius: Tyto Alba, 2003), 137.

11 The friction between Paleckis and Sniečkus was well known, documented by Sniečkus' stepson Aleksandras Shtromas, who witnessed that Sniečkus mocked Paleckis for his "soft spine" and lack of stamina. See also Tininis, *Sniečkus: 33 metai Valdžioje*, 44. In spite of these frictions, Paleckis kept his post as Chairman of the Supreme Soviet of Lithuania until 1967. However, his position was largely symbolic and while he exercised an important influence, especially in cultural matters, he did not have real decision power.

12 Vincas Justas Paleckis, Interview by author. Audio recording. Vilnius, April 10, 2012. See also Genovaitė Paleckienė in Alfonsas Bieliauskas et al. *Taurios Širdies Žmogus*, 273.

13 Vincas Justas Paleckis, Interview by author. Audio recording. Vilnius, April 10, 2012. While an independent account of this exchange could not be found, the passion with which Paleckis promoted the cause of Vilnius is entirely in keeping with his activities at the time. For additional materials on the conflict between Paleckis and Sniečkus drawing on Moscow-based archives, see Elena Zubkova, *Pribaltika i Kreml'*, 1940–53 (Moscow: Rosspen, 2008), 293–97.

14 Mark Mazower, "Reconstruction: The Historiographical Issues," *Past and Present* (2011 Supplement 6): 21–22.

15 Katerina Clark, "Socialist Realism and the Sacralizing of Space," in E.A. Dobrenko, and Eric Naiman, *The Landscape of Stalinism: The Art and Ideology of Soviet Space* (Seattle, WA: University of Washington Press, 2003), 3–18.

16 Katerina Clark, *Moscow, the Fourth Rome: Stalinism, Cosmopolitanism, and the Evolution of Soviet Culture, 1931–1941* (Cambridge, MA: Harvard University Press, 2011), 95–96.

17 Ibid.

18 Malte Rolf, "A Hall of Mirrors: Sovietizing Culture under Stalinism," *Slavic Review* 68.3 (Fall 2009): 612.

19 Theodore Weeks, "Remembering and Forgetting: Creating a Soviet Lithuanian Capital. Vilnius, 1944–49." *Journal of Baltic Studies* 39.4 (2008): 523.

20 Benediktas (pseudonym), "Naujojo Vilniaus istorija," *Vilniaus balsas* (July 10, 1940).

21 Weeks, "Remembering and Forgetting," 523.

22 Jūratė Markevičienė, "Vilniaus kultūros paveldo apsauga Lietuvos Respublikos (1939–40), Sovietų Sąjungos okupacijos bei aneksijos pradžios (1940–41 ir 1944–45) ir nacistinės Vokietijos okupacijos (1941–44) laikotarpiu," in Alma Lapinskienė, ed. *Vilniaus kultūrinis gyvenimas 1939–1945* (Vilnius: LTTI, 1999), 142–75.

23 Weeks, "Remembering and Forgetting," 526–27.

24 Arūnas Streikus, "Kierunki polityki pamięci na Litwie sowieckiej," *Politeja* 16 (2011): 281–307.

25 Marija Drėmaitė, "Naujas senasis Vilnius: senamiesčio griovimas ir atstatymas 1944–59 metais," in Giedrė Jankevičiūtė, ed. *Atrasti Vilnių: skiriama Vladui Drėmai* (Vilnius: Vilniaus dailės akademijos leidykla, 2010), 183–201.

26 Rasa Čepaitienė, "Tarybinės sostinės konstravimas J. Stalino epochoje: Minsko ir Vilniaus atvejai," in Alvydas Nikžentaitis, ed. *Nuo Basanavičiaus, Vytauto Didžiojo*

iki Molotovo ir Ribbentropo: atmintis ir atminimo kultūrų transformacijos XX–XXI a. (Vilnius: LII, 2011), 202.

27 Rasa Čepaitienė, *Laikas ir akmenys. Kultūros paveldo sampratos moderniojoje Lietuvoje* (Vilnius: LII, 2005), 236. The original copy of the letter is held at the Tolerance Centre of the Vilna Gaon State Jewish Museum.

28 Theodore Weeks, "Remembering and Forgetting," 523. Antanas Rimvydas Čaplinskas, *Vilnius Streets: History, Street Names, Maps* (Vilnius: Charibdė, 2000), 219.

29 See Rasa Antanavičiūtė, "Stalininis 'penkmetis': Vilniaus viešųjų erdvių įprasminimo darbai 1947–52 m." [The First Five Years Under Stalin: The Signification of Public Spaces in Vilnius, 1947–52] *Menotyra* 16.3–4 (2009): 150–69.

30 Weeks, "Remembering and Forgetting," 526.

31 Weeks, "Remembering and Forgetting," 523.

32 Mikučianis was born in 1913 in St. Petersburg into a family of Lithuanian communist émigrés, who participated in the failed attempt to create a Socialist Lithuanian Republic in the early 1920s. He received his degree in architecture in 1937 and worked in a design institute. In 1945, he was sent to Vilnius to work as a chief architect of the city, a position he kept until 1962 before joining the Vilnius Art Academy as a professor. He died in 2000 and his memoirs *Norėjau dirbti Lietuvoje* [*I Wanted to Work in Lithuania*] were published posthumously in 2001.

33 Vladislovas Mikučianis, *Norėjau dirbti Lietuvoje* (Vilnius: Vilniaus dailės akademijos leidykla, 2001), 55.

34 See Rasa Čepaitienė, "Tarybinės sostinės konstravimas J. Stalino epochoje: Minsko ir Vilniaus atvejai," *Nuo Basanaviciaus, Vytauto Didziojo iki Molotovo ir Ribbentropo: atmintis ir atminimo kultūrų transformacijos XX–XXI a.*, ed. Alvydas Nikžentaitis (Vilnius: LII, 2011), 171–224. Algimantas Nasvytis and Vytautas Brėdikis also recall that Mikučianis was receptive to the ideas of young Lithuanian architects.

35 Rasa Antanavičiūtė, "Stalininis 'penkmetis': Vilniaus viešųjų erdvių įprasminimo darbai 1947–52 m." [The First Five Years Under Stalin: The Signification of Public Spaces in Vilnius, 1947–52] *Menotyra* 16. 3–4 (2009): 150–69. Ūla Tornau, "Socialistinio miesto vizijos taikymas Lietuvoje: pokarinis Vilnius." *Europos erdvė: naujausios žinios apie genius loci* (Vilnius: Tarptautinės dailės kritikų asociacijos Lietuvos sekcija, 2004), 13–16.

36 *Tiesa* 143 (June 21, 1945): 1.

37 *Tiesa* 162 (July 13, 1946): 1.

38 *Tiesa* 161 (July 10, 1949): 1.

39 Many flags have been raised on the mountain of Gediminas,
   Our nation has seen many orders and governments.
   Where holy fire burned and the shrines of our forefathers once lay,
   Luxurious palaces, cathedrals and churches have since emerged.
   Honour to the gods was given through prayers and smoke,
   For people heavenly mist, and for nobles, paradise in palaces.
   Much blood flew into the Nėris from the streets and squares
   The Nėris remembers how the dukes were fighting,
   How the soldiers of Kutuzov chased after the Corsican,
   How Kalinowski was not afraid to die for the people,
   And how the red flag was raised in the struggle for freedom and song.
   For a time, Lithuanians suffocated without Vilnius,
   But now we speak with the Castle of Gediminas every day.
   Until recently, we visited Vilnius only in our songs,
   Now the songs of rebirth come to us from Vilnius.
   We did not come here to inherit bones or coffins,
   We do not wish to burn offerings on sacrificial fires.

We did not come to kneel at the gate of Ostra Brama,
Our generation is attracted by a different dawn.
Lithuanians have sworn not to relent without Vilnius
And through Vilnius they will be reborn in freedom:
We won Vilnius for ourselves in the name of Stalin
And engaged ourselves with a great new future.
"The streets are for you but the houses are for us"
The rich said to those who ate dry bread.
When Vilnius began to swell with the anger of many voices,
We learned that even the streets do not belong to the workers.
Here the true owner, who created and built it all,
For the past ten decades saw only the skeleton of poverty.
Now the times have changed in their essence:
Now the worker is the leader in life.
Who now is the owner of the streets and the houses?
A million voices respond – the worker!
All the riches of this land belong to him
Because it was created, because it was built by him.

Palemonas (Justas Paleckis), "Vilnius," *Pergalė* 7 (1949): 6. Translated by the author with permission.

40 See Venclova, *Vilnius, A Personal History* at 76 for a similar interpretation of Brazdžionis.

41 Vladas Grybas, "Vilnius," *Pergalė* 11 (1948): 53–54.

42 Tree planting was another prominent aspect of the reconstruction of Vilnius after the war. Contemporaries, especially those who came to Vilnius to study, remember participating in the tree planting campaign vividly. See for example "Atstatysim miestą Gedimino ... ", in Vytautas Merkys, *Atminties prošvaistės* (Vilnius: Versus Aureus, 2009), 90.

43 *Tiesa* 171 (July 25, 1945): 4.

44 In fact, the tradition originated in German-speaking lands and came to the Baltics via Estonia and Latvia in the late nineteenth century. The first such festival was held in Lithuania in Kaunas in 1924.

45 *Tiesa* 170 (July 23, 1946): 1.

46 *Tiesa* 169 (July 21, 1946): 1.

4   Engineers of urban souls

The damage done by the German occupant is now being redressed, and writers are invited to participate through the artistic representation of the process of reconstruction.

Kostas Korsakas[1]

The war devastated our cities, but it also destroyed the nerves and sensibilities of Lithuanians. They must be rebuilt by us, by writers. It is our task to rebuild peoples' minds.

Jovaras[2]

They [Soviet Lithuanian poets] have no regard for the nation. For a piece of silver they sell their pen, slander their homeland, soil the honorable name of Lithuania, desecrate their literature, and falsify their history.
Anonymous commentary from an underground anti-Soviet partisan newspaper[3]

The rebuilding of Vilnius went hand in hand with its symbolic representation in culture, and the Writers' Union was at the fore of Soviet cultural corps. The exceptional role of writers and other cultural figures in the building of Soviet socialism can be traced back to the creation in 1934 of the three major unions for writers, composers and artists. These came to serve as the principal channels through which the Party would patronize and, by the same token, exercise control over the arts.[4] At the time, Stalin called Soviet writers "engineers of human souls," adding that the "production of souls is more important than the production of tanks." This was no mere turn of phrase, but fundamental to the definition of socialist reconstruction, which began with the economic foundations and proceeded to the ideological superstructure.[5]

Archival evidence pointing to the inordinately huge amount of time that Stalin devoted to cultural matters would be hard to credit without an appreciation for how the arts had effectively replaced religion as a key institution during the transition from imperial Russian to Soviet rule.[6] Like the fascist dictatorships in Berlin and Rome during the interwar period, which made extensive and deliberate use of an ideological aesthetic to craft new forms of identity and politics, culture under Stalin served as "the critical interface between politics and mores in systematizing the value system and working out a code of values and behaviour."[7]

Little wonder then that the underprivileged and comparatively marginalized writers and artists in the interwar Lithuanian republic lobbied their government to emulate the corporatist cultural policies pursued in Berlin, Rome and Moscow. And little wonder that the intellectual elites in postwar Lithuania – those few that remained – were rather willing to accommodate themselves to the regime. In the command economy of Soviet Russia, the cultural intelligentsia came to form a privileged caste, receiving higher salaries, better apartments, and privileged access to special facilities and services.

From the mid-1930s onwards, the entire concept of being cultured took on a new importance in Soviet society, as it came to imply an entitlement to a prosperous life (*zazhitochnaya zhizn*) which had until recently been denounced as bourgeois.[8] Moreover, the tendency to provide exceptional privileges for the cultured elites only deepened in the postwar era of late Stalinism. Compared with the 1930s and the war years, the period from 1945 to 1953 witnessed a considerable increase in demands by cultural figures on the state to provide them with various benefits and privileges. Those in charge of the creative unions managed to broaden their power over the rank and file and to increase their autonomy from the Communist Party authorities.[9]

There was, of course, a price to be paid, as material rewards and ideological control went hand in hand. The doctrine for the new aesthetic was laid out in the tenets of socialist realism, the officially sanctioned method for the "truthful representation of Soviet reality in its revolutionary development."[10] Literature took pride of place among the arts of socialist realism for its ability to narrate the development of the personality over time, along the path towards ever-higher levels of socialist consciousness. Literature would become the most energetically promoted, as well as the most tightly controlled, form of cultural activity in postwar Soviet Lithuania.

Breeding literary offspring

The problem was that there were hardly any writers left after the war. The majority of the most famous authors of the interwar period like Vincas Krėvė or Bernardas Brazdžionis had emigrated to the West, and many of those who remained were killed or deported.[11] A small number of established writers like Balys Sruoga and Vincas Mykolaitis-Putinas (discussed in the previous chapter) had returned and joined the ranks of the Soviet Lithuanian writers, but they were considered less than fully reliable and – as distinct from architects – the authorities could not simply "parachute" reliable writers in from Moscow or Leningrad to solve the problem. If nothing else, the language barrier alone demanded the development of a new, indigenous corps of pro-Soviet writers.

The core of the initial literary cadres was drawn from among the left-leaning writers and intellectuals who were associated with the "Third Front," an antifascist, left-leaning literary journal published in Kaunas from 1930 to

1931. Kostas Korsakas (1909–86), Petras Cvirka (1909–47), Jonas Šimkus (1906–65), and Antanas Venclova (1906–71) would serve in turn as the first four chairman of the Lithuanian Writers' Union, which they founded during the first weeks of the first Soviet occupation in 1940.

Politically, they were a mix of romantic socialists and liberals, who looked during the interwar years to Soviet Russia as a progressive force and shared a hatred of the right-wing regime of Antanas Smetona. Recruited to high administrative positions in the Soviet hierarchy during the first occupation, they were evacuated to Moscow when the Germans invaded in 1941, continuing pro-Soviet agitation from there, and preparing for their eventual return to administer the new cultural institutions in 1944. Other prominent members of the Writers' Union included a younger group of Komsomol activists like Eduardas Mieželaitis and Alfonsas Bieliauskas, as well as established, popular writers with no socialist leanings like Vincas Mykolaitis-Putinas, Antanas Vienuolis, or Balys Sruoga, who were admitted "on probation" while they demonstrated their loyalty for the regime.

Transcripts from the early postwar meetings of the Lithuanian Writers' Union reveal an intense preoccupation with the *breeding* of young writers, in the literal sense of breeding literary "offspring" (*literatūrinis prieauglius*). The Writers' Union, along with the editorial boards of central and regional newspapers and magazines, the young writers' groups at schools, universities, factories and other institutions were to become "incubators" for new talent, where young writers would learn how to follow the ideological "furrows" of the new order and only then be allowed to address the public.

The implication that young writers could be bred like cattle or sown like wheat was not thought to be demeaning but simply reflected the Soviet rhetoric of production targets in agriculture and the rural origins of the young writers in question. The duty of literary mentorship went beyond young writers to embrace the battle for the hearts and mind of the next generation. According to Justas Paleckis, "The calling of the writer is to educate the young generation, which is surrounded by the spirit of clericalism, priests who are whispering and trying to seduce the young."[12]

Just as the reconstruction of the cities was viewed as a process of becoming "younger," the obsession with the cultivation of new talent reflected the legacy of Stalinist purges and the need to make an ideological break with the past. The purity of youth was to be preserved by "weeding out" aspiring writers who had compromised themselves by publishing in the Nazi press or through too close an association with "bourgeois" trends of the interwar period:

> Not all of our young colleagues are as young as they would like to be seen. Many have passed through Hitler's school and we find their names in the Nazi press. They cannot be allowed into our literature with this heritage, for the wounds of the German occupation remain in their consciousness.[13]

Given these constraints, the mentors and promoters of the new intelligentsia had to make difficult choices in the face of the urgency of fostering talent, the shortage of willing youth, and the political "unreliability" of writers with experience.

In some cases, the need for qualified literary cadres allowed those who had compromised themselves a chance at redemption. Kostas Kubilinskas (1923–62) was a talented poet who became one of the first heads of the young writers' section of the Union. But when his anti-Soviet satires published during the Nazi occupation were discovered, he was forced by the security services to prove his loyalty by infiltrating an underground partisan group, betraying it and personally killing one of its members, a fellow poet. However, such coercive measures were of no use when it came to the creation of a *new* intelligentsia. Immediate steps were taken to establish literary circles in gymnasiums, universities and other educational institutions, and to announce literary competitions to encourage the youth to publish in the local Soviet press. Those who did write were rewarded with flattery and various perks.

Indeed, the initial postwar years were a time of a great uncertainty, and many writers were still reluctant to have their name associated with the Soviet regime. Lithuanian émigré groups fanned expectations that America and the UK would liberate the Baltic States. For example, as late as 1952, the Voice of America broadcast an appeal by Vincas Krėvė, a famous writer and former foreign minister of interwar Lithuania who escaped to the West in 1944, assuring his fellow Lithuanians that the USA would come to their assistance and that "freedom was near."[14]

The resulting tendency to wait and see was fiercely attacked as the greatest of dangers by the leading figures of the Writers' Union and the Communist Party as a whole. As the military campaign against the resistance peaked in the late 1940s, Sniečkus issued a final warning to any wavering intellectuals:

> we must tear down the wall of silence and throw out everyone who is not with us ... We must give an opportunity for the intelligentsia to sort itself out so that we can see who is with us and who is against us.[15]

For their part, the partisans also tried to persuade the intelligentsia to take up the cause. Lionginas Baliukevičius-Dzūkas, an anti-Soviet partisan, writes in his diary:

> We sought urgently to publish a bulletin directed at the intelligentsia ... We had to address the indifference, passivity, sycophancy and exaggerated fear of the red horror displayed by members of our intelligentsia ... We wanted to transfer our enthusiasm and hoped that our words would move them to action.[16]

On the whole, these calls went unheeded, and very few intellectuals played an active role in the resistance. Moreover, defections to the Soviet side accelerated with the local launch of *Zhdanovshchina* in 1946.

Struggling to enforce a national boycott of Soviet institutions, the partisans equated publication of literary works with collaboration, and their bitterness towards "writers-collaborators" increased with time: "They have no regard for the nation's concerns. For a piece of silver they sell their pen, slander their homeland, soil the honorable name of Lithuania, desecrate their literature, and falsify their history."[17] Vladas Grybas, probably Soviet Lithuania's most famous young poet right after the war, constantly had to change his place of residence through fear of retribution, as did many other activists in the provinces.[18] About ten district newspaper editors were killed, and the partisans also targeted the heads of local reading rooms.[19]

But as Soviet power stabilized at the end of the 1940s, the Writers' Union managed to recruit more and more young people into its ranks. Material rewards played a role, as the honorariums for published articles were significant in the war-ravished country. The provision of housing for the more established writers, vouchers for stays at Writers' Union sanatoria on the coast of the Baltic Sea and all over the USSR, and innumerable other benefits had a decisive influence in an economy where the state had taken control of the redistribution of wealth.

And for rural youths of humble social origin, the honor of publication was a value in itself. In Lithuania, the role of literature and printed word in general was especially high due to the living memory of the press ban imposed by the Tsarist authorities until 1904, which prohibited printed materials in Lithuanian from using the Latin script. Among the rural population, literacy was still associated with a special moral quality or exceptional knowledge. Marcelijus Martinaitis recalls how his mother scolded him, insisting that writing was to be done by learned and holy men, and not people like him. "When I first saw my poem published, I felt above all a tremendous sense of honor. The payment seemed less important, for many of us the honor itself seemed more than enough."[20]

Less lofty motives also played a part, as Martinaitis recalls how he wanted to publish in order to impress the girls from his school. Similarly, poet Algimantas Baltakis notes the treatment he received during his first poetry reading in his native village of Leliūnai, including an enormous portrait of him hung on the wall, and a giant cake shared among the audience topped with his name written in icing.[21] Ultimately, the combination of moral and material incentives provided by the rapidly expanding infrastructure of the Soviet cultural machine won over a critical mass of creative youth.

The cult of youth

The sheer pace of social change was another factor driving the accommodation of Lithuanian youth to the Soviet regime. Sociologists have long argued that strongly marked generations tend to arise in societies where the values of the family or kinship unit have lost their relevance to the requirements of social advancement.[22] After 1789 in a rapidly modernizing Europe, for example, the opportunities presented to young men educated in universities and employed by bureaucracies gave them a sense of solidarity with their peers that took precedence over more traditional loyalties to family, clan or social estate.

Postwar Lithuania offers an extreme example of how rapid social change generates a sense of allegiance to a horizontal group of coevals looking towards the future. The generation of Lithuanians born around 1930 and who came of age during the onset of relative stability in the late 1940s were the first to benefit from the opportunities afforded by the postwar reconstruction. And because they were the first, they tended to occupy, and remain, in leading positions within the Soviet bureaucracy until the very end of the regime.

Given the rapid pace of change, their experience of war and the postwar period was markedly different from those who were just a couple of years older. Indeed, as pointed out by contemporaries, two people with basically the same background would often find it difficult to understand or relate to one another if they were separated by more than a few years of age. Other factors that marked writers as belonging to one group or another included when and where they first published, who and where they were during the first postwar years, and, of course, their social origin and how they were assessed by the authorities. The year of birth was not the exclusive factor in determining a person's generation, though. Some "fell out" of their generation because of political repression, and managed to reintegrate themselves into the system as ostensible members of the next generation. Others, like poet Vladas Grybas, succeeded in jumping ahead one generation by early entry into the world of communist activists and by not attending university.[23]

In general, those born before 1930 were much more likely to be drawn right into the violent vortex of the times, like Kostas Kubilinskas, born in 1923. Although Vladas Grybas was born later, in 1927, his professional career was launched before going to university and so he followed the path of those a few years his senior. He was quickly swept up by the demands of the Stalinist regime, wrote militantly ideological pieces and was rumoured to have been implicated in acts of repression.[24]

But after Stalin's death, that kind of hard-nosed militancy was no longer in strong demand, and Grybas was gradually shunned by his fellow writers. Although nobody expressed it openly at the time, in their recollections the highest-ranking members of the literary establishment viewed the likes of Grybas as "tainted" by the brutality of the early years of Stalinist occupation, and they did not wish to cast them as role-models for the next generation of Soviet Lithuanian youth.

For example, Antanas Venclova displays frequent indignation towards the young wartime generation of writers for their moral laxity, alcoholism and general debauchery.[25] He urged the Writers Union to use all means possible, "not to allow them [young writers] to perish" because "they are following the path whereby they will destroy their talent and themselves."[26]

He expressed similar concerns in his diary: "Jonynas, Macevičius and Pakalnis traveled to Marijampolė (Kapsukas) last week," Venclova records in his diary in 1956. "Macevičius was slightly drunk but Pakalnis could hardly stand on his feet and the public booed him of the stage. That is how our 'young friends' are raising the prestige of the Writers' Union."[27]

Notoriously, Kubilinskas and Grybas became degenerate alcoholics: the first literally drank himself to death one night at a writer's retreat in Moscow, and the second committed suicide in 1954. Reflecting on Grybas' suicide in his diary, Venclova blames not only alcoholism but "complete moral disintegration" and conveys that "it is probable" that Grybas' conscience was weighed by "some kind of crimes, even participation in executions."[28]

By way of contrast, Lithuanians born around 1930 were too young to be sent to the front in 1939, and so most of them witnessed World War II from the somewhat removed perspective of their poor, rural households. At fifteen or sixteen years of age, they were fully exposed to the trauma of the "war after the war" in the countryside. Indeed, virtually all those interviewed for this book who lived in villages during the insurgency recall this period as the most dramatic and traumatic time of their lives, noting that the city gave them a chance to escape and study at the rapidly expanding colleges and universities.

As a result, when they turned 18, they were the first generation to benefit from the stability after the defeat of the insurgency and the upward social mobility that came with postwar reconstruction. Instead of being pressed into service for the Soviets or the "forest brothers," they became students at university, a social status beyond their wildest dreams, and one that afforded the leisure and means to be young, to experience youth as a clearly defined phase of life.[29]

The Soviet Lithuanian authorities, like communist movements in general, cultivated youth as an ideal of change and modernization. Holding the promise of a brighter future, the young were seen to be superior to their parents in physical and moral terms. Unspoiled by bourgeois education, they were more receptive to progressive ideas and were more inclined to show initiative. The Soviets promoted a cult of youth in order to reshape young people in the image and likeness of the future, and by the same token to promote their role as harbingers of social change.

In the tumult of postwar Soviet Lithuania, young men who were born around 1930 and moved to the cities formed a remarkable group. The Thirties Generation, as they came to be called, included several of Lithuania's most successful and enduring cultural and political figures, such as Algirdas Brazauskas (1932–2010), the last leader of the Communist Party of Lithuania and first President of independent Lithuania, and Vytautas Landsbergis (b. 1932), the leader of the *Sąjūdis*, a popular movement against Soviet rule.[30]

Justinas Marcinkevičius (1930–2011), although little known outside of the country, was an iconic example of the progressive Soviet youth who would eventually rise to a status equal or superior to that of the nation's most popular political leaders. By the late Soviet period, he was commonly described as the conscience of the nation, much like the Czech Vaclav Havel.

Marcinkevičius was invited to open the founding meeting of Sąjūdis, and was later considered a serious candidate for President (though he never ran for office).[31]

Marcinkevičius and his peers, like Algimantas Baltakis (b. 1930) and Alfonsas Maldonis (1929–2007), were the poster children of this generation of writers, gaining rapidly in fame during the 1950s, and preserving their status at the

Figure 4.1 Algimantas Baltakis, Antanas Venclova and Justinas Marcinkevičius in Venclova's apartment. Vilnius, 1960

very top of the cultural hierarchy through to the end of the Soviet period. They were chosen as models for the Soviet youth and represented an entire social layer of Lithuanians who moved up to the forefront of the transformed society.

Little wonder that older members of the cultural establishment like Antanas Venclova and Justas Paleckis looked favourably at these youths as potential ideological role models for the next generations of Soviet Lithuanians. Their sporty, relatively sober lifestyles, handsome appearance and impeccable social origins in the Lithuanian village made them ideal figures for emulation. The image and reality of their success was only strengthened by way of contrast to the alcoholism, physical decline and moral compromise of those like Grybas or Kubilinskas, who had little chance to escape the grip of war and political repression. The exalted feeling of being privileged, young and able to enjoy it was thus a key dimension to the shared experience that defined the Thirties Generation.

Vilnius and the traumatic sublime

Katerina Clark describes the heady atmosphere of terror and elation felt by Russian intellectuals who were recruited by the Stalinist regime in the 1930s as the "imperial sublime." Raised by the state to the highest stations of fame and influence, they were at once completely dependent, trapped and enslaved by the system of privileges and subject at any time to arbitrary elimination.[32] A similar sense of fear and dread in the face of the destructive power of the Soviet regime, mixed with bewilderment and exhilaration at the adventure of the subject swept away by history, was felt by the young Lithuanians who moved to Vilnius after the war.

Nothing exemplifies the scale of cultural change more than the Lithuanization of the educational institutions in Vilnius. Vilnius University (which would be renamed in 1955 after the Lithuanian communist Vincas Kapsukas) opened its doors in October 1945 to over 800 students, with Lithuanians counting for 86 percent of all students. As one of the oldest and most prestigious universities in Eastern Europe, it was a bastion of Polish nationalism between the wars (when it bore the name Stefan Batory University) and was closed by the Lithuanian authorities when they annexed the city in 1939. The number of students rose rapidly from 800 in 1945 to 3,000 in 1950, with ethnic Lithuanians consistently making up for about 75–80 percent of the student population. In 1945, more than 2,000 students were registered at all Vilnius higher education institutes, of whom 1,620 were Lithuanians, 210 Poles, 140 Russians and 50 Belarusians. These numbers would multiply in the coming years, with Lithuanians always forming the great majority of students.[33]

An intense campaign to recruit young people from all over the country to join in the ranks of literary workers did not bypass the institutions of higher education. Young students at Vilnius University were quickly embroiled in the literary life of the new Soviet Lithuanian capital. They joined the young writers' section at the Lithuanian Soviet Writers' Union, published their poems in a high-circulation (5,000 copies) almanac dedicated to the literary works of young writers, poets, critics and translators called *Jaunieji*, and were taken under the wing of the older literary mentors.[34] The mode of poetry and literature in Lithuania during Stalin's time strictly adhered to the general canons of socialist realism. Draft literary works were subjected to intense criticism; authors were forced to correct mistakes of tone, of themes, of associations, until they attained the appropriate mix of ideological orthodoxy, optimism and militancy. Students were taught to emulate the propaganda slogans and odes of praise to party leaders in a Mayakovskian style with short and rough lines, and simple, almost childish rhymes.

The poster children of this lucky cohort, Marcinkevičius, Baltakis and Maldonis, all entered Vilnius University as freshmen in 1949. Each was the first of his family to get a higher education. At the time, the writing of poetry was an inseparable part of social interaction. Students would write couplets on the back of photographs or in messages to each other and kept special handwritten notebooks with excerpts from poems. One's performance in this area was a source of prestige and, most importantly, attraction to members of the opposite sex. Moreover, with the legacy of the press ban on writing in Lithuanian script still in people's living memory, writing and publishing in Lithuanian – no matter what the circumstances – was still felt as a patriotic duty.

When asked to describe his feelings at the time, Baltakis conveys a sense of exhilaration and pride: "We were young," he said. "We were happy that the war was over, that we could go to university." In spite of the difficult economic times and the grim political atmosphere, they nevertheless made a show of their new-found status as upwardly mobile urbanites:

> We bought hats, we rubbed our cloth shoes with chalk until they were shining white, and walked down the streets singing Lithuanian folk songs. Some Poles passed by us on the street and I heard them whisper: "the Lithuanians are singing."[35]

Such reminiscences display an acute awareness of being on the winning side of an historical struggle, and taking an active part in the formation of a common destiny. Indeed, the conflict with the Poles still simmered after the war. Vytautė Žilinskaitė recalls getting hit in the head by a stone thrown by a Polish youth, while she herself teased her Polish peers by referring to the Polish eagle as a chicken.[36] Marcinkevičius recalls the same singing as Baltakis, and links it explicitly to the achievement of widely felt national aspirations:

> When we had a break between lectures we, boys, went out into the university yard, sat down around the empty fountain and sang. When I think about it now, I wonder why we sang so much. Perhaps we intuitively felt that Lithuanians are singing here for the first time in their history, in the history of Vilnius.[37]

Nonetheless, the sense of historical triumph could not overcome the unease of displacement or the sense of cultural strangeness when faced with the concrete reality of Vilnius. Many were struck by the contrast between the image of the city they had formed in their minds as schoolboys in the interwar republic, and the reality that they encountered as young adults. For example, at primary school, like the rest of his generation, Marcinkevičius had memorized the patriotic couplets: "To Vilnius, to Vilnius, to our beloved land, there to the Gediminas mound, among our brothers." But upon his arrival, he was amazed and disappointed at the sight of Gediminas castle. Unlike his imaginary vision, the actual structure was quite diminutive and possessed a single rather humble tower. "I thought that there would be at least the palace of Dukes but I could not even find that."[38]

Similar references are made in the recollections of other aspiring young intellectuals after the war.

> I arrived in the train station and immediately got lost. From the hill I saw a beautiful image of the city – church peaks, towers, a castle. But when I walked down, I was overcome by horror. Ruins, dirt, the stench of herring in the stores, and nobody could converse in Lithuanian.

Such were the initial impressions of Vilnius as recalled by Martinaitis, who was especially struck by the contrast between Vilnius and the interwar capital Kaunas where "one could still sense the aura of former luxury – shiny store windows, ladies dressed from whatever was left from before the war, and gentlemen with canes and dogs."[39]

The new arrivals themselves stood out and were easily recognizable by the signs of their own distinct civilization:

> I took my first stroll down the main street of Kaunas decked out in the pants and jacket that my mother had sewn from coarse linen, carrying a wooden box that my father had made for me. Within a few minutes a pack of street kids followed after me calling: "Look at the peasant, look at the peasant!"[40]

In this context, the newly arrived bonded together from isolation as much as opportunity. As recalled by Marcinkevičius: "Perhaps it was the war or the terrible times that we had just lived through, but somehow we naturally bonded with each other. You could not call it a family but it was something like a family."[41] The elation caused by undreamed-of social advancement, of being the "masters" of the dream city of Vilnius and making an active contribution to the building of the nation combined with the dread of collaborating with a foreign occupation and the terror of arbitrary violence.

They all shared a strong reluctance to discuss the traumatic experiences they had escaped from in the countryside. "I do not recall anybody ever talking about the experience in the village. This was something that people simply did not talk about," recalls Algirdas Pocius, born in 1930, who arrived in Vilnius to become a radio journalist and one of the more prominent members of the Writers' Union. His words are echoed by Marcinkevičius:

> We never talked about the past, not even with friends. Of course, we had seen a lot. In the university choir where I sang, the two boys on each side of me in the bass section disappeared. They simply stopped coming to the rehearsals. Maybe they were tipped off about a deportation order, but we didn't talk about it. We just avoided that part of our lives, like a painful past that was buried somewhere.[42]

Each individual has his own story, but the common theme is that a move to the city was one of the ways to escape from the crossfire of the countryside – especially for those youngsters who were potential recruits for both sides. Even after the intense fighting stopped, the villages were desolate and increasingly impoverished, as collectivization took hold. It was obvious to many that to go and study was a way to escape this grim atmosphere.[43] For these young men who had just left the closely knit communities of their home villages, city life provided

Figure 4.2 Antanas Sutkus, *Greeting the New Year at the Writers' Union Club*. From left to right: Stasys Krasauskas, Alfonsas Maldonis, Algimantas Baltakis, Justinas Marcinkevičius. Vilnius, 1960
Courtesy of Venclovas House Museum.

their first experience of modern loneliness, as distinct from solitude, that can be found only in the impersonal urban environment, as well as a powerful sense of belonging and participating in a great historical project.

Notes

1 Kostas Korsakas, "Tarybinių rašytojų pareigos ir uždaviniai," *Tarybų Lietuva* 93 (8 October 1944). Lithuanian Archive of Literature and Arts, f. 34, a. 1, b. 1, 27.

2 Jonas Krikščiūnas (Jovaras), stenogram of a speech delivered on October 27, 1945 at the First Convention of the Soviet Lithuanian Writers Union. *Pirmasis Lietuvos Tarybinių rašytojų suvažiavimas, October 25–28, 1945.* Lithuanian Archive of Literature and Arts, f. 34, a. 1, b. 1, 56.

3 "Lietuvio poeto kelias" (The Path of the Lithuanian Poet)" *Laisvės balsas* (May 20, 1953). In *Partizanai apie pasaulį, politiką ir save. 1944–1956 m. partizanų spaudos publikacijos,* ed. N. Gaškaitė-Žemaitienė (Vilnius: Lietuvos gyventojų genocido ir rezistencijos tyrimų centras, 1998), 601.

4 Vera Tolz, "Cultural Bosses as Patrons and Clients: The Functioning of the Soviet Creative Unions in the Postwar Period," *Contemporary European History* 11.1 (2002): 87–105.

5 Oleg Khlevniuk, *Politbiuro. Mekhanismy politicheskoi vlasti v 1930-e gody.* (Moscow: Rosspen, 1996), 42, 112.

6 Katerina Clark, *The Fourth Rome,* 10.

7 Katerina Clark, *The Fourth Rome,* 10.

8 Sheila Fitzpatrick, *Everyday Stalinism: Ordinary Life in Extraordinary Times: Soviet Russia in the 1930s* (Oxford: Oxford University Press, 2000), 90–93.

9 Vera Tolz, "Cultural Bosses as Patrons and Clients: The Functioning of the Soviet Creative Unions in the Postwar Period," *Contemporary European History* 11.1 (2002): 87–105.

10 Katerina Clark, *The Soviet Novel: History as Ritual* (Chicago, IL: University of Chicago Press, 1981).

11 Aušra-Marija Jurašienė, "The Problem of Creative Artistic Expression in Contemporary Lithuania," *Lituanus* 22.3 (Fall 1976): 28–54.

12 Justas Paleckis, stenogram of a speech delivered on October 2, 1946 at a meeting of the Soviet Lithuanian Writers Union. *LTSR Rašytojų visuotinio susirinkimo stenogramos ir rezoliucija,* Lithuanian Archive of Literature and Arts, f. 34, ap. 1, b. 20, 112.

13 Kostas Korsakas, stenogram of a speech delivered on October 27, 1945 at the First Convention of the Soviet Lithuanian Writers Union. *Pirmasis Lietuvos Tarybinių rašytojų suvažiavimas, 1945 October 25–28,* Lithuanian Archive of Literature and Arts, f. 34, a. 1, b. 1.

14 "Vinco Krėvės kalba septyniasdešimtmečio proga," Amerikos balsas, Philadelphia, July 7, 1952. Lietuvos centrinis valstybės archyvas. Vaizdo ir garso dokumentų skyrius, Vilnius.

15 Vytautas Tininis, *Sniečkus: 33 metai valdžioje* (Vilnius: Lietuvos karo akademija, 2000), 99.

16 Lionginas Baliukevičius, *Partizano Dzūko dienoraštis* (Vilnius: LGGRTC, 2006).

17 Citation from "Lietuvio poeto kelias" (The Path of the Lithuanian Poet) *Laisvės balsas* (May 20, 1953).

18 For a detailed account of the struggle with collaborators, see Pocius, *Kita mėnulio pusė.* Rytis Trimonis, *Vladas Grybas* (Vilnius: Vaga, 1989), 57–58.

19 LSSR MGB 2-N valdybos 6 poskyrio viršininko kpt. Ščerbakovo 1947 m. gruodžio 12 d. pažyma "Apie banditinių išpuolių metu patirtus nuostolius nuo 1947.01.01 iki 1947.12.10" (On the damages incurred during bandit attacks from 1947.01.01

to 1947.12.10), Lietuvos ypatingasis archyvas, f. K-1, ap. 3, b. 31/12, l. 101. This information, drawn from a Soviet police report in the Lithuanian State Archives, was provided by historian Mindaugas Pocius.

20 Marcelijus Martinaitis, Interview by author. Audio recording. Vilnius, March 12, 2009.
21 In Valentinas Sventickas, *Paskui pėsčią paukštį* (Vilnius: Vaga, 1988), 13.
22 S.N. Eisenstadt, *From Generation to Generation. Age Groups and Social Structure* (London: Routledge and Kegan Paul, 1956).
23 Marcelijus Martinaitis, "Eduardas Mieželaitis, bet ne tas" in *Eduardas Mieželaitis: Post scriptum* (Vilnius: Rašytojų sąjungos leidykla, 2008), 31.
24 Marcelijus Martinaitis, Interview by author. Audio recording. Vilnius, November 12, 2008.
25 Antanas Venclova, Diary. (May 2, 1956): 33–34. Venclovas House Museum Archives, Vilnius.
26 Antanas Venclova, *Congress of Young Writers. May 12, 1951*. Lithuanian Archive of Literature and the Arts, f. 34, a. 1, b. 54, p. 35.
27 Antanas Venclova, Diary. (March 22, 1956): 9. Venclovas House Museum Archives, Vilnius.
28 Antanas Venclova, Diary. (May 2, 1956): 33–34. Venclovas House Museum Archives, Vilnius. Some émigré Lithuanians like Alexandras Shtromas held a significantly different opinion of Grybas, considering his alcoholism and suicide as testimony to the fact that he was never a true conformist, as opposed to Marcinkevičius and his peers. See Aleksandras Shtromas, "Official Soviet Ideology and the Lithuanian People," in Rimvydas Šilbajoris, ed. *Mind against the Wall: Essays on Lithuanian Culture Under Soviet Occupation* (Chicago, IL: Institute of Lithuanian Studies Press, 1983), 63.
29 Stephen Lovell, "Introduction," *Generations in Twentieth Century Europe* (Basingstoke: Macmillan, 2007), 5.
30 As mentioned above, Kaunas-born Landsbergis is the exception that proves the rule that the majority of the Generation of 1930 came from the villages.
31 Marcinkevičius became a national cult figure on the basis of the wild popularity of his works, especially the trilogy of dramas: *Mindaugas, Mažvydas* and *Katedra*, which were received as a kind of return of Lithuanian historical memory during the Soviet era. He died on 16 February 2011, and was given a state funeral that was attended by tens of thousands. In a coincidence felt by many Lithuanians as a sign of fate, February 16 is Lithuania's national holiday, marking the day when Lithuanian independence was first declared in 1918. Jonas Basanavičius, one of the leaders of Lithuania's national revival in the late nineteenth century and now known as the "Patriarch" of the Lithuanian nation, also died on February 16, 1927.
32 Clark, *The Fourth Rome*, 276–306.
33 Theodore Weeks, "A Multi-ethnic City in Transition: Vilnius' Stormy Decade, 1939–49," *Eurasian Geography and Economics* 47.2 (2006): 169.
34 Jonas Vosylius, ed. *Literatūra: dokumentų rinkinys* (Vilnius: Academia, 1991), 21.
35 Algimantas Baltakis, Interview by author. Audio recording. Vilnius, October 14, 2007.
36 Vytautė Žilinskaite, Interview by author. Audio recording. Vilnius, October 11, 2011.
37 Justinas Marcinkevičius, Interview by author. Audio recording. Vilnius, January 3, 2010.
38 Ibid.
39 Marcelijus Martinaitis, Interview by author. Audio recording. Vilnius, March 12, 2009.
40 Ibid.
41 Justinas Marcinkevičius, Interview by author. Audio recording. Vilnius, January 6, 2010.
42 Ibid. See also Violeta Davoliūtė, "Mūsų kursas buvo ypatingas – daug poetų, daug savižudžių" (Our Year was Special: Many Poets, Many Suicides. Interview with Justinas Marcinkevičius) *Kultūros barai* 2 (March 2011): 43–46.
43 Interviews with Pocius, Areška, Martinaitis, Baltakis, Marcinkevičius, personal communication with Bronius Raguotis and others.

5   Soviet Lithuanian renaissance

All I hear from you is modernism, modernism. So to hell with you: let there be modernism! Just make sure that it is our own, native, Lithuanian, Soviet modernism.[1]

Antanas Sniečkus

Stalin died just as Marcinkevičius and his cohort were graduating from university and beginning their professional careers. The authorities immediately allowed a greater degree of political, economic and cultural freedom, instilling hope for a new start, as well as some fear of uncertainty, throughout the Soviet Union. In his "Secret Speech" to the Twentieth Party Congress of the CPSU in 1956, Khrushchev condemned Stalin's use of terror as a criminal excess. Millions of prisoners and exiles were amnestied, and many returned home, including tens of thousands of Lithuanian deportees.

Meanwhile, the Hungarian Uprising had an echo of unrest in the Baltics. Moscow's decision to allow the deportees to return was taken without consulting the national communist leaders in the republics. In Lithuania, Antanas Sniečkus was taken aback and feared the political destabilization that the return of the deportees might cause. Indeed, the All Souls' Day tradition of lighting candles at cemeteries turned into mass protests in November 1956 as crowds of students in Vilnius and Kaunas sang patriotic songs and marched to the city centres, calling for independent Lithuania, for the departure of the Russians, and clashing with police.[2]

The protests were contained, however, and passed off as an act of ordinary hooligans. A few university officials were dismissed, but the broader process of cultural liberalization continued.[3] Previously banned works of literature, including several canonical texts of the national movement from the nineteenth century, were published. The publication of biographies of artists and writers from the interwar period "rehabilitated" many previously taboo names, thus serving to legitimate a large part of the cultural heritage of that period too.[4]

Important writers such as Antanas Miškinis (1905–83), Valys Drazdauskas (1906–81) and Juozas Keliuotis (1902–83) returned from Siberian exile and resumed creative work, although they were subjected to close monitoring and ideological pressure. The regime strove to incorporate elements of national

Lithuanian identity into Soviet historiography. This had begun already in 1949 with the first efforts to write a history of the LSSR, but the first significant result of this effort appeared only in 1957 with the publication of a history textbook for high-school children.[5]

In this dynamic, contradictory social context, an entire new class of young Lithuanian artists, writers and musicians went through their formative years. They were created through the patronage of a state that provided a guaranteed level of income and status higher than anything that previous generations of intellectuals could have expected.

De-Stalinization, however, did not spell an end to the goal of Sovietization through individual and social transformation. Instead, by renouncing terror as a tool of policy, Khrushchev hoped to revive popular support for modernization, to trigger reforms from below. The cultural Thaw was not anti-Soviet in inspiration but aimed rather at creating an authentic, grass-roots Soviet culture. The cult of sincerity, the expression of genuine feelings and emotions were part and parcel of what was described at the time as the "modernization" of Soviet literature, with lyrical poetry taking centre stage.[6]

In Lithuania, this process would be led by the new generation of postwar intellectuals. They absorbed and replicated the cultural models of the Thaw developed in Moscow and Leningrad, adapting them to the specific social circumstances of postwar Lithuania and blending them with the revival of interwar cultural traditions. In the decade after Stalin's death, the postwar intelligentsia would come into their own as the constructors of the modern, Soviet Lithuanian nation.[7]

After 1956, Lithuanian literature and other forms of cultural expression burst into the forefront of public discussion and progressive change, securing its position as *the* arena for serious exchanges of ideas that would be maintained until the collapse of the Soviet Union. After years of Stalinist repression, Lithuanian literature and the arts would go through a veritable renaissance, and it was in this new cultural sphere where the contours of the new Soviet Lithuanian identity were formed and disseminated.

The strength of national communism

The political and cultural effects of de-Stalinization were magnified in Lithuania by the strength and cohesion of the national communist leadership. Having served as the First Secretary of the Lithuanian Communist Party since 1927, Sniečkus exercised considerable authority in Moscow. He enjoyed the trust of Stalin and had proven his loyalty during the course of his long career as a communist, which had begun in Voronezh, the city to which he was evacuated during World War I along with the other pupils at the Vilnius gymanasium where he had been studying in 1915.[8]

There, among the large Lithuanian émigré community, Sniečkus became involved in leftist circles and soon became a committed communist, under the tutelage of Zigmas Angarietis, one of the leaders of the Lithuanian

Communist Party (CPL). His enthusiasm was such that he volunteered to join the Red Army in 1918 to fight in the Civil War. Given his age – a mere fifteen years – Sniečkus was encouraged instead to return to Lithuania as an agent of the Commintern.[9]

After his appointment as First Secretary at the age of 24, Sniečkus kept his position as the unchallenged leader of Soviet Lithuania until his death in 1972 and appears to have shielded Lithuania from excessive interference from Moscow. In sharp contrast to the communist party elites in the other national republics, the Lithuanian communists were never purged, and maintained an unusual level, by Soviet standards, of corporate autonomy in their affairs, especially as concerns cultural and economic matters.[10]

Sniečkus's ability to stay one step ahead of the policy process in Moscow was due in part to his readiness to clamp down well before being told to do so. For example, in April 1945, more than a year before Stalin and Zhdanov tightened the ideological screws, Sniečkus declared a war against "bourgeois nationalism" in history, literature and the arts: "We have to revise the cultural heritage of the Lithuanian nation and throw out everything that is reactionary."[11] He also benefitted from close relations with Mikhail Suslov, a frequent visitor to Vilnius as chair of the Central Committee bureau for Lithuanian affairs from 1944–46, and a key figure in the Kremlin in charge of foreign affairs and ideology until his death in 1982.[12]

In the spring of 1953, Lavrenty Beria and Georgy Malenkov launched an initiative to release state ministries from the interference of party functionaries. This coincided with the acceleration of the indigenization of local cadres. It was believed in Lithuania that Beria told Sniečkus and the Lithuanian leadership to "take the nationalization of politics … in their hands." Declassified MVD reports from the period reveal widespread expectations that all Russian communists would be called back to Russia, with Lithuanians taking their place.[13]

Beria was soon arrested and executed, but the indigenization of cadres in Lithuania proceeded unabated. Sniečkus took advantage of the leadership crisis, as well as the purge that accompanied Beria's liquidation, to advance more Lithuanians to high party and government posts. Thousands of Russian white-collar workers were repatriated from Lithuania: statistics of party membership from 1952 to 1956 show that membership in the CPL grew by 3,355 members, while 12,938 individuals joined the party during exactly the same period, meaning that some 9,000–10,000 members were either purged from the party or transferred to another jurisdiction.[14]

The second round of indigenization occurred between the Secret Speech and 1959. This wave of new Lithuanian recruits represented the new generation of graduates of Lithuanian universities and the advancement of the newly trained technical and cultural intelligentsia.[15] Young people were pushed to top posts at the expense of older Lithuanian and non-Lithuanian communists appointed under Stalin. From 1956 to 1959, the number of CPL members grew by 11,027, while 15,156 individuals joined the party, which suggests that once again the Lithuanian communists were able to purge Russians from their ranks by enforcing requirements that various functionaries and administrators know the native language. By 1959, the overwhelming majority of people in leading government and party posts were under 40, and mostly Lithuanian.[16]

And beyond the cultural elites, the mass migration of young Lithuanians to the cities was changing the face of Vilnius. Until the early 1950s, in-migrants from outside of Lithuania made up about half of the newly arriving population in Vilnius, with the other half coming from within Lithuanian territory. After 1950, an increasing percentage of new inhabitants of Vilnius came from within Lithuania: 60 percent between 1952 and 1957, and 73 percent between 1963–65. As recalled by Vilnius resident Vytautė Žilinskaitė:

> Nobody talks about this now but I personally saw how the city was becoming Lithuanian … We lived near Aušros Vartai [the Ostra Brama gate], where the Pedagogical Institute had a number of lecture halls. We saw a steady stream of girls going to the institute – very many of them. Their hands were worn from milking cows and other farm work. They were wearing slippers for lack of better footwear … They were all Lithuanians, so that was how it all started … This was around 1953.[17]

Critically, Lithuanians did not only become the majority in the city, but they were overrepresented in the spheres of technical engineers (57 percent),

Figure 5.1 Antanas Sutkus, *University.* Students signing up for entrance exams to Vilnius University. Vilnius, 1959
Courtesy of Antanas Sutkus.

enterprise management (67 percent) state administration (70 percent) and, most importantly, science, culture and education (80 percent). The only area where Lithuanians were under-represented was in the law-enforcement and secret services. Meanwhile, Poles were the least well represented in the intellectual fields.[18]

Indeed, the unspoken battle with Polish and Russian culture for dominance in Vilnius was acutely felt by Lithuanian intellectuals at the time. The demographic changes in favor of the Lithuanian population of Vilnius were clearly noticeable and a source of pride and excitement. A 1963 entry in the private diary of Valys Drazdauskas reflects a mood of cautious excitement in face of the ever-present reality of foreign occupation.

> Vilnius. Here, the fatal battle for Lithuania is taking place: to be or not to be. If Lithuanians will constitute 51 percent of the city's population in the next ten to fifteen years, the battle will be won. I believe that it will be won. The entire countryside is giving its best forces to Vilnius. Meanwhile, criminals and vagabonds are still arriving from Russia. Although we are still the minority in Vilnius, we are stronger intellectually and morally than the majority that has been thrown here from afar. Yes, the battle will be won, so long as there are no more deportations. But will there be no more deportations?[19]

Similarly, Justas Vincas Paleckis (the son of the Chairman of the Presidium Justas Paleckis) was working as a reporter for the youth daily *Komjaunimo tiesa* (*Truth of the Komsomol*). He was covering the development of factories in the Vilnius area and recalls the palpable demographic transformation of the city, as newly built factories were filled with Lithuanian rather than Russian-speaking workers and engineers. Later, as a student at the Diplomatic Academy in Moscow in the 1960s, during his weekend trips home to Vilnius, he would walk down a popular pedestrian street and tally how many passers-by were speaking in Lithuanian or Russian. "The proportion was always growing in favor of Lithuanian, and this immediately improved my mood."[20] Architects and urban planners like Vytautas Brėdikis and Algimantas Nasvytis also recall a sense that young Lithuanians in their fields of work were taking the lead from the older generation of "imported" specialists.[21]

The repression of the returnees

If the mass displacement of ethnic Lithuanians from the villages to the cities and their accomodation within the institutions of Soviet power had a transformative effect on mainstream Soviet Lithuanian society, other forms of displacement continued to relegate those real or imagined sources of resistance to the margins of society. Just as the deportees were created as a class by the initial act of displacement, their subsequent identity and place in society was shaped by their experience of return to a society that was completely different from the one they had left over a decade before.

During the five-year period after Stalin's death, about 4 million prisoners were released from the Gulag, shrinking the imprisoned population throughout the USSR by a factor of five. The problem of social reintegration for so large a population was felt throughout the Soviet Union, as local communities generally treated the Gulag returnees as criminals and pariahs, devising a multitude of measures to ensure their continued marginalization, in spite of directives from Moscow stating that they were to be given housing and employment within two weeks of their return.[22]

Former deportees started to return to Lithuania in 1956, with the initial release of about 17,000 people. These numbers grew after 1958 to reach a total of 80,000 by 1970.[23] The communist Lithuanian leadership and the local security services were strongly against Khrushchev's decision to amnesty and to allow their return. Sniečkus was livid at what he described as the careless experimentation of Khrushchev. A declassified report of the local KGB complains that the deportees were "erroneously and prematurely released from incarceration." The security services believed they "had not renounced their hostile views of Soviet power" and "exerted negative influence on unstable segments of the population," and that they would resume "their efforts to form an anti-Soviet nationalist underground."[24]

As a result, the returnees were subject to ongoing surveillance, they were allowed to travel abroad only in exceptional cases, and their movements within the LSSR were often watched. If there was any suspicion of involvement in subversive activities, the deportees were often subjected to public denunciation and compromise in the local press, reinforcing their exclusion from society.[25]

Notably, the exclusion faced by returnees was not only or even primarily imposed from above, but also very much a Lithuanian affair; although the one does not exclude the other. The social vulnerability of some deportees increased their vulnerability to manipulation and coercion by the security services. In exchange for an offer to erase the stigma of deportation from their official documents, a number of deportees, and even the children of deportees who had never been imprisoned, agreed to serve as KGB informants.[26]

When the deportees began to come back after the death of Stalin, the communities to which they returned were not the same as before. Already in 1946, Algimantas Indriūnas, who returned illegally to Lithuania even before the death of Stalin, wrote: "Having returned to Lithuania I felt that here life moved a couple decades ahead, while I did not even stay in the same spot but moved some decades back."[27] Indeed, both groups had undergone a profound transformation; one might say there were now two nations of Soviet Lithuania, both shaped by displacement.

Those who returned in the 1950s or later felt the social schism in even stronger terms. The deportees were often met with broad suspicion and were seen as a source of unnecessary trouble. People were afraid that the returnees would lay claims to their former property, thus disrupting the stability that had recently been established. There was also a widespread fear of the criminal ways that the deportees had allegedly adopted during their incarceration; they were seen as no better than the criminals whose company they had kept.

The social stigma of criminality extended even to the children of deportees. Joana Jakštaitė-Kurmelavičienė, who was deported with her family and returned in 1958, recalls how many parents would complain at meetings that the school "took in all sorts of bandit families, and now they will harm our children." Algirdas Janulevičius describes how the *propiska* system of registering one's place of registration was abused to keep returnees marginalized: "I could not register for half a year. I did not register because I was not employed, and yet nobody would employ a deportee because he wasn't registered. ... We were treated as lepers although we were not told so directly."[28] Some were forced to move or were recruited to work outside of the LSSR, like the family of Birutė Mickevičiūtė-Bičkauskienė, deported in 1947 as a teenager. After an unsuccessful attempt to integrate in Lithuania after her return in 1952, she had to settle with her family in Kaliningrad.[29]

Indeed, a report of a commission sent by the USSR Council of Ministers to investigate the integration of returnees took note of the extent to which Lithuanian municipalities created artificial administrative barriers to the reintegration of Gulag returnees. Similar measures were noted in Gorky, Baku and Yerevan, but the Lithuanian municipalities were singled out in this report for the range of measures they deployed. Duplicating the function of the existing police passport bureau, special municipal commissions were created to review requests for registration. The minimum "sanitary norm," or minimal living space per person, was arbitrarily raised, and many returnees were issued only temporary registration instead of permanent cards that were necessary to secure employment.[30]

Poetry and patronage

Notably, the social marginalization of the former deportees took place against the background of the increasingly broad accommodation of mainstream Lithuanian society to Soviet rule, and the growing confidence among the intellectuals that their choice to work within the system would not be in vain and could make a contribution to the development of the nation. The strength of institutional nationalism in Soviet Lithuania allowed for a broad and far-reaching compromise between the rulers and the ruled; and between the Lithuanian communist party leadership and the creative elites in particular. In exchange for displays of loyalty and membership in the communist party, intellectuals were left free to preserve and advance Lithuanian culture.[31]

It is in the context of this relatively liberal political environment and increasing assertiveness of the Lithuanian cultural elites that its postwar generation became the active constructors of a new Soviet Lithuanian identity. Cultural achievement gave them a sense of fulfilment, and allowed them to put aside the sense of guilt that weighed upon the older generation that was scarred by the years of war: "The Thaw gave more than this minimum. It consolidated their sense of belonging to a distinct generation and the idea that they perhaps are starting a new era."[32]

In practical terms, the development of the new class of Soviet Lithuanian intellectuals followed a pattern similar to that described by Barbara Walker and other students of the Russian intelligentsia, which involved a "complex pattern of networking and clientelist behavior which centred on the intelligentsia circle or *kruzhok.*" The state distributed its resources through these circles and the resulting patron–client relationships created cliques of intellectuals that had an enduring and strong corporate personality.[33] In the post-Stalin era, one of the most important circles of intellectuals was formed by Eduardas Mieželaitis as the "patron," and Marcinkevičius, Baltakis and Maldonis as the "clients."

The relationship was one of creative as well as political tutelage. For example, shortly after the student demonstrations of 1956, Baltakis recalls how Mieželaitis advised him and his peers against indulging in either protest or passivity.

> Miežis brought a bottle, he sat us down. We were like his team. "I see through you as if with an x-ray," he said. "I see that you are still waiting for something, hesitating, hoping that there will still be something different here. But look. There was the forest, and who helped? Nobody. Now in the middle of Europe, they beat up the Hungarians. And who helped? Nobody. I'm telling you, Soviet power is here to stay, for as long as you'll live. If you want to do something, you have to make the Party Lithuanian. We should be the bosses here, and not some outsiders."[34]

Mieželaitis was indeed a pivotal figure in the development of the postwar literary intelligentsia. Born in 1919, he was older than the Generation of 1930, but still considerably younger than leaders of the cultural *nomenklatura* like Antanas Venclova (1906–71) or Kostas Korsakas (1909–86). Mieželaitis joined the communist underground during the interwar period, but he was really more of a romantic socialist. His literary formation was influenced by the famous interwar poetess Salomėja Nėris (1904–45), known for her emotional poetic style and melodic rhymes. In terms of his age, temperament and ideology, he served as a bridge between the interwar and the postwar generations of writers.

Mieželaitis was already an old hand in the complex politics of Soviet Lithuanian culture, and his emergence as a figure of influence during de-Stalinization was representative of the times. In 1946, he was caught up in the *Zhdanovshchina* and was scandalously reprimanded for his collection of poems called *The Wind of the Homeland*, which combined Soviet motifs with a folksy, neo-romantic Lithuanian poetic mode usually associated with the last decade of the interwar period in Lithuania.[35] He was temporarily "excommunicated" from the fold of acceptable writers and went through a period of "repentance," writing children's poetry as well as strictly orthodox Stalinist works, all the while drinking heavily.

Nonetheless, Mieželaitis not only survived but re-emerged as a "progressive" cultural figure during the time of the Thaw, when the "modernization" of culture became the new orthodoxy. After Stalin's death, he staged a political and literary comeback with the rehabilitation of *The Wind of the Homeland* and the publication of a new collection of poetry called *My Nightingale* in 1956. Young Lithuanian writers, starving for anything aside from hymns of praise to Stalin and the Party, devoured this work, which they saw as organically connected to the prewar poetic tradition of using folklore in modern poetry. Mieželaitis quickly became the leader of the literary circle (*kruzhok*) to which the poster children of the postwar era – Baltakis, Maldonis and Marcinkevičius – belonged. At the same time, his official status as the leading Soviet Lithuanian writer was firmly established with the award of a Lenin Prize for his cycle of poems entitled *The Man* in 1962.[36]

Algirdas Julius Greimas, the renowned French semiotician of Lithuanian origin, noted how Mieželaitis' poetry revived the spirit of the interwar avant-garde, particularly the Four Winds movement of the mid-1920s: "The same search for a person, the world, and for the literary form, the same hysteria and shouting. I checked the date of publication several times: indeed, it was not 1926, but 1962."[37] Younger members of the cultural elite recall the exceptional role that Mieželaitis played in breaking down the barriers to modern, global trends in culture.[38] But while Mieželaitis rose to the very peak of official Soviet Lithuanian culture, the appeal of his modernist work did not extend to the broad populace. Instead, it would be the next generation that grew up under his wing that would make a genuine connection with Lithuanians at large.

The twentieth spring

Indeed, by the time Mieželaitis was awarded the Lenin Prize and was informally crowned the "Prince of Poets," it was increasingly clear that Justinas Marcinkevičius was emerging as the most authoritative representative of Soviet Lithuanian culture and identity with deep appeal among the reading public.

Marcinkevičius continued the trend that Mieželaitis started of reconnecting with the poetic tradition of Lithuanian folklore with the publication of his first collection of poetry in 1955, *I Plead for a Word*. A year later, the publication of *The Twentieth Spring* would propel Marcinkevičius to the peak of literary popularity, especially among the youth. With its overt reference to the hope unleashed by Khrushchev's historic intervention at the Twentieth Party Congress, *The Twentieth Spring* was awarded a state prize in 1957 and published (and republished) in many thousands of copies.

In-depth reviews published in practically every regional journal and newspaper in the country heralded *The Twentieth Spring* as marking the birth of a new generation of Soviet Lithuanians. Structured as an epic poem and written in an easy, lyrical manner, it combines folk songs, feuilletons and propagandistic couplets into a naïve, melodramatic plot about the journey of a young

Lithuanian man who goes from his village to Vilnius to study – a story of survival and arrival that resonated strongly with the experience of many Lithuanians at the time.

The original edition, enhanced by a handsome photograph of the author and illustrated with stylized folk lithographs made by a local artist, testified to Lithuania's book-publishing renown within the Soviet Union. It was genuinely popular and a much-loved work, especially among the youth, many of whom memorized the poem in its entirety.[39]After years of dreary Stalinist imitations of Soviet classics, it was not only the first popular work that tapped deeply into the folksy traditions of Lithuanian literature, but also the first to represent what Marcinkevičius and so many Lithuanians were living through at this time, namely, dislocation from the country to the towns.

The exemplary biography was the heart of the Socialist Realist narrative, a means of making the abstract principles of Marxism-Leninism concrete and comprehensible to the average citizen. The dogma of historical progress was embedded in a narrative of initiation whereby the individual hero is received into the great Soviet family – a *Bildungsroman* that would transform its readers by inscribing them into the master narrative of history. Over time, the socialist realist novel acquired a number of standard plots. The most common works were production novels, where the main drama concerns the fulfilment of the plan or the completion of a construction project. Other less common variants focussed on a historical theme, a worthy intellectual or inventor, war or revolution, a villain or a spy, or the West. In all cases, the hero passes from a state of lower to higher consciousness, following a path of moral and political growth and task fulfilment.[40]

In the case of Soviet Lithuanian literature, Marcinkevičius built the exemplary biography around the passage from the countryside to the Soviet city. Like Viktor Ehrenburg's *The Thaw* or Ivan Dudintsev's *Not by Bread Alone* in Soviet Russia, *The Twentieth Spring* depicted the "exemplary biography" of Soviet Lithuanian literature in a way that best responded to the ideological demands of the Khrushchev era.

The protagonist, the nineteen-year-old Simas Kairys, is the first of his kin to get an education. But while Vilnius is the destination of the voyage and setting for the subsequent action, the focus of the poem is on the subjectivity of the migrant, his rite of passage into urbanity and adulthood at the same time. After his arrival in Vilnius, Kairys makes friends, meets a girl, and is caught up in the struggle between the Soviet mode of thinking and that of the underground anti-Soviet resistance. Kairys ends up choosing the correct, Soviet path, and in doing so he rejects not only the clearly wrong path of the armed resistance, but also the naïve, apolitical and misguided, but in reality very attractive, "middle way," supposedly typical of the mentality the Lithuanian village. Critically, the young man learns to recognize and orient himself among the confusing mass of urban signs, to find a way through the unfamiliar and often deceptive urban environment.

While the plot sounds trite today, it was by the standards of the day a realistic portrayal of the dilemma faced by Lithuanians during the partisan war against the Soviet occupation. Moreover, even as the text fulfilled the ideological function of guiding Soviet Lithuanian youth along the path from their apolitical rustic origins towards socialist commitment in the city, it implicitly exposed the complexity of this path. By inscribing the paradigmatic, teleological narrative of Socialist Realism in the traumatic context of the postwar years, Marcinkevičius endowed the stock Soviet genre with a distinctly Lithuanian flavor.

This literary work was crucial for yet another reason. In *The Twentieth Spring*, the poet's voice actively encourages the formation of a cohort mentality among young Lithuanians, a sense of participation in a great historical endeavour. "My generation," he says, is wonderful: "it lived through storms and winds, but did not break, it survived / now it walks, lively, young / foot to foot, with a song."[41] As such, the *Twentieth Spring* probably was the first work of Lithuanian literature to succeed at creating a credible archetype of the new Soviet Lithuanian: educated, determined and poised for upward mobility; a Soviet man whose identity was credibly rooted in the common experience of many Lithuanians.

Echoes of anti-cosmopolitanism

Marcinkevičius would publish his next "blockbuster" novella in 1961, entitled *The Pine that Laughed*, at a time when conservative forces in the USSR were asserting their influence and trying to roll back the Thaw. By this time, his Russian coevals: *shestidesiatniki* like Yevgeny Yevtushenko, Andrey Voznesensky and Bela Akhmadulina, had reached the apex of their popularity and influence. Their poetry readings were filling football stadiums, and the 1961 publication of Yevtushenko's "Babi Yar" (critical of Soviet distortions of the Holocaust) in *Literaturnaya gazeta*, and a day later in the *New York Times*, attested to the agenda-setting power of the intelligentsia at home and abroad.

Khrushchev had backed the intelligentsia insofar as their activities supported his concept of reform and undermined the Stalinist old guard. But when they began to display what he viewed as an excess of cultural and social autonomy, he showed a very different face, announcing an abrupt turn of cultural policy in late 1961 during a visit to an exhibition of modern art in Moscow. "As far as art and music go," he pronounced at the time, "we have the same views as Stalin had. We will support those who are close to us. As for the others, we will strangle them."[42]

Flanked by the Kremlin's chief ideologist Mikhail Suslov, the KGB chief, the minister of culture and a few conservative artists, Khrushchev toured the paintings on display at the Manezh, calling each of the artists out one by one, dressing down each in turn. The following abusive address to one artist was repeated with variations several times as Khrushchev walked up and down the aisles:

You're a nice-looking lad, but how could you paint something like this? We should take down your pants and set you down in a clump of nettles until you understand your mistakes. You should be ashamed. Are you a pederast or a normal man? Do you want to go abroad? Go on, then; we'll take you for no charge right up to the border. Live out there in the "free world." Study in the school of capitalism, and then you'll know what's what. But we aren't going to spend a kopeck on this dog shit. We have the right to send you out to cut trees until you've paid back the money the state has spent on you. The people and government have taken a lot of trouble with you, and you pay them back with this shit. They say you like to associate with foreigners. A lot of them are our enemies, don't forget.[43]

While Khrushchev may have been improvising and expressing his views in a characteristically impulsive way, he confirmed the new approach to the arts and to the creative intelligentsia at a subsequent meeting on December 17, to which he had invited some 400 artists, writers, filmmakers and culture officials. He opened the meeting by taking credit for the publication of *A Day in the Life of Ivan Denisovych,* and praised Aleksandr Solzhenitsyn for his representation of the simple Russian *muzhik.* He then launched into a long, rambling attack on the young, cosmopolitan, elitist and Westernized cultural vanguard, positioning himself as a defender of the simple, working-class Russian.

Much to the dismay of the liberal intelligentsia, Khrushchev's diatribes were supported by a significant majority of the members of the creative unions and the cultural bureaucracy. Forced to go through a humiliating process of "self-examination" and institutionalized confession, liberal intellectuals felt isolated, marginalized, and began to despair about their place in Soviet society. Some emigrated, others were radicalized into dissidents, but many more conformed to the new demands for obeisance. Over the next year, reformist bureaucrats in the Writers' Union and other cultural institutions lost their jobs and were replaced by Stalinist stalwarts and a new generation of cultural traditionalists.[44]

Khrushchev's anti-cosmopolitanism campaign had an echo in Lithuania, but the recollections of Lithuanian intellectuals emphasize the relative leniency of the campaign. For example, Sniečkus called the leading intellectuals and cultural officials to a meeting where he intended to put them in their place as Khrushchev had done in Moscow. But when he began to imitate Khrushchev's rant about cosmopolitanism and libertinism, the audience reacted with suppressed laughter rather than acclamatory applause.[45]

The fact is that Lithuanian artists and intellectuals had already become accustomed to a specific mode of ritual criticism where those delivering and those receiving the criticism viewed the exercise as a necessary procedure, after which they would frequently sit behind a table with a bottle of cognac and have rather friendly discussions. Sniečkus himself liked to have an occasional drink with the leading writers and artists, and is said to have exclaimed after a long debate: "All I hear from you is modernism, modernism. To hell with you: let there be modernism! Just make sure that it is our native, Lithuanian, Soviet modernism!"[46]

Similarly, Algimantas Apanavičius recalls frequenet meetings with Sniečkus during presentations of TV programs and films at the Lithuanian film studio, where the communist leader would frequently invite the entire production staff, including light and sound technicians, for a glass of cognac in a relaxed, "completely non-Soviet" atmosphere.[47]

Rimtautas Šilinis remembers vividly a meeting of the Central Committee—with representatives of the creative unions in the late 1960s, in which he took part.

> One of the officials, I think Kuzmickas, launched a vicious attack on Vincas Kisarauskas, an abstract artist, for not conforming to the conventions of the socialist realism. Sniečkus was to speak after Kuzmickas, closing the meeting. He walked up to the podium slowly, waving a paper folder in his hand. "Dear comrades, the department of culture wrote me a speech, but I will not read it," he said placing the folder aside. "I will say simply: which one of us was not young? Which young person does not make mistakes? And who can condemn us for the mistakes of our youth? We have to look at life simply. Everybody has his area and we have to perfect it as much as we can. Of course, critique is necessary but it must not be done in the tone used by the previous speaker."[48]

Some members of the creative intelligentsia then went to a restaurant for a drink, and were joined by a good-spirited Sniečkus. Reflecting on this episode, Šilinis expresses a commonly held opinion among the Soviet Lithuanian elites that Sniečkus grew increasingly tolerant in his old age.

At the same time, the relative autonomy that Sniečkus was able to secure for the cultural establishment in Soviet Lithuania was predicated on the willingness of this establishment to side with the authorities against one of its own in order to "keep the peace." Marcinkevičius's *The Pine that Laughed* appeared in this highly ambiguous political environment, continuing with the discursive construction – and discipline – of the new Soviet Lithuanian subject.

In the preface, Marcinkevičius's emphasizes the continuity of his interest in "the birth of the new personality" that he began in *The Twentieth Spring*.[49] While the action of *The Twentieth Spring* takes place in 1948–49, when his generation was moving from the country to the city, the action of *The Pine that Laughed* takes place around 1960, that is, after the new urban communities had been formed and the postwar generation was trying to define and express itself in the new social context.

The narrative is centered on the personal development of Romas Staugaitis. As distinct from Kairys, the hero of *The Twentieth Spring*, Romas is not a peasant youth, but a 23-year-old aspiring artist.[50] The son of a famous professor, an expert on Lithuanian philology, Romas lives very comfortably in the Lithuanian capital with every possible privilege of modern Soviet life, like a shiny new motorbike. Well educated and talented, he also demonstrates a passion for idealist philosophy and the latest intellectual trends in the West. He is especially interested in the ideas of the philosopher "Oscar Badler" (a *non de clef* for Oswald Spengler) and he shares his fascination with his friends – a *kruzhok* of young artists and intellectuals. The plot is intricate, with unexpected turns and intrigues in the relationships between Romas and his father, his stepsister, and his friends.

The book is written in a crisp style and fascinated young Lithuanian readers by giving them a window into the world of Romas and his friends – the "golden youth" of a modern Soviet city. And while the drama is really about Romas and his efforts to express his personality and find his place in the Soviet world, his tortured and conflicted character is juxtaposed against the simple virtue of his fellow student from the Art Institute – Gailiūnas. Gailiūnas is a village youth who recently moved to the city, but who seems untroubled by the transition and maintains a telluric connection to the land: "Gailiūnas was from the village. He loved the earth in a pantheistic fashion and knew how to draw it in all seasons ... He was tall, very naïve, and very good."[51]

Throughout the text, Gailiūnas serves as a kind of ethical standard or a moral compass which helps the young reader to understand the development of Romas. For example, when Romas and his refined friends expound bombastically on esoteric topics of art and philosophy, they are dumfounded by Gailiūnas' simple, direct questions, which they are surprisingly unable to answer. His earthiness unmasks the pretensions of the urban snobs and exposes their shallowness.

Later, Romas makes a kind of pilgrimage to the collective farm, experiences a revelation about the spirituality of working the land, and develops a deeper emotional closeness to people who work in a factory. The dichotomy between the "impure urbanite" and the "pure villager" carries through to the last line of the story: "Everything was washed away, all of the dirt, garbage and useless chatter, and the earth was so intelligent as not to resist."[52]

Like its predecessor *The Twentieth Spring*, *The Pine that Laughed* was genuinely popular among young Lithuanian readers, in part because of the elements of romance and hints of eroticism contained in several passages, which broke with the extreme prudishness of the Stalinist era and the complete absence of boulevard literature.[53] For others, it was the "hint of complexity" underlying the characters and their actions which distinguished these works against the otherwise gray mass of Soviet Lithuanian literature of the time.[54]

Moreover, the work was strongly supported by the cultural establishment. It was printed in an initial run of 15,000 copies, and was distributed and reviewed throughout the country. Influential critics hailed Marcinkevičius as "the spiritual leader" of his generation.

> Now we can see in an especially pronounced manner the coming to life of a new generation ... Justinas Marcinkevičius feels the greatest responsibility for his generation. Not every writer could become the spiritual

leader of his generation, but the author of *The Twentieth Spring*, *Blood and Ashes*, and *The Pine that Laughed* is such an author.[55]

Justas Vincas Paleckis, who began his studies at Vilnius University in 1959, recalls the effect that the two texts of Marcinkevičius had on him and his peers, noting that they were "exactly the generation of Lithuanians who were targeted by these works." He says they made such a strong impression because they conveyed a new level of authenticity that he had not encountered before: "reading these works, the youth felt that they had finally found what they were searching for, not some imagined scheme, but reality." The new standard of realism also served to strengthen Lithuanian sense of belonging to the new Soviet order: "We felt and could directly relate to the optimism that underlay these texts, to the sense that we can do something to improve our society."[56]

But although the majority of young Lithuanian readers may not have paid it much attention at the time, the text does express a rather blatant ideological message criticizing the individualism and cosmopolitanism of Western liberalism and particularly of the incipient dissident groups that were forming in Soviet Lithuania during the Thaw. According to statements first made by Tomas Venclova in 1991, Marcinkevičius was "commissioned" by the authorities to write the story as a *roman-a-clef* designed to intimidate the young generation of "decadent" urban intellectuals who identified with the Western-leaning views of Romas.[57]

One such group at the time was led by none other than Tomas Venclova, whose social position as the son of Antanas Venclova was very similar to that of the protagonist of *The Pine that Laughed*. Moreover, Venclova's *kruzhok* included a number of children of leading members of the highest Soviet Lithuanian *nomenklatura*. Pranas Morkus was the stepson of Kazys Preikšas, a Stalinist official who left a heavy imprint during the time of *Zhdanovshchina*, and whose mother was a theatre actress and winner of the Stalin Prize. Aleksandras Štromas was a lawyer whose parents were killed in the Holocaust, escaped from the Kaunas ghetto in 1943 and was adopted and raised by the family of none other than Antanas Sniečkus.

Other members of this elite group included Ramūnas Katilius, the son of professors at the Pedagogical Institute, who went on to become a well-known Lithuanian physicist, his brother Audronis, and Juozas Tumelis, another philology student at Vilnius University. Tumelis was actually the only one who came from a more humble social background and, owing perhaps to his lack of strong family connections among the *nomenklatura*, the only one to have suffered direct consequences from his involvement in the group (aside from interrogation by the police) insofar as he was expelled from university.[58]

According to Venclova, Marcinkevičius based some of the facts of the story on notes and materials seized in a police raid of Venclova's circle. Marcinkevičius denied any direct commission or that *The Pine that Laughed* had anything to do with Venclova. Whatever the facts, the story nonetheless clearly reflects the growing friction and competition that existed between the different groups of the cultural elites and their respective visions of community. The anti-cosmopolitan message of the novel could well have been inspired by Khrushchev's campaign, but it could also have been an expression of the indigenous nativism of Marcinkevičius and his peers of humble social origins. For them, Venclova belonged to a different social category with a completely different biographical experience, set of values and outlook on the world – a social distinction as clear in reality as the fictional opposition of Romas and Gailiūnas.

Interestingly, in the recollections of contemporaries, this distinction was not so much political as it was social. The younger members of the postwar intelligentsia like Martinaitis (b. 1936), Romualdas Granauskas (b. 1939) and Viktorija Daujotytė (b. 1945), who as political non-conformists subscribed to Tomas Venclova's views and admired his work as a poet and scholar, felt an insurmountable personal distance between themselves and Venclova due to his social position – they referred to him as a "lord" (*ponas*) only half in jest.[59]

The high official position of his father Antanas also alienated Tomas Venclova from more nativist Lithuanian dissident circles, such as the "cultural soirees" organized by Meilė Lukšienė, at which Gulag deportees could find a venue to speak about their experiences. Although Venclova had close relations of confidence with leading dissidents in Moscow and Leningrad, this did not in itself bring him closer to certain dissidents in Lithuania, who kept him in a so-called "zone of silence," meaning that one should not speak of sensitive issues in his presence.[60]

During the Brezhnev years, the tension between the appeal of an urban, modern and cosmopolitan way of life, on the one hand, and the heritage of traditional, rural communities on the other would grow into a veritable *Kulturkampf* between the progressive and conservative wings of the Soviet intelligentsia (to be discussed in Chapter 7). Within the LSSR, this tension would eventually resolve firmly on the side of tradition and cultural nativism, but until the mid-1960s, the Soviet Lithuanian intellectuals maintained their efforts to explore the progressive, positive aspects of Soviet modernism and its manifestation in the new forms of urban life.

Notes

1 Jonas Mackonis, *Boružės odisėjos* (Vilnius: Tyto Alba, 2003), 161.
2 Thomas Remeikis, *Opposition to Soviet Rule in Lithuania, 1945–1980* (Chicago, IL: Institute of Lithuanian Studies Press, 1980), 275–78; R. Misiūnas and R. Taagepera, *The Baltic States, Years of Dependence, 1940–1990* (Berkeley, CA: University of California Press, 1993), 136; Amir Weiner, "The Empires Pay a Visit: Gulag Returnees, East European Rebellions, and Soviet Frontier Politics," *The Journal of Modern History* 78 (June 2006): 333–76.
3 Romuald J. Misiūnas and Rein Taagepera, *The Baltic States, Years of Dependence, 1940–1990* (Berkeley, CA: University of California Press, 1993).
4 Works by Maironis, Vincas Krėvė, Balys Sruoga, Juozas Baltrušaitis, Marius Katiliškis and others were published with ideologically correct Marxist introductions. Vytautas Kubilius, *XX amžiaus literatūra* (Vilnius: Alma Littera, 1996), 511–12.
5 Arūnas Streikus, "Kierunki polityki pamięci na Litwie sowieckiej," *Politeja* 16 (2011): 281–307.

6 Emily Lygo, *Leningrad Poetry 1953–1975: The Thaw Generation* (Bern: P. Lang, 2010), 13.
7 Hilary Pilkington, *Russia's Youth: A Nation's Constructors and Constructed* (London: Routledge, 1994).
8 For the full biography of Sniečkus, see Vytautas Tininis, *Sniečkus: 33 metai valdžioje* (Vilnius: Lietuvos Karo akademija, 2000).
9 Elena Zubkova, *Pribaltika i Kreml: 1940–1953* (Moscow: Rossiiskaya akademiya nauk, Institut rossiiskoi istorii, 2008), 264–65.
10 Romualdas J. Misiūnas and Rein Taagepera, *The Baltic States, Years of Dependence, 1940–1990* (Berkeley, CA: University of California Press, 1993), 142.
11 *Tarybų Lietuva* (April 24, 1945), 1.
12 Tininis, *Sniečkus: 33 metai valdžioje*.
13 Amir Weiner, "The Empires Pay a Visit: Gulag Returnees, East European Rebellions, and Soviet Frontier Politics," *The Journal of Modern History* 78 (June 2006): 333–76. For a detailed account of the origins and demise of Beria's *indigenization* policy in Lithuania, see Elena Zubkova, *Pribaltika i Kreml: 1940–1953* (Moscow: Rossiiskaya akademiya nauk, Institut rossiiskoi istorii, 2008), 320–37.
14 Thomas Remeikis, *The Lithuanian Phoenix: Studies and Essays, 1940–1990* (Vilnius: Vytautas Magnus University, the Lithuanian Emigration Institute, 2009), 134.
15 The memoirs of Algirdas Brazauskas frequently evoke the collective "we" of this generation of the technical intelligentsia. *Ir tuomet dirbome Lietuvai: faktai, atsiminimai, komentarai* (Vilnius: Knygiai, 2007).
16 Remeikis, *The Lithuanian Phoenix*, 134.
17 Vytautė Žilinskaitė, Interview by author. Audio recording. Vilnius, October 11, 2011.
18 Liudas Truska, "Ilgas kelias į Vilnių," 58–65.
19 Valys Drazdauskas was a member of the leftist literary movement "Third Front" and the communist underground between the wars. He spent the war in the USSR working for a Soviet newspaper, and was put in charge of a literary publishing house from 1944 until 1949, when he was arrested and deported to the Gulag until he was amnestied and returned to Lithuania in 1956. "Rytoj važiuoju į Vilnių!," *Kultūros barai* 12 (2001): 77.
20 Vincas Justas Paleckis, Interview by author. Audio recording. Vilnius, April 4, 2012.
21 Vytautas Brėdikis. Interview by author. Audio recording. Vilnius, March 12, 2013. Nasvytis, Algimantas. Interview by author. Audio recording. Vilnius, May 14, 2012.
22 Marc Elie, *Les Anciens détenus du Goulag: Libérations Massives, Réinsertion et Réhabilitation dans L'URSS Poststalinienne, 1953–1964* (Paris: Ecole des Hautes Etudes en Sciences Sociales, 2007).
23 Kristina Burinskaitė, "KGB prieš buvusius politinius kalinius ir tremtinius," *Genocidas ir rezistencija* 2.24 (2008): 121–26.
24 In Amir Weiner, "The Empires Pay a Visit: Gulag Returnees, East European Rebellions, and Soviet Frontier Politics," *The Journal of Modern History* 78.2 (2006): 333.
25 For example, the authorities published an article in the local newspaper harshly criticizing the character of Dalia Grinkevičiūtė, a deportee who returned to Lithuania to work as a village doctor, and who also engaged in dissident activity. The story of Grinkevičiūtė's return to Lithuania from the Gulag and her encounter with Marcinkevičius will be discussed in Chapter 8. Marija Vitkevičienė, "Dėmės baltame chalate" [Stains on a White Robe], *Artojas* 67 (June 11, 1974): 3–4.
26 Weiner, "The Empire Pays a Visit," 369. Kazys Saja depicts the harshness of the local Lithuanian authorities towards the returnees in "Lietuvos Antigonė," *Lietuvos aidas* (October 7, 1995), 5.
27 Algimantas Indriūnas, *Nelegalios karjeros metai* (Vilnius: Gairės, 2005), 133.
28 In Marija Marcevičienė, ed. *Atmintis: tremtinių atsiminimų rinkinys* (Kaišiadorys: Kaišiadorių muziejus, 2003), 101–105, 81.

29 Marija Marcevičienė, ed. *Atmintis: tremtinių atsiminimų rinkinys* (Kaišiadorys: Kaišiadorių muziejus, 2003), 52. See also the study by Roberta Drąsutytė, "Senyvo amžiaus moterų trauminių prisiminimų rekonstrukcija", unpublished M.A. thesis, VDU, Department for Social Work, 2012.
30 Report dated 25 March 1958. GARF R-8131/32/5600/11, in Elie, *Les Anciens détenus du Goulag*, 269.
31 Donatas Sauka, *Fausto amžiaus epilogas* (Vilnius: Tyto alba, 1998), 234.
32 Sauka, *Fausto amžiaus epilogas*, 234.
33 Barbara Walker, "*Kruzhok* Culture: The Meaning of Patronage in the Early Soviet Literary World," Contemporary European History 11.1 (2002): 108.
34 Algimantas Baltakis, Interview by author. Audio recording. Vilnius, March 8, 2011.
35 In a speech to a meeting of the Writers Union, where the crackdown on the *Zvezda* and *Leningrad* literary journals was replicated in the Lithuanian context, Zhdanov's role was played by Kazys Preikšas, the head of the Lithuanian Communist Party Central Committee Propaganda Section. Preikšas accused Mieželaitis of writing "the most repulsive obscenities." He was referring to a poem about a young lad who talks to a mare after he was rejected by a girl and gives the mare a kiss. Tomas Venclova commented that Preikšas' indignation was so extreme that he seemed to imply some kind of zoophilic perversion on the part of Mieželaitis. Tomas Venclova, Interview by author. Audio recording. Vilinus, June 22, 2009.
36 This was the only Lenin Award ever granted to a Lithuanian poet. Mieželaitis was Chairman of the Writers Union from 1959 to 1970, a member of the CC of the Lithuanian Communist Party from 1960–89, and a deputy to the Supreme Council of the USSR from 1962 to 1970.
37 Algirdas Greimas, "Apie Mieželaitį ir jo Paryžių" in Algirdas Greimas and Saulius Žukas. *Iš arti ir iš toli: literatūra, kultūra, grožis* (Vilnius: Vaga, 1991), 479–80.
38 Interviews with Baltakis, Sutkus, Saja and others.
39 *The Twentieth Spring* is hardly studied or even read in Lithuania today, relegated to the "ideological" phase of Marcinkevičius' work. Nonetheless, contemporaries recall the personal significance that it had for them as youths. Romualdas Granauskas says that he memorized the poem "instantly" and can recite it from memory to this day. Romualdas Granauskas, Interview by author. Audio recording. Vilnius, June 3, 2011.
40 Katerina Clark, *The Soviet Novel: History as Ritual* (Chicago, IL: University of Chicago Press, 1981), 265.
41 Justinas Marcinkevičius, *Dvidešimtas pavasaris: poema* (Vilnius: Valst. grož. lit. l-kla, 1956), 23. Translated by the author with permission.
42 *Encounter* (London), April 1963, 102–3.
43 Ibid.
44 Vladislav Zubok, *Zhivago's Children: The Last Russian Intelligentsia* (Cambridge, MA: Belknap Press of Harvard University Press, 2009).
45 Jonas Mackonis, *Boružės odisėjos* (Vilnius: Tyto Alba, 2003).
46 Ibid., 161.
47 Algimantas Apanavičius, Interview by author. Audio recording. Vilnius, April 10, 2012.
48 Rimtautas Šilinis, Interview with author. Audio recording. August 2, 2012.
49 Justinas Marcinkevičius, *Pušis, kuri juokėsi: apysaka* (Vilnius: Valstybinė grožinės literatūros leidykla, 1961), 2.
50 Contemporary critics spoke of Romas as the Hamlet of his time and compared the novella to similar Soviet works on the existential challenges facing the younger generation, notably Vasily Aksyonov's *Ticket to the Stars*. Critics also noted the special affinity between the character of Gailiūnas and Marcinkevičius himself. Jonas Lankutis, "Ginčas dėl gyvenimo prasmės," *Pergalė* 2 (1962): 137–45.

51 Justinas Marcinkevičius, *Pušis, kuri juokėsi: apysaka* (Vilnius: Valstybinė grožinės literatūros leidykla, 1961), 21.
52 Ibid., 156.
53 Interviews with Marcelijus Martinaitis, Romualdas Granauskas, Algimantas Baltakis, Vacys Reimeris, Vytautas Rubavičius.
54 Vytautas Rubavičius, personal communication, October 2, 2012.
55 Jonas Lankutis, "Ginčas dėl gyvenimo prasmės," *Pergalė* 2 (1962): 137–45.
56 Vincas Justas Paleckis, Interview by author. Audio recording. Vilnius, April 10, 2012.
57 Tomas Venclova said this on the television programme *Krantai* in 1991 together with Aleksandras Štromas, forcing a stormy debate in Lithuania among the older generations of the elites that lasts to this day. Whatever the truth of this allegation, the parallels between Romas and Venclova are striking, though they probably would not have had much significance to the vast majority of the book's young readers when it was first published.
58 Tumelis was later allowed to re-enroll in the Faculty of History, from which he graduated only in 1972.
59 Romualdas Granauskas, Interview by author. Audio recording. Vilnius, June 3, 2011. Marcelijus Martinaitis, Interview by author. Audio recording. Vilnius, November 12, 2008. Viktorija Daujotytė-Pakerienė, Interview by Valdemaras Klumbys. Audio recording. Vilnius, September 10, 2004. Recording provided courtesy of Valdemaras Klumbys.
60 Ingė Lukšaitė, Interview by Valdemaras Klumbys. Audio recording. Vilnius, July 7, 2002. Recording provided courtesy of Valdemaras Klumbys.

6 Soviet modernity and its limits

By the mid 1960s the Soviet Union was nearing the peak of its power and influence. The economy was growing, consumer products were increasingly plentiful, and the Soviet armed forces were well on their way towards nuclear parity with the United States. A Soviet citizen, Yuri Gagarin, had been the first man to reach orbit in 1961, and the USSR was projecting its image as a force for progress, an alternative and entirely credible route to modernity.

In spite of its small size, Lithuania gained renown for its high productivity in agriculture, modern light industry, and above all its contributions to Soviet culture and the culture of progressive internationalism. In 1965, the Lithuanian Soviet Socialist Republic celebrated the twenty-fifth anniversary of its incorporation into the USSR, and was itself awarded the Order of Lenin that year for its contribution to the construction of socialism.

This was the Golden Age of Soviet Lithuania, if ever there was one. The state-sponsored effort to cultivate a Soviet Lithuanian intelligentsia could be declared a success, and the leading members of the newly formed Lithuanian elite began to enjoy the status of celebrities beyond their native republic, reaching the "all-Soviet" level and beyond, into the expanding world of progressive internationalism cultivated by the vast machine of Soviet international cultural relations.

In fact, the Soviet Baltic republics as a whole were rapidly gaining a fashionable status as the "Soviet West" – a place where the leading members of the Soviet intelligentsia could benefit from the familiar and the unfamiliar at the same time.[1] But while the framework of Soviet modernity and internationalism propelled certain members of the intelligentsia to previously unimaginable heights, their ambitions to secure recognition for Lithuanian culture in the cosmopolitan West were ultimately disappointed, precipitating a return to the more traditional sources of national culture.

National achievements

In addition to writers like Mieželaitis, Marcinkevičius and Baltakis, the graphic artist Stasys Krasauskas (1929–77) was in high demand to illustrate all-Union bestsellers.[2] The sculptor Gediminas Jokūbonis (1927–2006) was awarded the

Figure 6.1 Raimondas Urbakavičius, Neringa Café after renovations that restored the original design of the 1960s. Vilnius, 2000

Lenin Prize for his rendering of "The Grieving Mother of Pirčiupiai," a large statue of a grieving woman clothed in folk attire, placed on a memorial site commemorating the burning by the Nazis of the village Pirčiupiai. The statue was widely imitated, and Jokūbonis was commissioned in 1967 to make the monument to Lenin on none other than Il'ich Square in Moscow.[3]

A number of Lithuanian actors like Regimantas Adomaitis, Juozas Budraitis, Donatas Banionis, Laimonas Noreika and others became super-stars of the Soviet cinema, greatly respected across the whole Soviet Union, often playing leading roles in the most famous productions made in Moscow, especially the roles of "fascist Germans" or other stock "foreigner" types. Writer Mikhail Iossel recalls from his youth in Leningrad how: "There was something special about them, perhaps these huge, immobile, but very expressive facial features. They were and are still greatly admired in Russia to this day."[4] At the same time the native Lithuanian cinema was also entering a new age as a crop of talented graduates from the best cinema institutes of the USSR returned to the LSSR to develop the genre in their homeland.[5]

In 1966, an action film made by Algirdas Žalakevičius (1930–96) called *Nobody Wanted to Die* was released to a tremendous reception throughout the USSR. Notably, the film stunned non-Lithuanian audiences for its portrayal of real conflict *after* the Soviet victory in the Great Patriotic War. To be sure, the film depicted the postwar struggle in the Lithuanian countryside from the Soviet point of view, but with a degree of sophistication that set it apart from the typical war films of the time, drawing Soviet-wide attention to a practically unknown chapter of recent Soviet history.

As recalled by Aleksei Venediktov, Editor in Chief of the Ekho Moskvy radio station:

> For people of my generation, the history of the Molotov–Ribbentrop pact began with the film *Nobody Wanted to Die*. I watched it when I was 10, 12, even 14 years old, and could never really understand what was happening. Which side was our side, which side were we against? Where were the fascists, and where were we, the Soviets? How could this be?[6]

Khrushchev's Thaw was marked not only by internal liberalization but efforts to engage with the West in terms of cultural, scientific and person-to-person exchanges. Khrushchev set a personal example as the first Soviet leader who travelled extensively, seen to partake in the local culture and rituals, admittedly of the more populist kind, like eating hot-dogs in America. A major 1955 Geneva conference of leaders from both sides of the Iron Curtain made some ground-breaking agreements in the area of tourism, trade and culture. The "spirit of Geneva" was key to normalizing cultural and scientific relations in subsequent years, leading to sharp increases in foreign exchanges as well as tourism both into and from the Soviet Union.[7] The Moscow International Youth Festival of 1957, which had thousands of young people visiting Moscow, marked a watershed in the opening of Soviet culture to the West and the effort to put a distinctly Soviet stamp on the emerging world culture.[8]

The Soviet Lithuanian intelligentsia participated fully in such exchanges, travelling abroad and – after 1959, when Vilnius, Riga and Tallinn were added to the list of cities that foreigners could visit – by hosting foreign delegations. Given their European character and relatively advanced infrastructure, the capital cities of the Baltic republics were used by the authorities in Moscow as showcases for the achievements of Soviet science, culture and industry, and by implication the Soviet nationalities policy as well.[9]

At the same time, the exposure to international currents in the arts empowered the Soviet Lithuanian intelligentsia to chart a distinct national course in the broader Soviet context. A new cohort of Lithuanian architects entered the stage, including such prominent figures as Algimantas and Vytautas Nasvytis (twin brothers born in 1928), Vytautas Brėdikis (b. 1930), Vytautas Edmundas Čekanauskas (b. 1930) and others. In 1954, a delegation of young Lithuanian architects led by Justinas Šeibokas (b. 1929) made a number of trips to neutral Finland and Sweden to see the latest developments of regional architecture and urban planning.[10] Inspired and influenced by the Nordic schools of architecture, they developed a distinctive Soviet Lithuanian architectural style that soon gained international recognition. Designs for the first new postwar suburb of Lazdynai in Vilnius were completed in 1966 and construction began in 1969 to produce the first work of residential construction to be awarded the All-Union Prize for architecture in 1974.[11]

The opening in Vilnius of the Neringa Café, designed by the Nasvytis bothers, was celebrated as reflecting modern European trends in architecture and seen as a revival of the Kaunas school of modernism that was launched during the interwar period. The interior design with its original layout of small tables

Figure 6.2 Soviet Stamp Image of Gediminas Tower
Depositphotos. Nikolay Neveshkin.

and large frescoes with stylized folk motifs was striking for the times, to the point of intensely irritating the more orthodox Stalinist branch of the Lithuanian intelligentsia. Teofilis Tilvytis (1904–69), a Stalin Prize winner and mentor to the more conservative and ideologically rigid flank within the

Writers' Union, for example, refused to step into the building because he "could not stomach the far too modern frescoes."[12]

The café was also subject to a stiff critique from Moscow in the form of an article published in *Izvestiia*, just a couple of weeks after it opened on 6 November 1959. The author made a fuss over the café's extravagant design, noting the extraordinary cost of constructing a venue that could hold a mere 200 visitors. Such conservative protests came to nothing, however, and the Nasvytis brothers were later invited by none other than Aleksey Adjubey, Khrushchev's influential son-in-law and Editor-in-Chief of *Izvestiia* (from May 1959 to October 1964) to redesign the newspaper's flagship building on Pushkin Square in Moscow—an offer they scandalously refused.[13]

Nonetheless, the cafe quickly gained recognition as one of the most fashionable haunts in the USSR, and was frequented by top members of the political and cultural elites, especially from the more modernist branch of the Soviet intelligentsia. In time, the venue became the spot where members of the gilded cohort socialized among themselves and with the most prominent Soviet intellectuals of the Thaw period like Bella Akhmadulina, Vasiliy Aksyonov, Robert Rozhdestvensky, Andrei Voznesensky, Yevgeny Yevtushenko, and others.

These famous *shestidesiatniki* visited Lithuania quite frequently, taking in the more relaxed, quasi-Western atmosphere with its opportunities to shop and to drink, and would invite their Lithuanian peers to the most fashionable events in Moscow. On one such visit Andrei Voznesensky gave Baltakis a signed copy of his collection of poetry *Mozaika* with the inscription, "To Algimantas, the first Cuban I have ever met," as recognition of the sense of liberty and the power of the young generation that emanated from the Baltics. "We felt like we were in the centre of Europe. This was our time."[14]

Baltakis recalls how around 1965, he felt that he virtually reached the peak of his achievements – he had an apartment, a car, was part of the prestigious literary *nomenklatura*. As the editor of *Pergalė*, his lifestyle could even be described as lavish:

> I would get a phone call from Robert Rozhdestvensky in Moscow. He would tell me that this or that restaurant there has a new dish, a new drink. I call Stasys [Krasauskas], who works in the institute, teaches there. "Shall we go?" "OK, let's go … " So we fly there, have lunch and come back. At the time, it didn't cost that much.[15]

Even staunchly anti-Soviet émigré groups in the United States acknowledged that Soviet Lithuanian intellectuals were genuinely proud of their achievements. According to a *samizdat* report by the dissident Eitan Finkelstein:

> De-stalinization provided the opportunity for the Lithuanian creative intelligentsia to create in their native language and, utilizing national themes, to immerse themselves in the studies of national culture and history … This up-to-then unheard of opportunity became a source of

unique euphoria for a large part of the intelligentsia and its intensity was raised to a high degree by the rapid expansion of cultural and scientific centres in which Lithuanians occupied the principal positions.[16]

Indeed, the memoirs of contemporaries reveal an intense sense of pride at the recognition they were getting at the all-Union level. Setting their sights even further, the Lithuanian intelligentsia was gaining the confidence to assert its identity and to seek a place for Lithuanian culture in a global, and not just Soviet context.

Mieželaitis' award-winning poem *Man* was presented as a *chef d'oeuvre* of world literature, and was praised by artists throughout the progressive world: "I love you, Mieželaitis," effused the exiled Turkish poet Nazim Hikmet.[17] Mieželaitis travelled extensively throughout Europe, Africa, Latin America, the USA, Japan and India, where he:

> voraciously absorbed the artistic experiences contained in the museums of the world, and in his work recorded the architectural rhythms of big cities, images of a world transformed by civilization, the new sensations he felt while looking out of the wings of an airplane.[18]

He received the Lenin award at a pompous evening gala in 1962, where speakers emphasized the significance of this prize as the highest possible recognition of the achievements of "Soviet Lithuanian literature and culture."[19]

Not all were impressed with such cosmopolitan flights, particularly among the older and more worldly generation of the literary elite. Antanas Venclova found Mieželaitis' habit of undersigning his poems as though they had been composed in Paris, London or New York to be "very provincial."[20] His remarks were echoed by Aldona Liobytė, a translator and writer of children's literature and one of a handful of Lithuanians born and raised in the relatively cosmopolitan environment of Vilnius between the wars. "I just read the new book of poetry by Mieželaitis," she wrote to a friend.

> Oh, the pleasures of a poor man who has been raised to the nobility. Just imagine what happiness! He flies in an airplane to South America. He drinks coffee. He talks to the famous American poet [Robert] Frost. He howls with the not so famous beatnik [Allen] Ginsberg. He is indignant with the dictator who prevents him from stepping off the plane in Spain. He understands contemporary music, he knows about art ... and only a couple of sincere lines without posing and empty chatter.[21]

It would not be until the time of Lithuanian independence that former Soviet Lithuanian readers would be exposed to the writings of Algirdas Julius Greimas, a prominent French semiotician of Lithuanian origin, who mocked the representation of Paris provided by this this well-traveled Soviet intellectual. Greimas does not blame Mieželaitis for not knowing Paris, but rather for the pretentious way in which he describes the city.[22] But even this pretentiousness cannot be blamed on Mieželaitis alone – in many ways it was an indelible part of an environment where travel was special privilege of a few and almost a necessary trait of an official Soviet "literary genius."

That said, their interactions with the wider world, beyond the congratulatory atmosphere of progressive internationalism, were characterized by greater cultural friction, revealing certain limitations and weaknesses in the Soviet Lithuanian model. Greimas, for example, met a group of Lithuanian intellectuals visiting Alexandria in 1957, where he worked as a teacher at a French boarding school for girls. He was struck by their strong sense of patriotism – not Soviet, but national – as well as by how many features they shared with his father's generation of interwar Lithuanians. These included a pronounced sentimentality, a special pride in the Lithuanian landscape ("the Mediterranean is not as beautiful as our Baltic coast"), the enhancements made to the capital of Vilnius, and the same uneasy attitudes towards the Poles ("we received them so well in Lithuania and they still dare to criticize our culture!")[23]

By all accounts a sympathetic observer, Greimas nonetheless found the young Lithuanian intellectuals to be culturally isolated, their pretensions to cosmopolitanism naïve. They were fiercely proud of Lithuania's cultural achievements: its poetry, art, drama, architecture and even basketball and paper manufacturing, but equally ignorant of cultural developments in the Western world. He noted their strong cohort mentality, speaking of "our" achievements in various areas of endeavour, but he was also bemused by their assertion that the translation of Shakespeare into Lithuanian was a great step forward for de-Stalinization and Lithuania's integration into world culture. He feared that isolation from the West would continue to act as a serious limitation on Soviet Lithuanian culture, though he was equally confident that their provincialism would prove to be a sufficient brake on the feared loss of national identity through Russification.[24]

Cosmopolitan fantasies

Within Lithuania itself, the rapid growth of the cities reinforced the contemporary rhetoric of human mastery over the environment, be it the vast expanses and natural resources of northern Siberia, the cosmos, or the cityscape. "It seems that we stepped out of the room into the street, into a large city," Tomas Venclova wrote in a 1962 book called *Rockets, Planets and Us* which extolled space travel as a new "post-colonial" form of scientific exploration and expansion that would set a new standard for human civilization, transcending the greedy imperialism of past empires:

> The travellers of the past were attracted not only by adventure. They were lured by the colonies and gold, their heroic actions were accompanied by robbery. People from communist society who conquer the cosmos will not

and cannot have selfish goals. Instead of colonies, scientific bases will be created. Rocket trips will serve knowledge and peace.[25]

Similarly, debates on city planning and design were couched in metaphors of backwardness and progress where the village frequently stood as a synonym of parochialism. Urban developments that followed the Khrushchevian ideology of "faster, cheaper, more functional" aimed to provide comfort at a low cost, and succeeded in increasing the availability of cheap housing. The interiors of apartments were also changing rapidly, as the traditional wooden chests and dressers brought to the city by the new arrivals from the villages gradually gave way to a light and functional, if highly standardized and uniform design.[26]

The press was delighting in fantasies about plastic houses with plastic furniture, and even plastic cities that could be built in a blink of an eye. "You will see. The time will come and such houses will be built not only in Vilnius but also in the other cities of our republic," Jonas Tamošaitis assured his Lithuanian readers in his fantasy about the city of tomorrow, the city of the Sun.[27] These debates were joined by other writers: in the lead article of a 1967 issue of *Literatūra ir menas* entitled "How should cities develop: As Cities or as Large Villages?," Albinas Žukauskas exclaimed: "Enough of the village. The buildings of our cities should be higher and higher!"[28]

The creative works and memoirs of the intelligentsia from this period, especially those with the reputation of being literary "modernizers," display a concerted effort to find new means of artistic expression that would match the spirit of the times. Baltakis' diary from July 19, 1960 reads:

> My greatest ambition is to write poetry that expresses the self-perception and worldview of the individual of our times – the one who lives in the city. I have to create a certain style, not a traditional one that was born in the village, but a new one – dynamic, angular ... URBAN [sic].[29]

In this context, Baltakis and his peers faced the challenge of ensuring that their writing kept up with the times. Their chief concern was to rise above their rural upbringing, to be more up-to-date and up-to-speed in a rapidly changing and increasingly modern world. The new intellectuals saw it as their mission to "take poetry out of the village" and to "register" it in the city. Baltakis expresses this intent in the preface to a collection of poetry:

> For many years our poetry lived in the village without stepping out of it anywhere. Perhaps this is because our nation was born not in the city castle but in simple huts covered in hay. And only recently, with cities growing ever faster, the centre of our life started moving from the village to the city. From my very first book I was consciously trying to become an urban poet. I sprinkled some urban poems in all my collections; however, I did

not become a truly urban poet. And perhaps it will never happen. Nonetheless, our poetry will register in the city one day. If not today, then tomorrow.[30]

However, this intention was often frustrated by the friction of the passage between two separate worlds, two value systems and two perspectives on their surroundings. In a poem published in 1967 entitled "First Generation from the Plough," Baltakis captures the plight of the post-war generations taking up new professions and identities in the city:

> From Leliūnai, Gargždai, from Žagarė
> We are the first generation from the plough.
> Engineers, party activists, poets
> Half city and half village.
> Like asphalt tar in tire treads
> We have soil beneath our nails.
> The hand that remembers the shaft of the scythe
> Flits across Whatman paper like a meadow.
> Like a strange, heavy rake
> Crude fingers grasp a pen.
> …
> Even if we reach the Arctic with turbogiants
> in our dreams we are still harnessing a horse.
> From Leliūnai, Gargždai, from Žagarė
> We are the first generation from the plough.
> In us the earth remains unsettled
> Half city and half village.[31]

Marcinkevičius was driven by similar ambitions and anxieties. In 1961 he wrote an epic poem called "Publicistic poem" which echoed the widespread fascination with Walt Whitman's poetry, and showed the intent to communicate philosophical ideas through modern means like *vers libre*. Contemporary critics pointed out how fragments from Whitman's poetry used in the opening of the work revealed a poet seeking to inscribe his oeuvre into world culture, of an ambition to speak about issues of universal importance to the world, assuming the position of a "true internationalist."[32]

Similar efforts were continued in Marcinkevičius' epic poem from 1965 entitled *The Wall*, subtitled *An Urban Poem*. Named after the 1939 story by Jean-Paul Sartre, the poem clearly aspired to bring Lithuanian literature up to speed with the leading trends of modern world literature and philosophy.[33] Critics were falling one over another in praising this work as a new radical turn in the development of Lithuanian culture. It was praised for its philosophical scope, intellectual depth, innovation in form, and uniqueness of expression.[34] Even Russian critics writing in the metropolitan journals joined in its praise.[35]

A lyrical voice intones at the beginning of the poem: "The cracked wall of the house is like a grey screen, telling the history of a person through sparse, modern means."[36] The city in the poem has no particular name or features, it is simply "the city" and is symbolized by a wall casting a shadow over a court-yard. The wall is joined by several other abstract figures: a woman, repre-senting fate, destiny, historical continuity; a beast representing fear; a man who lost his legs, a symbol of war; and several other, equally abstract figures.

The poem inspired and was cited in the opening images of a cutting edge 1968 documentary by Almantas Grikevičius (1935–2011), one of the up-and-coming directors of the new Lithuanian cinema. Entitled *Laikas eina per miestą* (Time walks through the city), the film juxtaposes scenes of modern, bustling Vilnius with "flashbacks" to the memory of war and fragments of Lithuania's conflict-ridden history, evoked through scenes of churches, med-ieval military fortifications, mass tombs and forests, accompanied by eerie modern music alternating between religious and warlike themes.

Marcinkevičius himself pointed out on many occasions that he was striving for an innovative, avant-garde way of exploring existential questions regarding the flow of history and human fate. He consciously sought to exclude those "national attributes" that were so dear to him and characteristic of his work (for example, in his poem *Donelaitis*) because they would have interfered with his effort at the time to "search for universality in thought and creativity."[37]

Marcinkevičius also described *The Wall* as the first effort of a man who "is rooted in the village, in its customs, in its landscape ... to touch upon the urban phenomenon and an existence rooted in the city."[38] He imagined the city as a milieu that did not and could not generate its own folklore, as the village did, and so he took it upon himself as a writer to "look at the city through various genres: to compose a city poem, a city fairy tale, a city drama, and so on." In the end, he admitted the artificiality of this approach, which turned out to be a disappointment and yielded only about 200 lines that he worked into the poem.[39] *The Wall* was outwardly praised, but also criticized in private for its artificial schematics and "literariness."[40]

The reference of *The Wall* to the famous French existentialist philosopher was not coincidental. Sartre was at the peak of his renown among Eastern bloc intellectuals after he refused to accept the Nobel Prize for Literature, awarded to him in October 1964, so as not to take a side in the cultural struggle between East and West.[41] To Lithuanians, his works were readily available in Russian and in Polish translations. He was very much respected and even adored in Lithuania.[42]

Accordingly, Sartre's five-day visit to the country in 1965 was seen as the cultural event of the decade, as proof of the cultural achievements of Soviet Lithuania and most of all its integration into the larger universe of cosmo-politan culture. He had traveled many times already to various parts of the USSR (including the Baltics), but it was the first time that Soviet Lithuania had received a guest of such international renown. Vilnius was already established as a fashionable place for the Moscow intellectuals to visit, but now it was to be visited by the most illustrious western intellectual.[43]

Sartre and Beauvoir arrived in Vilnius on July 26, 1965 and stayed for an entire week on a program designed to show them the republic's most significant sites. They traveled through the three major urban centres of Vilnius, Kaunas, and Klaipėda, the popular seaside resort town of Palanga as well as Nida, an exclusive retreat reserved for the highest party functionaries. The tour finished at the World War II monument near Pirčiupiai, a village burned by the Nazis and a key site of official Soviet memory signifying the sacrifices made by the Soviet people during the Great Patriotic War in Lithuania. The story of the burned village was also immortalized in a much-venerated poem by Marcinkevičius called "Blood and Ashes," written in 1960. The poem was the foundational work depicting the trauma of World War II in Lithuania, reproduced in textbooks and memorized by virtually every schoolchild.[44]

For Lithuanian intellectuals, the importance of Sartre's visit was beyond measure, one they had anticipated with great trepidation. The welcoming team was carefully selected and the choice to greet and accompany the famous guests throughout their visit became a reason for intense friction and bitterness among the local elites. Mieželaitis and the novelist Mykolas Sluckis,[45] two of the younger breed of literary innovators, were chosen to lead the welcoming team and to accompany Sartre and Beauvoir throughout their visit, along with a young Lithuanian photographer, Antanas Sutkus.[46]

Antanas Venclova, the dean of Soviet Lithuanian writers, a well-travelled man who had long served as Lithuania's cultural ambassador to the world, complained to his diary that he was not among those selected to meet personally with the French existentialist – in contrast to his friend, Kostas Korsakas, who hosted the French writer in his dacha. For Venclova, who in marked contrast to the new generation of power-brokers within the Writers' Union, knew French, this was yet additional evidence of the hidden battles in the ranks of the Lithuanian literary establishment and a sign of how the older generation was being pushed to the margins.[47]

Korsakas later poured salt on Venclova's wounds coming round to visit his home and enthusiastically describing Sartre's habits, interests and the like in great detail. "But I already knew all this," concludes Venclova, closing this clearly unpleasant topic in his diary.[48] In turn, the literary critic Vytautas Kubilius poked fun in his diary at both of his colleagues from the old establishment, pointing out that Venclova talked with tears in his voice that Sartre did not visit him, and Korsakas "got into the picture and is shining because now he can enter the Pantheon."[49]

Due to the overwhelming importance of the visit as perceived from the perspective of the local cultural context (Sluckis took down a verbatim account of virtually everything Sartre said), the encounter was perhaps destined to disappoint. From the remaining records it seems that while the French couple was trying to show a polite interest in everything they were being shown, the establishment artists and intellectuals of Soviet Lithuania were grasping for signs of recognition that would validate their achievements.

In his memoirs, the Lithuanian painter Augustinas Savickas describes his encounter with the French intellectuals in a section entitled "Shirt Stuck to the Body," conveying the nervousness and excitement he felt when Sartre and Beauvoir were brought to see his works. Throughout the viewing, Sluckis and Mieželaitis repeatedly asked the guests whether the painter's perspective on reality and his relationship with time was "contemporary," and they sighed with relief when they finally received a positive answer, as if Savickis, and by extension Lithuania, had just passed some important exam.[50] Beauvoir would later record a lack of enthusiasm for the modern art that she saw during the trip, noting that she found the folk art more appealing.[51]

For their part, the Lithuanians were perhaps even more disappointed in the lack of glamour surrounding the French visitors. They were taken aback by Sartre's humble presence: he seemed diminutive, withdrawn, tired and unattractive – a sharp contrast to the tall and handsome Mieželaitis, who accompanied him throughout the trip.[52] The attire of Beauvoir was also unimpressive, and Sluckis had to explain to the Soviet Lithuanian ladies, bewildered at the sight of her worn-out shoes, that intellectuals of this calibre do not pay attention to matters such as physical appearance.[53]

In general, the visit stirred passions and was the source of much jeering, and innumerable anecdotes. There was much gossip about how Mieželaitis

Figure 6.3 Antanas Sutkus, *Sartre in Lithuania*
Nida, 1965. Courtesy of Antanas Sutkus.

was enraged that Sartre did not give much consideration to his literary genius (which was so obsessively praised within the USSR), or offer to popularize his poetry in France. Just a few years later, after Sartre fell out of favor with the Soviet authorities for his support of Mao and his opposition to the invasion of Czechoslovakia, Mieželaitis published a sarcastic poem featuring a conversation between "the snob Sartre" and a *rūpintojėlis* – a traditional folk Lithuanian wooden sculpture of the Christ figure, a clear symbol of two worlds that are destined not to understand one another.[54]

From discovery to disillusionment

The sense of disillusionment arising from this highly charged encounter of Soviet Lithuania with a paragon of Western culture was of greater consequence than the disappointment of personal ambitions. A subsequent 1967 meeting between Sartre and Marcinkevičius, who at this point was already gaining stature as the most popular writer of the nation, provides an even clearer picture of the failed cultural encounter between the ambitious nationalism of a Soviet Lithuanian and the cosmopolitanism culture of the metropolitan West.

Marcinkevičius was not in Lithuania to take part in Sartre's 1965 visit, but he made up for the lost opportunity during his visit to Paris in 1967, upon the invitation of a French writers' society. After the critical success of *Blood and Ashes* and *The Wall*, Marcinkevičius was using his growing prominence in the USSR and beyond to promote Lithuania on the world stage. In particular, he had a plan to use UNESCO as a publishing house for the literature of small nations and a means of securing international recognition for Lithuania's unique language and culture.

In his numerous accounts of the meeting, written and told on several occasions to various interlocutors (including this author),[55] Marcinkevičius admits that he was nervous about how it would go, and spent a lot of time in preparations. He was pleased that Sartre proposed to meet for dinner at his favorite café, and especially glad when Sartre arrived with Simone de Beauvoir. He had just read a translation of her book, *Les Belles Images*, and so he felt more secure about his ability to carry on the conversation, in spite of the awkwardness of speaking through an interpreter.

They covered a range of topics over dinner and Marcinkevičius slowly gathered courage to make his UNESCO proposal. But instead of replying directly, Sartre shifted the conversation to the works of James Joyce. Marcinkevičius was initially at a loss and thought perhaps the interpreter was leading him astray, but after a few minutes he realized what Sartre meant to say. Just as the Irish author wrote in English, Sartre was implying that Lithuanians who wanted to reach an international audience should write in Russian, and abandon their attempts to elevate their own language and literature to the level of world literature.

Marcinkevičius was utterly shocked and dejected by this reply, feeling that his ambitions and those of his peers to find a place for Lithuanian culture in the wider world had been completely misguided. He was dismayed by what he felt to be an insurmountable cultural distance between himself and the idolized French intellectual:

> After the meeting with Sartre I was hit as if by lightning, by the revelation that nobody in the world cares about us and our tiny Lithuania. I felt like a completely superfluous person. This was a brutal discovery. Sartre is not guilty; it was merely the passing of my blindness. I realized that all what was left was this small plot of land, on which I remain to this day. As Voltaire wrote in the last line of Candide: "We must cultivate our own garden, gentlemen!"[56]

When he returned to Lithuania from Paris, Marcinkevičius set off to a writers' retreat and began to work on the first part of what would become a fantastically popular trilogy of historical dramas focussed on the turning points of Lithuania's medieval history. The first, *Mindaugas*, published in 1968, is about the medieval duke who unified Lithuanian lands and thus laid the first foundations for the Lithuanian state. The second, *Katedra*, published in 1971, is about the construction of the Great Cathedral of Vilnius as the symbolic heart of the nation's capital. The third, *Mažvydas*, published in 1977, is about the Lutheran pastor who is credited with the publication of the first printed Lithuanian text.

Marcinkevičius' dramas harked back to the interwar effort to define collective identity through the search for the key transformative historical points in the development of the nation. The story of the medieval duke Mindaugas, who sacrificed what was near and dear to himself for the sake of the Lithuanian state, tells of a territory consecrated with the blood of its people. The play about the Great Cathedral or *Katedra* of Vilnius, closed by the Soviets in 1949 and later converted into an art museum, evokes the spiritual, redemptive foundation of the community. The third drama about the Lutheran pastor Mažvydas who sacrificed his life for the printed Lithuanian word and enlightenment, dramatized the spread of culture and literacy, and the birth of an enlightened nation.

Indeed, during Soviet times, passages from these texts would be chanted in unison by audiences in theatres, such as the closing refrain from *Mažvydas*, where the main protagonist, the sixteenth-century Lithuanian Protestant priest, prompts the audience:

> We shall try to say our first word.
> Listen to it well … Listen with your heart!
> When you pronounce this word
> You will taste honey and blood on your lips,
> You will hear orioles calling before the rain,
> You will smell hay and linden trees,

You will see the frightened shadow of a cloud
Scurrying across the field …
So let us try.[57]

The choir then loudly recites the word *Lietuva* (Lithuania) pronounced in three syllables, each with heavy emphasis: "LIE-TU-VA, LIE-TU-VA." Some years later, at the peak of the popular movement against Soviet rule, these same refrains would be chanted by hundreds of thousands of ecstatic Lithuanians gathered in public protests, a phenomenon that astounded and puzzled foreign observers like the journalist and historian Anatol Lieven, who described these highly theatrical rallies as something of a cross between a communist convention and a Catholic mass.[58]

Between the meeting of Marcinkevičius and Sartre and the popular movement, Lithuanian society underwent a profound transformation. In retrospect, some people like Regimantas Adomaitis, a famous theatre actor, trace the beginnings of the popular movement against Soviet rule to this period.

For me *Sąjūdis* started in 1969 with the production of *Mindaugas* and then some time later, *Mažvydas*. These performances allowed us to express what was latent in our hearts, our minds, our souls. … They were a social event that woke us up, united us. I remember an incredible atmosphere of unity and solidarity among all who were on stage and those who were in the audience.[59]

Similarly, the respected theatre critic Antanas Vengris confided to Aldona Liobytė that he could not keep himself from crying throughout a reading of *Daukantas*, another historical epic by Marcinkevičius.[60]

These dramas gave their author the status of a national icon and cult figure – *the* national poet. Characterizing his own self-development, Marcinkevičius said that after his meeting with Sartre, he became a poet "with the land," shifting his focus from cosmopolitan breadth to national depth. His subsequent works were infused with a folkloric lyricism and moral categories like spirituality, simplicity, sincerity and tradition. He asserted the act of writing in Lithuanian as his mission and destiny – abandoning the language would have meant a betrayal of the national cause.[61]

For all of the individual drama of this revelation, Marcinkevičius was far from alone in turning away from the forward-looking attitude and preoccupation with the idea of progress and modernity. As his friend and course mate Algirdas Baltakis recalls, "I consciously tried to make myself an urban poet but it came to nothing. In any case, this village route is buried deep inside of me, God damn it, and that's all there is to it."[62] At some point in the mid-1960s, the tenor of Lithuanian culture made a significant shift. Instead of looking forward to the future of life in the modern city, it turned backward, and began a profound reflection on what was being lost during the transition.

Notes

1 See Anne Gorsuch's description of the Estonian SSR as the"Soviet Abroad" in Chapter 2 of *All This Is Your World: Soviet Tourism at Home and Abroad After Stalin* (Oxford: Oxford University Press, 2011), 49–78.
2 Krasauskas illustrated Mieželaitis' *The Man*, Robert Rozdestvensky's *Requiem*, and many other books. Krasauskas had personal exhibitions throughout the Soviet bloc and beyond, in East and West Germany, Bulgaria, Yugoslavia, India, and so on.
3 Jokūbonis' other important works include statues of Lenin in Klaipėda (1976) and Panevėžys (1983), the opera singer Kipras Petrauskas (1974), the historian Simonas Daukantas (1977), and the poet Adam Mickiewicz (1984) in Vilnius as well the poet and priest Maironis (1977) in Kaunas. Prestigious commissions continued in the post-Soviet era with the statue to Martynas Mažvydas on the 450th anniversary of the publication of the first Lithuanian book in 1997, and the Center of Europe monument in 2004.
4 Personal communication with Mikhail Iossel. Vilnius, August 12, 2011.
5 Marijonas Giedrys (1933–2011), Robertas Verba (1932–94), Almantas Grikevičius (1935–2011), Raimondas Vabalas (1937–2001), Arunas Žebriūnas (1930–2013), and others.
6 In Elena Zubkova, *Pribaltika i Kreml'*, 1940–53 (Moscow: Rosspen, 2008), 192.
7 Vladislav M. Zubok, "Soviet Policy Aims at the Geneva Conference," in *Cold War Respite: The Geneva Conference of 1955*. Ed. Gunter Bischof and Saki Dokrill (Baton Rouge, LA: Louisiana University Press, 2006). According to Intourist figures, 1 million foreign tourists visited the Soviet Union between 1957 and 1969, and 560,000 Soviet citizens travelled abroad each year starting in 1956, doubling to a million by 1965. Anne E. Gorsuch, *This is All Your World: Soviet Tourism at Home and Abroad After Stalin* (Oxford: Oxford University Press, 2011).
8 Pia Koivunen, "The 1957 Moscow Youth Festival: Propagating a New, Peaceful Image of the Soviet Union," in *Soviet State and Society under Nikita Khrushchev*, ed. Melanie Ilic and Jeremny Smith (London: Routledge, 2009).
9 Anne E. Gorsuch, *This is All Your World: Soviet Tourism at Home and Abroad After Stalin* (Oxford: Oxford University Press, 2011), 24.
10 Vytautas Brėdikis, "Kelionių žavesys ir skurdas (b)" in unpublished memoirs (Vilnius, 2013).
11 Marija Drėmaitė, Šiaurės modernizmo įtaka "lietuviškajai modernizmo mokyklai (1959–69)," *Menotyra* 18.4 (2011): 308–28. See also the unpublished memoirs of Vytautas Brėdikis.
12 Antanas Venclova, Diary (November 22, 1961): 41. Venclovas House Museum Archives, Vilnius.
13 Nikolai Konovalov, "Soshestvie bogov," *Izvestia* 274 (November 19, 1959): 4. Sniečkus, who had testy relations with Khrushchev, was upset with the Nasvytis brothers for not having consulted with him before refusing Adjubey's invitiation. Algimantas Nasvytis, Interview by author. Audio recording. Vilnius, May 14, 2012.
14 Algimantas Baltakis, Interview by author. Audio recording. Vilnius, February 22, 2010.
15 Algimantas Baltakis in Aistė Krasauskaitė, *Juoda ir balta: Prisiminimai apie Stasį Krasauską*. Vilnius: Tyto Alba, 2004, 153. Algimantas Baltakis, Interview by author. Audio recording. Vilnius, February 22, 2010.
16 *Akiračiai*, June 1977. See also Donatas Sauka, *Fausto amžiaus epilogas* (Vilnius: Tyto alba, 1998), 175.
17 *Literatūra ir menas* 16.24 (June 1962).
18 Elena Baliutytė, "The Evolution of Eduardas Mieželaitis' Creative Work from the 1960s to the 1980s: From Prometheanism to Quixoticism," in Elena Baliutytė

and Donata Mitaitė, eds. *Baltic Memory: Processes of Modernisation in Lithuanian, Latvian and Estonian Literature of the Soviet Period* (Vilnius: Institute of Lithuanian Literature and Folklore, 2011), 180.

19 *Literatūra ir menas* 24 (June 16, 1962).

20 Antanas Venclova, Diary (January 15, 1965): 41. Venclovas House Museum Archives, Vilnius.

21 R.Z. Saukienė, ed. *Šmaikščioji rezistentė Aldona Liobytė: publicistika, laiškai, atsiminimai* (Vilnius: Lietuvos rašytojų sąjungos leidykla, 1995), 140.

22 Algirdas Greimas, "Apie Eduardą Mieželaitį ir jo Paryžių," in *Iš arti ir iš toli* (Vilnius, 1991), 478–82.

23 Algirdas Greimas, "Medžiaga sovietinio lietuvio fenomenologijai" [Material for a phenomenology of the Soviet Lithuanian], in J. Algirdas and Saulius Žukas, *Iš arti ir iš toli: literatūra, kultūra, grožis* (Vilnius: Vaga, 1991), 141–44.

24 Ibid.

25 Tomas Venclova, *Raketos, planetos ir mes* (Vilnius: Valstybinė grožinės literatūros leidykla, 1962), 164.

26 For a Soviet Lithuanian view on the changes of the *habitat* of the urban residents see the study by A. Daniliauskas, *Lietuvos miesto gyventojų materialinė kultūra XX a.* (Vilnius: Mokslas, 1978). See also Dangė Čebatariūnaitė, "Ideologija fizinėje erdvėje: butų interjerai sovietinėje Lietuvoje 'atšilimo' laikotarpiu," in *Naujasis židinys-Aidai* 8 (August 2006): 329–38 and Regina Lakačauskaitė, "Miestiečio butas Sovietų Lietuvoje: ideologijos atspindžiai gyvenamojoje erdvėje: 1944–90," *Naujasis židinys-Aidai* 1–2 (February 2010):13–22.

27 Jonas Tamošaitis, "Kaip augs miestai," *Pergalė* 10 (1962): 140.

28 Albinas Žukauskas, "Miestai ar didkaimiai?" *Literatūra ir menas* 6.1 (January 1962): 1.

29 Algimantas Baltakis, *Gimiau pačiu laiku: iš dienoraščių, 1960–1997* (Vilnius: Tyto alba, 2008).

30 Algimantas Baltakis, *Požeminės upės (Underground Rivers)* (Vilnius, 1967), 45.

31 Algimantas Baltakis, *Keliaujantis kalnas: eilėraščiai* (Vilnius: Vaga, 1967). Translated by the author with permission.

32 The poet was quickly translated into Russian by Robert Rozhdestvensky. Whitman became something of a literary guru for Soviet writers when his poems started appearing in *Innostrannaja literatura* during Khrushchev's time in the Soviet literary milieu. See Yassen Zassoursky, "Whitman's Reception and Influence in the Soviet Union," in Sill, Geoffrey M., ed. *Walt Whitman of Mickle Street: A Centennial Collection* (Knoxville, TN: University of Tennessee Press, 1994), 42–49. In Lithuania, Whitman was much admired and imitated, notably by Eduardas Mieželaitis. See Dovydas Judelevičius, "Apie žodžius, laiką ir save" *Pergalė* 9 (1962): 144–56 and others.

33 Sartre's *The Wall* was published in Lithuanian translation in 1965.

34 Jonas Lankutis, "Žmogus ir dinozauras," *Pergalė* 2 (1966): 89–100; Dovydas Judelevičius, A. Rabačiauskaitė, Jonas Lankutis, R. Pakalniškis *et al.*, "Literatūrinis *Pergalės* antradienis," *Pergalė* 2 (1966):181–83.

35 "I solntse podnialos' iz za steny," *Literaturnaya gazeta* (February 28, 1968): 6.

36 Justinas Marcinkevičius, *Siena: miesto poema* (Vilnius: Vaga, 1965), 309.

37 Justinas Marcinkevičius, "Literatūrinis *Pergalės* antradienis," *Pergalė* 2 (1966): 182–83. *Donelaitis* was published in 1964, about an eighteenth-century Lithuanian priest and poet, and the author of one of the first works of classical Lithuanian literature called *The Seasons*. In *The Seasons*, Donelaitis depicts the lives of simple Lithuanian peasants living in East Prussia, where Lithuanians were subject to colonization and assimilation by Germans. In his play, Marcinkevičius extols the poet-priest as a savior and the very manifestation of the nation, explaining that his aim was to depict the physical annihilation of a part of the nation and its spiritual immortality.

38 Fifty years later, Marcinkevičius would recollect *The Wall* as his contribution to the all-union debate among "lyricists" and "physicists," the essence of which was the relation of nature and civilization. His idea was to introduce a model of the city which was not separated from nature, but created in the likeness of the Lithuanian urban areas, which were something in between a village and a city. Justinas Marcinkevičius, Interview by author. Audio recording. Vilnius, January 6, 2010.

39 Justinas Marcinkevičius, "Literatūrinis *Pergalės* antradienis," *Pergalė* 2 (1966): 182–83.

40 For example, this critique is frequently expressed in the diary of Antanas Venclova, who generally felt a strong liking for Marcinkevičius and his circle.

41 Sartre's star with the Soviet authorities would soon be tarnished by his support for the Prague Spring in Czechoslovakia and Mao's Cultural Revolution in China.

42 Marcinkevičius said that at the time he considered Sartre and Camus to be the greatest minds of the era. Justinas Marcinkevičius, Interview by author. Audio recording. Vilnius, January 3, 2010.

43 Much of the following account of Sartre's visit to Lithuania is indebted to Solveiga Daugirdaitė's study "1965-ųjų akimirkos su Simone de Beauvoir ir Jeanu Pauliu Sartre'u," *Colloquia* 21 (2008): 96–113.

44 Mykolas Sluckis, a contemporary of Marcinkevičius, told of the impression it made on him: "I felt that it raised Lithuanian literature to a completely different level. He was like a Soviet Maironis." Mykolas Sluckis, Interview by author. Audio recording. Vilnius, November 10, 2008. Maironis (Jonas Mačiulis, 1862–1932) is one of the most famous Lithuanian romantic poets.

45 Sluckis was born to a Jewish family in Panevėžys (Ponevez) and lost both his parents and most of his family in the Holocaust. After the war, Sluckis became one of the first members of the Soviet Lithuanian Writers Union and a classic author of Soviet Lithuanian literature, writing only in Lithuanian (somewhat rare for the Jewish community which at that time comprised mostly of Yiddish, Polish, and Russian speakers).

46 Sutkus' recollections of the trip and collection of photographs were published in *Sartre & Beauvoir: Cinq jours en Lituanie* (Latresne: Le Bord de L'Eau, 2005).

47 Antanas Venclova, Diary. Book IV (August 1, 1965): 233–34. Venclovas House Museum Archives, Vilnius.

48 Antanas Venclova, Diary. Book IV (August 11, 1965): 236. Venclovas House Museum Archives, Vilnius.

49 Vytautas Kubilius, Janina Žėkaitė, and Jūratė Sprindytė, *Dienoraščiai 1945–1977* (Vilnius: Lietuvos literatūros ir tautosakos institutas, 2006), 324.

50 Augustinas Savickas, *Žalia tyla* (Vilnius: Tyto Alba, 2002), 222–23.

51 On the significance of the "contemporary style" (*sovremenny stil*) to Soviet artists during the Thaw see Susan E. Reid, "Modernizing Socialist Realism in the Khrushchev Thaw: The Struggle for a 'Contemporary Style' in Soviet Art," in Polly Jones, *The Dilemmas of De-Stalinization: Negotiating Cultural and Social Change in the Khrushchev Era* (London: Routledge, 2006), 209–30. Simone de Beauvoir, *Tout Compte Fait* (Paris: Gallimard, 1972).

52 Almost fifty years later, Marcinkevičius still remarked on what he perceived at the time as Sartre's lack of grandeur, charisma or presence. Justinas Marcinkevičius, Interview by author. Audio recording. Vilnius, January 6, 2010.

53 Solveiga Daugirdaitė, "1965-ųjų akimirkos su Simone de Beauvoir ir Jeanu Pauliu Sartre'u," *Colloquia* 21 (2008): 88.

54 Eduardas Mieželaitis, "Medžio grimasos," *Nemunas* 3 (1970): 10–12.

55 For example, see Justinas Marcinkevičius, *Dienoraštis be datų* (Vilnius: Vaga, 1981), 111, and Valentinas Sventickas, "Išsaugoti – žmones, kūrybą, Lietuvą: poetą Justiną Marcinkevičių kalbina Valentinas Sventickas 2005.III.3," (Interview with Justinas Marcinkevičius) *Literatūra ir menas* (11 March 2005).

56 Mindaugas Kvietkauskas, "Triūsas savo sode" (Labor in your own garden). Interview with Justinas Marcinkevičius. *Metai* 3 (2000): 98–102.
57 Justinas Marcinkevičius, *Mažvydas: trijų dalių giesmė* (Vilnius: Vaga, 1977). Translated by the author with permission.
58 Anatol Lieven, *The Baltic Revolution: Estonia, Latvia, Lithuania, and the Path to Independence* (New Haven, CT: Yale University Press, 1993), 109. In this respect, Lieven's flippant presentation of these specific lines from *Mažvydas* as "stomach-turning stuff" fails to convey their importance to the audience in question and thus weakens his insightful argument about the "Wilhelmine" fusion of Soviet and nationalist styles in the Baltic literatures and art of the period (127–29).
59 Regimantas Adomaitis, *Sąjūdis ateina iš toli* (*Sąjūdis* comes from afar) (Vilnius: Margi raštai, 2008).
60 R.Z. Saukienė, ed. *Šmaikščioji rezistentė Aldona Liobytė: publicistika, laiškai, atsiminimai* (Vilnius: Lietuvos rašytojų sąjungos leidykla, 1995), 161.
61 Mindaugas Kvietkauskas, "Triūsas savo sode" (Labor in your own garden). Interview with Justinas Marcinkevičius. *Metai* 3 (2000): 98–102.
62 Onė Baliukonytė, Interview with Algimantas Baltakis "Ir pats stipresnis," *Moksleivis* 2 (1980): 14–15.

7   The rustic turn

The connection between the personal and artistic transformation of Marcinkevičius and his peers in the 1960s and the emergence of the popular movement *Sąjūdis* in the 1980s is captured in the concept of the rustic turn. The rustic turn was a broad cultural reaction to the failure of Soviet modernity, which gathered speed through the 1970s and was expressed as a return to the rural, pre-modern roots of identity. It began as a vague sense of nostalgia for the lost way of life and grew into a politically explosive discourse of collective trauma.

The rustic turn is perhaps best understood as a local, peripheral and by the same token highly accentuated expression of the "return of memory" which took place throughout Europe in the later twentieth century; a transnational process that for Pierre Nora was based on the "acceleration" and "democratization" of history, generating abrupt changes in mass consciousness. In France, for example, the growing awareness among urbanites of the passing of the traditional way of life in the village created a sense of being cut off from the past. Nora writes that this led to the widespread sense of "a tradition from which we would be forever separated, one that would thereby become precious, mysterious, and imbued with an uncertain meaning, which was our task to recover."[1]

The same feeling of separation and loss was felt throughout the Soviet Union, only much stronger, insofar as the leap from a pre-modern, agrarian way of life to the modern industrial existence in the metropolis occurred over the space of a single generation. According to Geoffrey Hosking, the progressive, forward-looking impulse of modernism and its specific expression in Socialist Realism was abruptly reversed around 1965. "At a stroke the Promethean Soviet drive towards the future had been inverted, had become the worship of a lost Golden Age."[2] In his description of the cultural precursors to the cataclysmic changes that would rock the Soviet Union in the mid-1980s, Hosking points to the emergence of a genre of literature called Village Prose, which he interprets as a sign of a paradigm change in Soviet culture and mentality.

Russian village prose was inherently critical of the modernizing agenda of Soviet power, provoking a reaction among liberal cosmopolitans and Marxist-Leninist ideologists alike. Emerging as a widespread, grass-roots cultural phenomenon, it was also selectively co-opted by the Kremlin, which increasingly came to rely on Russian national sentiment to bolster its waning socialist legitimacy. As great-power chauvinists gained ground in the political and cultural bureaucracies, the Soviet state stepped up the pressure on dissidents, liberals and manifestations of non-Russian nationalism, notably in Ukraine.

In Soviet Lithuania, by way of contrast, the strength of the national communist leadership and the cohesiveness of the cultural elites focussed the repressive energies of the regime onto the local liberals, cosmopolitans and dissidents, leaving the rustic turn to grow in the shade, as it were, of the quasi-official Russian nativist movement. What began as a seemingly apolitical revival of folk heritage grew into a widespread ethnographic movement that articulated standards of cultural authenticity that were implicitly anti-Soviet. Activists mobilized the youth through various forms of expeditions, folk rituals and performance focussed on individual and collective self-transformation. Artists and writers crystallized the widespread but vague nostalgia for the lost way of life into an increasingly politicized discourse of traumatic displacement that held Soviet-style modernity to be the source of contemporary malaise.

Peasant metropolis

The rustic turn was rooted in the profound social changes caused by rapid urbanization in the Soviet Union; specifically, the creation of large urban populations of individuals who had recently migrated from the villages. As an unintended by-product of the Stalinist model of modernization through forced collectivization and industrialization, the explosive, uncontrolled growth of Soviet cities combined aspects of urban and rural life in a complex cultural synthesis that has fascinated Western observers since Walter Benjamin coined the phrase "rural metropolis" during his visit to Moscow in 1926–27 and described in his *Moscow Diary*.[3]

Benjamin is perhaps the most celebrated but certainly not the first foreigner to focus on this aspect of Soviet life. In 1922 the American journalist Louis Fischer already noticed that Russian "cities seemed to be filled with people fresh from the forests and wheat fields."[4] In equally picturesque but bitterly ironic terms, Russian observers who actually lived through this period like Vasily Grossman remind us of the traumatic, "urbicidal" cost of such rapid social transformation:

> the movement of millions of people resulted in that bright-eyed, high-cheekboned provincial people who filled the streets of Leningrad, while in the labour camp barracks Ivan Grigorievich encountered more and more of those sad Petersburgeans with their French sounding 'r's.[5]

Demographic statistics bear out these literary impressions. By Western standards, the USSR as a whole was urbanized belatedly and rapidly. In 1917 less than one in six residents of the Russian Empire lived in cities, compared to three out of four in Great Britain and about half of the residents in

Germany or the United States. Between 1926 and 1939, an estimated 23 million Soviet peasants moved permanently to the cities, a rate of rural-to-urban migration that David Hoffman claims was unprecedented in world history. By the end of the 1930s, he writes, 40 percent of the Soviet urban population consisted of former peasants who had moved from the countryside over the past decade, turning Moscow into a "peasant metropolis" together with other large Soviet cities.[6]

After the mass destruction and urbicidal effects of World War II, rapid urbanization would resume in the 1950s and 1960s, driving the city population of Soviet Russia up to 62 percent in 1970 and 72 percent in 1985. In Soviet Lithuania, collectivization and the brutal counter-insurgency coincided with postwar reconstruction to drive urbanization at a rate much higher than the postwar Soviet average, and even higher than Soviet Russia in the 1930s, matched in the postwar era only by Moldova and Belarus and, presumably, Western Ukraine – i.e., those territories on the European periphery with the lowest initial rates of urbanization that were incorporated into the Soviet Union after World War II and subjected to reconstruction, forced industrialization and collectivization at the same time.

After the death and displacement of World War II, only 15 percent of Lithuanians lived in cities in 1945, about the same level as the Soviet Union in 1917, and this figure still included the 170,000 Poles who would be "repatriated" to Poland in 1946. But by the time the next census was taken in 1959, the urban population had almost tripled in size (375,000 to 1,025,000), with the inflow of ethnic Lithuanians from rural areas accounting for the majority of the increase. By 1989, urbanization in Lithuania exceeded the Soviet average and was comparable to that of Russia and the other Baltic States.[7]

Meanwhile, collectivization and rural depopulation had left the villages in a half-deserted and decrepit state. Most of those who left for the cities were from the younger generations, leaving the villages populated mostly by older people. Even after collectivization was complete, the rural population was subjected to incessant waves of "reforms" imposed from above.

In the mid-1960s, a "melioration" campaign was launched to improve the living conditions of the rural population. Starting in 1966, people living on individual homesteads were transferred to villages of some 200–300 inhabitants. But just a few years later, the directive was changed and the normative size of the new villages was to be no less than 1,000 inhabitants, which resulted in the repeated relocation of one third of those who had already moved.[8] Taken together these repeated relocations had the social and psychological effect of a second collectivization.

The ongoing dislocations in the countryside, coming on top of the mass migration of the young to the cities, had a destabilizing effect on the rural communities, especially the elderly, for whom the amenities of Soviet mass housing projects provided cold comfort after the traumatic experience of being forced from the homes they inhabited since the interwar period. Indeed, many families had lived in the same locality for several generations, if not centuries, meaning that melioration put a sudden and literal end to the most significant *lieux de mémoire* of traditional Lithuanian society. The campaign eliminated the single-family homestead as a social structure, leaving the countryside dotted with abandoned cemeteries, wooden houses and barns leaning into the ground, the yards overgrown with high grasses and bush – a semi-erased map of a lost world.

Similarly, the extremely rapid in-migration of people from the countryside left the new urban population in a state of psychological and cultural disorientation. In a prophetic 1970 essay that accurately identified the social causes of Soviet collapse, Russian dissident and historian Andrey Amal'rik highlighted the social effects of collectivization and rapid urbanization:

> The "proletarianization" of the countryside has created an "alien" class that is neither peasant nor worker. They have the dual psychology of the owners of tiny homesteads and of farm hands working on gigantic and anonymous farms. How this class views itself, and what it wants, is known, I think, to nobody. Furthermore, the mass exodus of peasants to the city has created a new type of city dweller: a person who has broken with his old environment, way of life, and culture, and who is finding it very difficult to discover his place in his new environment and feels ill at ease in it. He is both frightened and aggressive. He no longer has any idea to what level of society he belongs.[9]

These reflections were echoed later in a 1992 interview by the Lithuanian writer Romualdas Granauskas, who describes the root causes of social malaise in Soviet Lithuanian cities with an almost anthropological detachment and attention to everyday detail:

> He got lost. Pushed out of his village, his field, his rivulet by the campaign of melioration … having left behind his neighbors who had become like relatives over time, he bought an apartment in the city, moved into the multi-story building without any idea where to put his butter churn or his oak barrel. After having moved in, he nevertheless would get up with the dawn, observe the weather through the window, gauge the wind. After coming home from some job to which he was assigned by the state, he had nothing to do, nothing to undertake, because he was used to working until late. And out of this disorientation many started to drink … [10]

Russian village prose

Russian intellectuals who sought to represent and give voice to this new category of *homo sovieticus* gathered around the themes and motifs of village prose, which grew to become the most prevalent genre of literature of the Brezhnev era. Geoffrey Hosking draws an analogy between the emergence of village prose and the Victorian period of English literature, when novelists like Charles Dickens portrayed the contagion of moral and spiritual disorder that spread through the teeming industrial towns, reasserting the values inherited from an earlier, ostensibly more stable and human era.[11]

The genre is considered to have developed from Valentin Ovechkin's essays published in the early 1950s on the problems faced by the collectivized villages. His example was followed by a group of writers called the *ocherkisty*: the novels and stories of Ovechkin (*Trudnaya vesna*, 1956), Efim Dorosh (*Derevenskiy dnevnik*, 1958) and Aleksandr Iashin ("Rychagi," 1956), all of which brought to public attention the damage collectivization had done to the village and to the religious values and traditions of the peasantry. The genre matured through the 1960s and 1970 in the works of Fyodor Abramov, Viktor Astaf'yev, Vasily Belov, Viktor Likhonosov, Vladimir Lichutin, Yevgeny Nosov, and many others.

Village prose writers emphasized the connection of Russians with nature and the soil by glorifying the peasant way of life in the countryside. The countryside was portrayed as pure and unsullied, in stark contrast to the cities, which were defiled by technology and so-called progress. Village prose was more than a literary theme; it was an ethical programme and a manifesto. The accusation that the Soviet system had destroyed the environment and alienated Russians from their primordial connection with the land was ever present, if only by implication.

Initially, the village prose movement received only oblique and selective support from the authorities, starting with Khrushchev's decision to allow the publication of *One Day in the Life of Ivan Denisovych* in 1962 in the literary journal *Novy Mir*. Solzhenitsyn's groundbreaking novel was not a work of village prose, but contemporaries note that Khrushchev's support for it was driven by his sympathy for the protagonist as a simple *muzhik*.[12] Aleksandr Tvardovsky, the editor of *Novy Mir*, was himself the son of a peasant who had been persecuted as a *kulak*. He strongly encouraged the publication of village prose works, and his journal was an important base for village prose writers with a liberal orientation in the early 1960s.

Later, with the ouster of Khrushchev and the installation of Brezhnev in the Kremlin, the conservative journals *Veche* and *Molodaia gvardia* began to publish village prose works, but they now took on more of a Russian nationalist and occasionally anti-Semitic or even neo-Stalinist slant. Russian patriots emerged in the 1970s as a growing network of intellectuals and artists. They published programmatic articles, revived Slavophilism and criticized the cosmopolitan, Westernized Soviet intelligentsia. Some even urged the authorities to take measures to save the peasantry and the foundations of national culture, to purge "cosmopolitan" (i.e., Jewish) intellectuals like the Polish regime had done after March 1968. They applauded the crushing of the Prague Spring and were critical of détente with the West.[13]

As argued by historian Vladislav Zubok, the gradual politicization of Russian village prose literature in a nationalist direction was an outcome of a *Kulturkampf* between conservatives and liberals amid the ideological wreckage of communism. De-Stalinization had undermined established ideological certainties and it uncovered traumatic memories of the past, generating divergent and incompatible martyrologies. Liberals who supported the Thaw progressed from the de-Stalinization promoted by Khrushchev to a more comprehensive critique of the Soviet system and the communist idea as a whole. The conservatives who reacted cautiously or who were directly threatened by Khrushchev's reforms also sought to articulate new forms of collective identity that would survive the wreckage of the Soviet model.[14]

On the left, artists and intellectuals focused on the political tyranny of Stalin, the mass purges of the urban elites in the late 1930s, on the anti-cosmopolitan/ anti-Semitic campaign of the late 1940s, on the destruction of the best and the brightest of the Russian and Soviet intellectual elites in general. Initially, they sought to revive utopian ideals of socialist community, with high culture and the traditions of the urban intelligentsia as the source of a social revival. After the Soviet invasion of Czechoslovakia in 1968 and with the demise of any hope for "socialism with a human face," they turned increasingly to Western models of modernization that emphasized democratic development, universal human rights and cosmopolitan citizenship. Those who engaged in dissent were subject to continual harassment; many chose to emigrate or were forced into exile.

The martyrology of the right focussed on collectivization and the destruction of the peasant way of life. In this narrative the heroes were not Mandelstam and Pasternak, but the simple, uneducated peasant, while Khrushchev came across as no less a villain than Stalin. Khrushchev's "hare-brained schemes" and disastrous agricultural reforms, his vision of various nationalities merging into a cosmopolitan Soviet nation, and his dogmatic persecution of religious belief, which resulted in the demolition or closure of over 10,000 Orthodox churches, provoked an irrational but powerful nostalgia for the halcyon days of social conservatism under Stalin. Rather than turn to the West, the Soviet right rejected modernization altogether, seeking to develop an alternative set of values based on the nation's spiritual links with the natural world, on folk culture and tradition.

Further echoes of anti-cosmopolitanism

The *Kulturkampf* between the liberals and conservatives reached a turning point in 1972 with the publication of a long, two-page broadsheet article in *Literaturnaya gazeta* called "Against Anti-Historicism," signed by one "Doctor of Historical Sciences A. Yakovlev," which subjected the views of several dozen Russian village prose writers, poets, critics, and historians who sought the sources of national identity in the rural tradition to a withering ideological critique.

The article caused an immediate sensation, as all could easily surmise that the real author was none other than Aleksandr Nikolayevich Yakovlev, head of the Kremlin's Department of Ideology and Propaganda.[15] Cultural conservatives feared the publication marked the beginning of a witch-hunt, making ironic comparisons to the infamous report denouncing Akhmatova and Zoshchenko published in *Pravda* in 1946, which launched the *Zhdanovshchina*.

Only now the attack appeared to be coming from the liberal, cosmopolitan left, couching its anti-nativist thrust in the doctrinal internationalism of Marxism-Leninism. In the article, Yakovlev accused those seeking to revive the traditional culture of the village of "de-facto taking issue with the dialectical Leninist view of the peasantry, and with the socialist practice of reforming the village." By invoking the name of Lenin, Yakovlev was making a serious accusation, and the article did not hesitate to name the names of a few dozen of the worst offenders.

> Proponents of the theory of "sources" hold that it is not the city but the village, moreover, of the old type that exists primarily in their imagination, the old *aul*, the lost *khutor* or *kishlak*, preserving stagnant traditions of everyday life, which is the main breeding ground for national culture, for some kind of "national morality." And by this they cultivate an admiration for the patriarchal way of life, for family tyranny as the basis of national values. Naturally, from this point of view, socialism and the changes that it has brought to our lives over the past half century, the social practices of Soviet society and the nascent communist morality must seem like an artificial innovation, an unjustified disruption of their accustomed way of life.[16]

In subsequent interviews and in his memoirs, Yakovlev describes the article as the culmination of a personal campaign waged against the chauvinism, neo-Stalinism and anti-Semitism that was gaining ground in journals like *Oktyabr'* and *Molodaia Gvardia*.[17] He dismisses the communist vocabulary of the piece as a mere formality that was necessary to ensure publication and to protect his position, but the text is actually an extremely coherent expression of the cosmopolitan, urban vision of community common to the modernizing ideologies of liberalism and Marxism alike.

That said, this was no coordinated campaign against the conservatives, but a quixotic attempt by one man to stem the tide. Indeed, with the publication of this article, Yakovlev had come about as close as one could get to freelancing in the Kremlin by pushing the article through the vetting process against the advice of his colleagues and superiors. As the subsequent wave of complaints mounted, including letters of outrage from such established cultural figures as Mikhail Sholokhov, author of *Quietly Flows the Don*, Brezhnev decided that Yakovlev had gone too far, exceeded his rank, and needed to be brought down to size.[18] He was dismissed from the CPSU Central Committee, and sent into "exile" to Canada as the Soviet Ambassador in 1973.[19]

By this point, Yakovlev's orthodox Marxism was already out of touch with the Kremlin's *de facto* policy of co-opting Russian nationalism as an alternative source of legitimacy for the regime.[20] All of his attempts to defend his position with reference to socialist doctrine were dismissed out of hand.[21] Moreover, Yakovlev's doctrinal support for communist cosmopolitanism was also out of touch with Brezhnev's approach to the nationalities question, which had recently (at the XXIV Party Congress in 1971) abandoned the goal of "merging" (*slianie*) the various nations of the USSR, pursued by the Soviet nationalities policy under Khrushchev, and celebrated instead the fictitious "unified Soviet people" (*yediny sovietsky narod*) as an accomplished fact.

(A joke from the period captures Brezhnev's approach to such problems: Stalin, Khrushchev and Brezhnev are together in a train which breaks down. Stalin orders the conductor to be shot, but the train does not move. Khrushchev orders the conductor to be rehabilitated, but the train still does not move. Brezhnev then reaches to draw the curtains, turns on the gramophone and exclaims, "There, moving at last!")

Notably, the reference in "Against Anti-Historicism" to "stagnant traditions" singles out three non-Russian types of rural settlement to amplify the idea of backwardness and tribalism: an *aul* is a fortified village typical of the Caucasus; a *khutor* is homestead settlement typical of Ukraine and southern Russia, and the term was also used to refer to homestead settlements in the Baltics. Finally, a *kishlak* is a rural settlement typical of the semi-nomadic peoples of Central Asia – the term means "wintering place," derived from the Turkic *qış* – winter.

With such references, Yakovlev was only giving expression to the chauvinism implicit in Soviet nationalities policy, which presumed that non-Russian nationalities would gradually assimilate to Russian culture – an implicit but fundamental point of Soviet nationalities policy. Not surprisingly, letters of complaint from the Ukrainian and Uzbek writers' unions were organized by the Communist Party leaders in each republic and they too were used by Kremlin conservatives to force Yakovlev's ouster.[22]

Naturally, Yakovlev's departure to Canada did nothing to help the cause of the non-Russian republics. Petro Shelest, leader of the Communist Party of Ukraine, was also dismissed in 1972 (as was the leader of the Georgian Communist Party) and the Ukrainian intelligentsia subjected to a deep purge. Hundreds of dissidents, including many artists, writers and intellectuals, were targeted with prosecutions, and a number of writers including Zinoviy Krasivsky and Anatoly Lupynis were forcibly committed to psychiatric clinics.[23] Within Russia, the liberal and dissident-nationalist wings of the Russian village prose movement were suppressed through the suspension of the journal *Veche* and the exile of Solzhenitsyn in 1974.

Meanwhile, nationalist members of the Soviet Russian cultural establishment were advanced to leading positions and Russian village prose came to be associated with cultural and political conservatism.[24] Yakovlev's quixotic attempt to mount a campaign "against anti-historicism" ended up provoking another wave of anti-cosmopolitanism and great-power chauvinism.

In this context it is striking that even after the 1972 self-immolation of Romas Kalanta (1953–72) in Kaunas and an eruption of mass demonstrations, there was no real purge of the leadership or brutal crackdown on the intelligentsia in Lithuania. A student in his early twenties, Kalanta died after setting himself ablaze in the square adjoining the theatre in Kaunas where Soviet power was first proclaimed. Aside from a note he left on a nearby bench that read "blame only the regime for my death" (the contents of which became known to the public only after the opening of the KGB archives in the 1990s), he left no other explanation for his act.[25]

News of his act spread by word of mouth, provoking a public demonstration in Kaunas the next day by some 3,000 people, mostly youths chanting "Freedom for Hippies, Freedom for Lithuania!" The police broke up the demonstration, provoking violence and sporadic fighting that led to the death of a police officer and some 400 arrests. Smaller demonstrations took place in other cities.[26] However, Sniečkus was able to convince Moscow that he had the situation under control, and although 20 percent of those arrested were members of the *Komsomol*, he explained that the outburst was exceptional, provoked by foreign radio broadcasts, and not indicative of social trends in the country. The suppression of Lithuanian dissidents and Catholic activists was intensified and many feared a broader crackdown, but the Lithuanian intelligentsia was as a whole spared any serious reprisals aside from a few harsh speeches and the shifting of a few editorial positions.[27] By deflecting the blame for the outburst of social dissatisfaction to the work of nefarious radio broadcasts and the corrupt Western influence on the youth, Sniečkus retained the trust of the Kremlin, and the exploration of national identity in folk culture was less tainted with the brush of "bourgeois nationalism" as it was, for example, in Ukraine.[28]

As a result, in Lithuania the rustic turn was able to develop relatively unhindered, in the shade, as it were, of the officially sanctioned nativist movement in Soviet Russia. This immunity did not apply, however, to Western-oriented, cosmopolitan intellectuals like Tomas Venclova who, over and above his increasingly dissident politics (he was among the founders of the Lithuanian branch of the Helsinki movement in 1976), was fully engaged in the *Kulturkampf* waged between the liberals and the conservatives in Moscow and Leningrad at the time. A friend of Joseph Brodsky and with close relations to other leading Russian dissidents, he was a genuine urbanite and cosmopolitan, a Soviet "aristocrat," and in this respect he stood out from the majority of his Lithuanian colleagues.

Like Yakovlev, Venclova was a vocal critic of the rustic turn in Soviet culture. His poetry and writings were erudite, and he consciously distinguished himself from his peers whose work drew on rural folk motifs.[29] Wary of the potential for the rustic provincialism of Soviet Lithuanian society to lapse into xenophobia, his personal identification with Lithuanian history and culture reached beyond the pre-modern legends of the Grand Dukes or the folk revival of modernity, but included the Polish "interregnum" of the renaissance and classical periods, which he appreciated and viewed as authentically Lithuanian. For example, in an article written in 1970, he wrote:

> We all are fascinated by folklore and folk art. The folk groups have plenty of members and the folk museums never lack visitors. But we sometimes act

as though we lived on a reservation, and forget the other dimensions of our culture. The national traditions of Lithuania include more than folk sculptures, songs and laments, but also Vilnius University, the architecture of Vilnius, the old and modern towns of Kaunas and Klaipėda, as well as the literature and music of the sixteenth and seventeenth centuries. Just as we defend folk art from unnecessary intrusions, so too should we defend even more passionately the monuments of professional art which are often still found in a very bad state.[30]

The article concludes with an appeal for a cosmopolitan conception of Lithuanian culture that would embrace the full heritage of Vilnius and other Lithuanian cities and promote the development of a genuinely urban culture. He emphasized that while Lithuania was becoming an urban country, city culture was not the same as technical culture. While Kaunas and Klaipėda were becoming technically more progressive, they still lacked the "the real urbanity that comes only from an immersion in the heritage of humanism."[31]

In the mid-1970s, Venclova's application to join the Lithuanian Writers' Union was rejected, and while the circumstances of the decision are murky, the probable reasons include not only his dissidence but also the social and cultural distance that separated him from the mainstream of the local cultural elites. Shortly thereafter, he would send an application to the Communist Party of Lithuania to be allowed to emigrate, which was granted in 1977. After establishing himself at Yale University, Venclova became one of the most prominent international advocates for human rights in the Soviet Union and a mediator between Soviet Lithuania and the West.

Venclova's exclusion from the Lithuanian Writers' Union and his subsequent emigration is symbolic of the direction that Soviet Lithuanian culture was taking. Shortly after he emigrated, he gave an interview to the American-Lithuanian journal *Akiračiai* (Horizons) entitled "About Cities, Villages, Freedom and Poetry." After a number of questions relating to the circumstances of his departure, his activities as a writer and dissident, and the strength of the resistance movement, Venclova was asked whether the Lithuanian village might once again, as it has throughout history, emerge as a wellspring of tradition to inspire a cultural renaissance in Lithuania.

Venclova's response was brusque. He asserted that if a national revival were to appear in Soviet Lithuania, it would come rather from the new culture that was emerging in the cities. Admitting that the Lithuanian village was in moderately better shape than in Soviet Russia, it too had been destroyed by collectivization and so would not make any contribution to a cultural or political revival. Quite the opposite:

The efforts of our writers to search for ethical or aesthetic values in the village seem pointless. It is not only Lithuanians who suffer from this disease, but also, for example, Solzhenitsyn. The center of Lithuanian culture is in the cities, of course. If there is anything interesting that can inspire hope in our culture, it is taking place in the city.[32]

Contemporary readers of this interview may well have been taken aback by Venclova's statement. Lithuanian émigrés in America, both liberals and conservatives, were nurtured on the classics of the national revival of the nineteenth and early twentieth centuries, which extolled the village as the source of national identity, and they were committed to preserving traditional Lithuanian customs in America. Venclova's likening of the revival of folk culture to a "disease" must have seemed harsh, and possibly even symptomatic of "Soviet thinking." His critical view of Solzhenitsyn, the winner of the Nobel Prize for literature in 1970 and author of the famed *Gulag Archipelago*, published in 1973, must also have seemed rather untoward.

But while Venclova and Solzhenitsyn were both committed dissidents and defenders of human rights, the fact is that they fell on opposite sides of the barricades of the emerging *Kulturkampf* to define the nature of post-Soviet society. In Russia, this process saw the resurfacing of the old cleavage between Westernizers and the Slavophiles. The first trend was strongest among the established urban intelligentsia, espousing values of liberalism, cultural cosmopolitanism and the need to "catch up" with the West. The second trend was fed mostly from the newer generation of intellectuals with roots in the village, espousing values of conservatism, cultural nativism and the need to "return" to the nation's roots in the village.

In Soviet Lithuania, the absence of an established urban intelligentsia and the disruption of continuity between the newly created postwar intelligentsia based in Vilnius and the interwar intelligentsia based in Kaunas meant that Venclova represented a small minority of intellectuals who were bred and educated in a culture of cosmopolitanism. Venclova was correct to say that the center of Lithuanian culture was located in the city, but only insofar as rapid urbanization in the postwar years had reached the point where a growing majority of Lithuanians resided in urban areas. The culture that took root in these growing urban conglomerations was increasingly preoccupied with the rustic cultural heritage of the village.[33]

The folk revival in Soviet Lithuania

Lithuania had, of course, seen periods of folk revival before, when urbanized intellectuals sought to appropriate elements of rural culture for the purpose of nation-building. During the Lithuanian awakening in the late nineteenth century, the recording, codification and standardization of peasant language and culture were key elements in the process of nation-building, the assertion of a national Lithuanian identity in a modern mode. Between the wars, the newly established urban intelligentsia in Kaunas also sought to build a sense of national belonging in part on the basis of peasant culture.[34]

Soviet nationalities policy under Stalin also promoted folk culture as a means of promoting Sovietized national identities, and while the rustic turn in Soviet Lithuania generated a number of distinct subcultures, it was also very much part of the cultural mainstream. The highest representatives of Soviet Lithuanian officialdom like Juozas Baltušis and Antanas Venclova, among others, supported and participated in the movement as a natural, positive and, to their minds, politically neutral cultural trend. In his private diary from 1967, for example, Antanas Venclova records his delight with a staged performance of a traditional peasant wedding:

> Yesterday, my wife and I experienced the rare joy of watching an amateur art group of the older generation, performing the ancient wedding ritual of the Kupiškis region. Real peasants were performing in authentic outfits, and in such a way as happens in real life. This kind of documentary realism made a huge impression on me. ... It is wonderful that the native customs of our fathers and forefathers, which seemed to be buried under the ashes of time, are in fact alive, interesting, moving. And how many such things are coming back to life in our times – songs, dances, and folk music – all of this is becoming part of our daily existence, our pride! What a strong connection links our times to the past! How lovely and how necessary![35]

The show that Venclova so enthusiastically describes was the opening performance of an ethnographic ensemble called *Kupiškėnų vestuvės*.

The popularity of *Kupiškėnų vestuvės* among elite figures like Venclova and common Lithuanians alike was significant and portentous of subsequent cultural developments. Aesthetically, the group's performances contrasted sharply with those of the standard Soviet folk ensemble. The leading troupe of the latter genre, *Lietuva*, was modeled after the professional folk ensembles developed by Igor Moiseyev in the 1930s. Moiseyev adapted folk dances for performance by professional dancers using techniques from classical ballet and gymnastics. Stalin was a great enthusiast, and so the genre quickly became the new orthodoxy throughout the USSR, as each republic developed its own version of such troupes.[36]

Lietuva was established during the first Soviet occupation in 1940, continued to perform during the first years of the Nazi occupation, and was again promoted heavily in the postwar era, participating in All-Union festivals and concerts given on significant holidays in Moscow and throughout the Soviet bloc. The elite performers were rigorously selected from scores of applicants and were all extremely good-looking and physically fit, the very model of Soviet youth.[37]

Meanwhile, the performances of *Kupiškėnų vestuvės* were based on a completely different aesthetic and standard of authenticity. The group consisted of elderly villagers who were not professional actors or singers. The

Figure 7.1 Viktoras Kapočius, Soloists of the *Lietuva* State Folk Dance and Song
Company. Vilnius, 1979
AFP Image Forum.

beauty and value of their performance were seen to derive from the fact that
they were representing traditions acquired during their childhood. They sang
in a local dialect and wore antique costumes that were handed down from
prior generations or were made using the strictest traditional methods and
materials. Every detail of the traditional ritual was followed; all stylization or
so-called improvements to the original were considered to be unacceptable.

This new, grass roots mode of authenticity swiftly gained official support and
came to be promoted as a manifestation of official Soviet Lithuanian culture.
The peasant wedding was performed in 1966 at Vilnius University and then at
the Lithuanian Academic Drama Theatre, a stronghold of high culture. On
April 25, 1967 it was performed at the Labor Union Palace and warmly
received by the Soviet Lithuanian establishment. This performance, the same
one that Antanas Venclova described so enthusiastically in his diary, was the
token of the highest official recognition.

From this point onwards, the members of the wedding group "received
generous hugs from the highest among the highest." Toasts were raised "to

the creativity of the people, to the manner in which pearls of artistic creativity emerge from its very roots, and how only the Soviet order could have opened such a miracle, which was its greatest merit."[38] Of course, there was nothing political in the motivation of the elderly performers, but the national flavour and enormous popularity of the group gave it a real social significance.

The group toured different regions of Lithuania relentlessly, filling Soviet Lithuanian Houses of Culture to overcapacity. "Whoever has not seen *Kupiškėnų vestuvės* is not a true Lithuanian," was a common saying at the time.[39] For many spectators, the group seemed to have come out of nowhere, and they would often describe the shows as some kind of miracle.[40] In fact, however, such ethnographic performances of traditional weddings first took place in the interwar period, in concerts organized and promoted by the Catholic Women's League of Lithuania, particularly through its regional branch in Kupiškis. They formed an integral part of the revival of peasant culture in line with the cultural policy of the interwar republic and of the Lithuanian awakening of the late nineteenth century.[41]

However, while the earlier folk revivals drew on romantic notions of the peasant as the keeper of an ancient heritage, they had also developed in the context of a modernist project, seeking to "raise" peasant culture to the level befitting a modern nation-state, be it the interwar republic or the postwar LSSR. The rustic turn of the 1960s and 1970s, by way of contrast, took place in a post-apocalyptic cultural atmosphere imbued with an overwhelming sense of nostalgia and trauma. Instead of seeking to "improve" local peasant culture and to "raise" it to some modern, international standard, the emphasis was on the postmodern impulse to "return" to the unsullied, pre-modern and pre-Soviet original.

Indeed, *Kupiškėnų vestuvės* assumed a much greater cultural and social significance during the Soviet period than it had during the interwar years. The performances were received in a highly emotional, often ecstatic manner. From personal experience I can recall how my grandmother Ona Inčiūraitė (Varslauskienė), forced out by the last melioration campaign from her native village of Šalnakundžiai in the Kupiškis region to the city of Panevėžys (and hating it thoroughly), would reach a state of ecstatic grief and joy as she watched the wedding performed on Soviet state television. The advanced age of the performers in the roles of a young bride and groom jarred the conventions of realism and embodied a deep sense of nostalgia for a culture and for rituals that no subsequent generation would be able to perform in the same authentic manner.

Over time, *Kupiškėnų vestuvės* and *Lietuva* came to be seen as two opposed paradigms of folk expression, and by extension, of national self-understanding. While the aesthetics of the amateur ethnographic ensemble were seen as an authentic manifestation of grass-roots culture, the stylized professionalism of *Lietuva* was increasingly felt to be inauthentic, false, and Soviet. As one folk revivalist recalled: "We hated the *Lietuva* ensemble, hated all these degraded, official folk bands … We were engaged in the search for authenticity – for authenticity in melodies, everywhere."[42]

Figure 7.2 Algirdas Tarvydas, *Robertas Verba filming Čiūtyta rūta.* Vilnius, 1967 Lithuanian Theater, Music and Cinema Museum. PV-6, N81. The roles of the young bride and groom are here played by actors in their sixties and seventies.

Cinema, photography and the aesthetics of loss

The deep but vague sense of nostalgia that inhered in the performances of *Kupiškėnų vestuvės* came to infect virtually all forms of artistic and social expression in Lithuania. Indeed, the new sense of cultural authenticity was most enthusiastically picked up by the quintessentially modern genres of Soviet Lithuanian cinema and photography.

In 1968 Robertas Verba made a film about the elderly folk performers, and the resulting documentary entitled *Čiūtyta rūta*, a non-translatable line of an old Lithuanian polyphonic song, focused on portraits of the old villagers and their insights.[43] The key to this documentary, which portrays fragments of the performance, is the way it contrasts the old and the new in a manner that is sometimes ironic and sometimes lyrical. But perhaps even more important is the way the film captures the reaction of the audience watching the live per-formance: deeply emotional, completely carried away and often reduced to tears.

The film was a continuation of the motif that Verba launched in 1965 with the production of *Old Man and the Land* – a documentary that was immediately recognized as an aesthetic breakthrough by contemporaries.[44] Echoing the title of Ernest Hemingway's *Old Man and the Sea*, the film focusses on the portrait of an old Lithuanian peasant who talks about his life and children as well as his recently deceased wife. On the surface, the old man's story is organized as a narrative of progress and enlightenment, showing the good that his sons – a teacher, a tractor driver and a professor – bring to their community. It shows how the children of a simple peasant could become members of the most progressive layers of Soviet society.

But under this surface of modernity, the setting of the story in the old village house, the sound of the old man speaking a regional dialect, his manner of speaking and idiomatic expressions were immediately recognizable as archaic and as dying away, generating a powerful sense of nostalgia. The seemingly innocent phrase of the protagonist, "nowadays people can make everything but they still cannot make the sun," signaled the limitations of modernity and progress. The slow movement of the camera, the broken montage, the strong visual symbolism and the juxtaposition of the modern and the archaic not only contrasted with the progress-driven and plot-centered documentaries of the time, but conveyed a palpable sense of trauma and loss.[45]

Verba's films were seen as establishing a new genre of film in Lithuania due largely to his skilful appropriation of cinematic innovations associated with the *cinéma vérité* movement in France, or the living camera movement in the United States. Before the use of synchronous sound became economical in the 1960s, visuals were typically filmed first and then music and voice-overs were added in the studio as a separate process. In the new mode of documentary filmmaking, the editing of footage with simultaneously recorded sound creates the impression of lived or real time. Events just "happen" in front of the camera, unleashing the power of performance by promoting a completely different apprehension of the speaking subject.[46]

By filming simple peasants and very old people, Verba was able to let his subjects speak and to express themselves in a direct and ostensibly transparent way that was not possible before. Using the techniques of *cinema vérité*, Verba represented the past through its traces in the present, not only topographically or archaeologically in the landscape, but physiologically and empirically, in the performance of the voices and bodies of speaking witnesses:

> Old village huts with fruit and flower gardens, old people who, it seems, have been living there forever. It seemed that there, on screen, the very essence of what we call Lithuania is grasped. When I happen to be in a village even now it seems to me that I am in Verba's film. And these films are not cinema but pieces of life.[47]

His films introduced, in a novel manner, the archaic figure of the ethnic Lithuanian autochthon, a character who "grows from the earth" like a tree, an immediately recognizable figure in Lithuanian culture, seen as increasingly anomalous in the all-too rapidly changing environment.

Verba worked closely with Lithuanian photographers who shared a similarly rustic aesthetic. As recalled by Antanas Sutkus, he and his generation of photographers, including Romualdas Rakauskas (b. 1941), Aleksandras Macijauskas

(b. 1938), Algimantas Kunčius (b. 1939) and Stanislovas Žvirgždas (b. 1941) among others, were lucky because the traditional Lithuanian village had still not entirely disappeared when they came into the profession.[48] Influenced by the humanism of the Edward Steichen (1879–1973) and Henri Cartier-Bresson (1908–2004), as well as the ethnographic realism of the interwar Lithuanian photographer Balys Buračas (1897–1972), they developed a unique style which was recognized in the Soviet context as "distinctly Lithuanian."[49] One of the striking motifs of this school was the focus on the individual who emerged and appeared inseparable from the rural landscape.[50]

Figure 7.3 Antanas Sutkus, *The Last Summer*
In *People of Lithuania*, 1959–. Zarasai, 1968. © Antanas Sutkus.

Figure 7.4 Romualdas Rakauskas, *Blooming*. Dzūkija district, Lithuania, 1974–1984

Performing Lithuania

Algirdas Tarvydas, a photographer and film director who worked as an assistant to Verba in the making of *Čiutyta rūta* and *Šimtamečių godos*, emphasizes the close engagement of their work with contemporary social and cultural developments in Lithuania. "It was right at this time, starting in 1962 that the ethnographic societies and folk ensembles were being founded ... People in the cities started to sing ancient village songs ... It was all in the atmosphere ... Verba collected this all in his documentaries."[51]

The yearning for a new standard of authenticity was the implicit driving force of an ethnocultural movement that embraced several forms of activity, including folklore groups, hikers clubs and cultural monument preservation groups (*paminklosaugos draugijos*).[52] The groups and their respective memberships varied, but their motivation and intentions were interrelated. The common concerns of these groups with cultural authenticity became increasingly focussed on the act of self-transformation and collective becoming through the performance of ethnic culture.

The cultural project to preserve and recover the dying remains of a lost civilization strengthened during the 1970s as an idea that began to unify the intelligentsia with a new sense of purpose. Professional ethnographers from Vilnius University played an important role in this process, notably the philologist Norbertas Vėlius, who organized student expeditions to the villages to collect and codify songs, riddles, tales and other forms of oral tradition.

Since the mid-1950s, the Department of Lithuanian Philology had grown into one of the most prestigious areas of study. It had dozens of professional ethnologists and folklorists who directed the national preoccupation with the collection, classification, and publication of Lithuanian folklore. This professional work was popularized among students, including those specializing in engineering, scientific and other fields.[53]

The stated goal of the hikers' club, for example, was "to learn about the country, to preserve cultural monuments, to cultivate oneself physically and spiritually and to seek enlightenment." Another group called *Romuva* was torn by internal tensions and ideological diversity: one branch was focussed on preserving historical monuments, another on reviving the pre-modern, pagan roots of ethnic culture. These two branches were more or less acceptable to the authorities, while yet another section viewed Christianity as the source of Lithuanian national identity and had close ties with the anti-Soviet Catholic underground.[54]

On the surface, however, they were difficult to distinguish, since their activities all incorporated the singing of folk songs, going on hiking trips and celebrating traditional festivities. Some members emphasized the collection of folklore, others put more emphasis on bringing enlightenment to the rural areas, others on bringing village culture to urban milieux, and still others delved in mystical explorations of the national ethos. But regardless of their differences or their level of accommodation or opposition to the authorities, all were involved in the search of an authentic self.

According to Ainė Ramonaitė, the ethnographic movement formed a "parallel society" along with the Catholic Church that was opposed to the Soviet system. Noting that the KGB closely monitored and even prosecuted some of its members, she attributes a distinctly anti-Soviet ethos to the movement as a whole. "During Soviet times," she writes, students and ethnographers would travel to villages spread over the forests of Dzūkija and other regions, in order to experience their own, non-Soviet, order. They would go to villages which preserved their own unique style of living, traditions, and everyday life, ancient songs and songs of partisans, natural interpersonal relations and trust in people.[55]

Debates about the significance of each of these groups continue to rage and have become highly politicized in today's Lithuania, with each current and sub-current claiming to have been the real source of popular resistance that would later surface during the popular movement. However, this retrospective and idealized view of the movement probably overstates the distinction between official and unofficial culture, as well as the political dimension of the movement in its early stages. It also seems to ignore the fact that similar movements emerged throughout the Soviet Union at this time.[56]

Other Lithuanian scholars like Nerija Putinaitė have argued more convincingly that the ethnographic movement was opposed to modernization but not the Soviet regime as such, insofar as it lacked any clear political objectives and was generally compatible with the Soviet worldview.[57] In a similar vein, Arūnas Streikus argues that the authorities promoted an interest in paganism and Baltophilism as a means of undermining the position of the Catholic Church.[58] Although the regime was suspicious of the ethnographic movement and sought to ensure that it remained under control, he claims the Soviets also used the movement to promote a "sterilized" form of ethnicity and to pit this against more vital Christian traditions.[59]

Whether official or underground, apolitical, dissident or merely nonconformist, each trend within the movement was nurtured on a common apprehension of cultural loss and a desire to recover elements of ethnic authenticity as a means of living differently. The focus on personal transformation through the enactment of authentic culture was paramount. In spite of the post-Soviet temptation to interpret the ethnographic movement in Lithuania as self-consciously anti-Soviet, or cleverly co-opted by an omniscient Soviet regime, it is perhaps better understood as part of a pan-Soviet cultural reaction to the experience of rapid modernization, with parallels to similar movements in other countries throughout the twentieth century.[60]

The pratice of leaving the city and traveling across the landscape as a ritual of individual and collective self-discovery was articulated as a sort of pilgrimage, a means of witnessing a past otherwise obscured by the veneer of Soviet modernity. As recalled by the philosopher and signatory of Lithuania's Declaration of Independence Romualdas Ozolas, he started to travel across Lithuania in the 1970s, to reflect on "how the hills, roads and homesteads are arranged," and in so doing, "to witness the manifestation of history in concrete objects: old huts with no foundations, homesteads where only old trees remain, little double roads, and so-on." His objective was to uncover

"Lithuanianness in its entire ethnographic and ethnological worldview" in the landscape as a means of individual and collective self-transformation.[61]

Similarly, Algirdas Patackas, another hiking enthusiast and a dissident, explains that travelling to the countryside was part of a long tradition of "going to the people" in the manner of nineteenth-century Russian populist intellectuals. He recalls how in his efforts to attain "a state of higher knowledge," he "turned himself into a villager" through language, by acquiring a dialect that he had rarely heard as the child of educated professionals in Kaunas.[62]

The urge to trace history across the land as a means of personal and collective self-transformation took on an increasingly public and quasi-official character, as demonstrated by his extraordinary journey on a horse-drawn carriage made by Petras Vasinauskas (1906–95), a Soviet Lithuanian agronomist, across Lithuania. Vasinauskas was an unusual personality. An established professional during the interwar republic, he remained in Lithuania to work for the Soviet state. He was highly respected by communist officials and personally by Antanas Sniečkus.[63] This made his journey to raise public awareness about Lithuania's agricultural heritage into a rather well publicized and highly significant social act.

Vasinauskas had been a strong proponent of collectivization, even during the interwar years, but he resisted innovations that were imposed for purely ideological reasons. He defended the wisdom and objective rationality of traditional agricultural practices that had developed over the centuries, and viewed them as a key element of Lithuanian cultural heritage and of civilization in general. The Soviet drive to mechanize all aspects of agriculture and to abandon the use of horses on the farm struck him as excessive and bordering on the barbaric. His performative critique of this policy took the unusual form of a thousand-kilometre, 43-day trek through the country on a horse-drawn carriage. The awareness-raising campaign seemed especially eccentric against the background of Soviet consumerism, where people were kept on waiting lists for years to get a car, and the acquisition of a new *Moskvich* or *Volga* was the dream of the average Soviet family.

The illustrious agronomist sought to draw attention to the fact that modernization was destroying not only centuries-old traditional forms of agriculture but also an entire layer of human culture. For him, the horse became a symbol for an endangered way life, a heritage preserved in the very language of the equestrian tradition with its rich vocabulary and expressions relating to each detail of horse tack and the symbols, rituals and customs that pertained to the animal and its use by humanity. His ideas resonated with the cultural intelligentsia, many of whom took part in the voyage, accompanying him for stretches of the journey, writing stories and articles about it, and participating in the making of a documentary film entitled *Will You Carry Me, a Young Lad* (*Ar nuneši mane jauną*).[64]

The film delivered a profoundly anti-modernist message by persistently juxtaposing images of horse-drawn carts with those of tractors, buses and the multi-storey buildings of the capital of Vilnius. Together with the soundtrack based on a lyrical folk song sung in an "authentic" rustic style, these images contribute to an ironic mood of tragic nostalgia. The film was also translated into Russian and distributed across the USSR, with a new Russian title *1,500 Miles Through a Life*, a title that sought to dilute the anti-modernism of the story by posing as a biography of Vasinauskas himself. This group initiative to record the journey of an agronomist in journalism and film represented the beginnings of an alliance between the technical and the creative intelligentsia as a force for cultural and social change, one that would take on a more obvious and political significance under *glasnost'* a decade later.

Literature and the discourse of displacement

The discourse of trauma and deracination was expressed most explicitly and forcefully in works of literature, and it was through literature that the alternative aesthetics of authentic identity would reach the greatest number of Lithuanians. From the mid-1960s, at about the same time when the Soviets pushed forward with the melioration of the countryside that destroyed the last remaining homesteads, the most popular works of Lithuanian literature expressed a lament over the separation from the land that with time grew in intensity until it emerged as a widely shared vision of cultural apocalypse and national disaster. By the early 1980s, well before the onset of *glasnost'*, this discourse of physical and cultural displacement had started to sensitize Lithuanians to the trauma of deracination as a basic condition of Soviet modernity.

Lithuanian writers never used the term "village prose" to describe a discrete school of Lithuanian literature. Novels by authors like Mykolas Sluckis (*Steps to the Sky*, 1963), Vytautas Petkevičius (*On Bread, Love and the Gun*, 1963), Jonas Avyžius (*The Village at the Crossroads*, 1964) focussed on the "class struggle" in the countryside during the collectivization campaign. Later works by Juozas Aputis, Romualdas Granauskas, Bronius Radzevičius, Henrikas Čigriejus, Vytautas Bubnys and others explored the trauma of deracination that accompanied the transformation of the countryside. The concern with the tectonic cultural changes involved in the process of rapid urbanization was not a discrete literary movement but rather the pervasive cultural background to creative pursuits of all kinds.

Moreover, after the departure of Tomas Venclova, the rustic turn never turned into a divisive issue between Lithuanian liberals and conservatives in the way that Russian village prose eventually came to be seen as the preserve of the nationalist camp. Granted, a certain rift developed between the Generation of 1930 and the next generations of writers like Martinaitis (b. 1936) and Sigitas Geda (b. 1943), who added a political stance of non-conformism to their avant-garde aesthetics and viewed their "elders" (who were just a few years older but occupied a significantly different niche in the cultural mosaic) as cultural and political conservatives.[65]

The very ubiquity of the rustic turn in Soviet Lithuania is attested by the way in which it became a staple not only of cultural conservatives, but of the younger generations of cultural innovators and political non-conformists, and how broadly it permeated not only literature but music, cinema and art to form a powerful cultural synthesis. Sigitas Geda's first collection of poems entitled *Pėdos* (Footsteps) in which expressionist images and colors imitate the simplicity and freshness of folk language and a mythological perspective of the nation, provided a creative impulse for an entire plethora of avant-garde works in music, painting and other forms of cultural expression.[66]

His next major work, *Strazdas*, evoked the legendary figure of the Catholic priest and poet of the late eighteenth century who deliberately partook of the difficult life of Lithuanian serfs. This text blended violence, eroticism, religion and mythological archetypes onto a surrealist canvas that simultaneously conveyed a subversive political message: Antanas Strazdas (Antoni Drozdowski, 1760–1833) was the first Lithuanian poet to be censored by the Russian imperial authorities, and the implied comparison with the Soviet period was sufficiently clear.[67]

The poem was adapted as a theatre play in Kaunas in 1984, and later in 1990 as a feature film. The play was set to the music of the minimalist composer Bronius Kutavičius, who in his turn was inspired by Geda's poetry to compose the *Pantheistic Oratorio* (1970), and *Last Pagan Rites* (1978), valued as among the most important and influential Lithuanian contemporary music works.[68] Contemporaries recall that they listened to Kutavičius' *Rites* with its incantations of Geda's poetry in a very literal sense, as a ritual of self-transformation: "We listened to this music with our entire bodies, with sweet bumps which started at our foot soles and went up under our ears ... its power passing over us, it empowers us, our spirit, our language, our listening," recalls literary critic Viktorija Daujotytė.[69]

That said, Daujotytė also emphasizes that it was literature that played the leading role in the renewal of culture through the revival of archaic and mythological themes.[70] Moreover, the discursive nature of literature allowed avant-garde poets such as Martinaitis in the cycle of poems *Kukučio baladės* (1977) to ground such themes in a narrative of the transition from the country to the city. The lyrical hero Kukutis (the name is derived from cuckoo bird) is a complex and enigmatic character embodied in a simple peasant who represents the spirit of a dying agrarian civilization. As a village fool, a simpleton, an idiot and a clever and persistent trickster, he represents a figure familiar from folklore, and yet reflects something much darker and doomed. His carnivalesque appearances in the modern context of Soviet Lithuania impart the shock of anachronism. Kukutis brings a chaotic inconvenience to the well-ordered structure of modern Soviet society, evoking the return of repressed memories and visions and an unsettling sense of trauma.

For example, in a poem called "Kukutis Dreams up Žuveliškės Village on Cathedral Square," a chaotic stream-of-consciousness description of village life is juxtaposed to clean and well-proportioned space in the center of the modern capital. Dizzy from the summer heat, Kukutis lays his head on a loaf of bread and conjures his home village on the central square of Vilnius through a dream:

> Like after the great flood out of Noah's saved ark into the square pour forth flocks of sparrows and dogs bloated cows one year old calves and girls surrounded by bulls with wreaths braided of the first dandelions of the year on their heads at the end of the Cathedral Square leaning on a pitch fork Mr. Little Fish happily stares at a lamb in front of the bell tower showing off a sheepskin coat the entire square becomes crowded with Žuveliškės from all corners something live comes crawling out hurrying everything starts to bellow moo cackle oink whistle crow crackle neigh squeal bellow quack hiss cluck bleat cock a doodle doo howl yelp cackle and smell like a cattle yard's warmth in a manure wagon's wheels the coolness of a hundred year old pantry the hot depths of vodka unclean old people's words from the tower to the Vilnelė river Žuveliškės sets itself up with the cow's footpath stretching right through the very center of the Cathedral and after an afternoon's nap the historical chickens suffocatingly cluck with Antose on the hay wagon and her firmly pressed-together breasts.[71]

The vision of Kukutis gets him into trouble with a police officer who notes that cars are stopping with people viewing the disgraceful scene. The complaints continue, an official delegation is due to arrive, and Kukutis is ordered to stop dreaming of "abolished farmsteads that the engineer has already crossed off his list." Eventually a fire brigade armed with water-hoses comes to chase the apparition that has "risen from the dead" back into the ground. The absurdity of Kukutis' statements and appearances has something involuntary and obsessive about them, like the flashbacks of traumatized memory. Notably, in Martinaitis' poetry, Vilnius has lost its romantic and idealized quality and stands for the oppressively ordered presence of power, the new urbanity in which there is no place for the "crossed-out" but lively chaos of the "regressive" agricultural past.

However, nobody articulated the sense of trauma in more explicit and apocalyptic terms than novelist Romualdas Granauskas in *The Homestead Under the Maple Tree*. Published in instalments in *Pergalė* over the course of 1986, it was perhaps the culminating work of the discourse of traumatic displacement. The novel evoked the same existential concern with questions of ethics and repentance, collective identity and ecology that was erupting throughout Soviet literature at the time, such as Chingiz Aitmatov's *Plakha* (*The Executioner's Bloc*) published in *Novy Mir* that same year. It also echoes the classics of Russian village prose like Valentin Rasputin's *Farewell to Matyora* or Solzhenitsyn's *Matryona's House* by portraying an old woman, the last resident in an abandoned village, as the sole survivor of a vanished world, with a deep sense of attachment to the land, an idealized ethical commitment to communal relations, and centuries-old traditions in the context of social destruction and degradation.

Granauskas pushed the limit of literature towards its breaking point in the direction of social and political critique, focussed on the tragedy of collectivization, urbanization and melioration:

> We have seen many wars and upheavals, fires, floods and plagues. Our lives and destinies are in flux, but one thing never changes. Come what may, your patch of land will not burn. It cannot be arrested or deported, or blown to pieces. Come what may, you can rest yourself upon it, it may be small and infertile, but still you wrap your arms around your children, pressing their small heads to your chest, and calmly watch how the world is thundering and trembling all around you.[72]

He wrote the book over the course of a month, almost in a single draft. Somewhat raw as a literary text, it was highly effective in capturing and transmitting the cultural mood of the time. First published in serial form in 1986, it provoked a steady stream of essays and discussions on ecology, tradition, language and the village. The apocalyptic sensibility of this text, together with an autochthonous sense of national identity based on a post-traumatic attachment to and identification with the land, became a core element of Lithuanian cultural and political discourse in the late 1980s. Arvydas Juozaitis, one of the founding members of the popular movement, told Granauskas that he wrote the speech for the founding session of *Sąjūdis* "in a single breath," the moment he had finished reading *The Homestead Under the Maple Tree*.[73]

By instilling an intense nostalgia about the village as an alternative source of authentic feeling and identity, the rustic turn amounted to nothing less than a cultural revolution that stood the modernism of the Soviet Lithuanian renaissance on its head. The process of urbanization, which for a time inspired the creative classes to participate in the creation of a cosmopolitan culture, came to be seen as one of several manifestations of the trauma of displacement. The abandoned homestead, overgrown with trees, was a silent witness to the trauma of deracination, of occupation and the brutality of the postwar years – a *lieu de mémoire* that expressed an autochthonous vision of collective identity based on the nation's origins in the land.

Notes

1 Pierre Nora, "Reasons for the current upsurge in memory," *Eurozine.com* (April 19, 2002).
2 Geoffrey Hosking, *The Awakening of the Soviet Union* (Cambridge, MA: Harvard University Press, 1990), 23.
3 Walter Benjamin and Gary Smith, *Moscow Diary* (Cambridge, MA: Harvard University Press, 1986).
4 Louis Fischer, in R.H.S. Crossman and Arthur Koestler, *The God That Failed* (New York: Harper, 1950), 203.
5 Vasilii S. Grossman, Anna Aslanyan, Robert Chandler, and Elizabeth Chandler, *Everything Flows* (London: Harvill Secker, 2010).
6 David Hoffman, *Peasant Metropolis: Social Identities in Moscow, 1929–1941* (Ithaca, NY: Cornell University Press, 1994), 1–2.

7 Goskomstat SSSR, *Demograficheskiy yezhegodnik SSSR 1990* (Moscow: Finansy i statistika, 1991), 11. In 1959, Lithuania's urbanization rate was still just 39 percent, well behind that of Estonia or Latvia at 56 percent, or the RSFSR at 52 percent, or 48 percent for the USSR as a whole. By 1989, Lithuania's urbanization rate was 68 percent, higher than 65.9 for the USSR as a whole, about 71 for Estonia and Latvia, and 73.5 for the RSFSR.

8 By the early 1970s, the average age of those employed in agriculture was 45 years old, and only one fifth were below the age of 30. Two thirds of all pensioners lived in the country, and one third of rural households did not have a single male worker in the "able bodied" category of 16–55 years of age. Benedict V. Maciuika, "Contemporary Social Problems in the Collectivized Lithuanian Countryside," *Lituanus* 20.3 (Fall 1976): 5–27.

9 Andrei Amal'rik, *Will the Soviet Union Survive Until 1984?* (New York: Harper & Row, 1970), 62–63.

10 Interview with Romualdas Granauskas, *Vakarinės naujienos* (October 2, 1992). Similar points were made later by Leonidas Donskis in "Miesto likimas komunistinėje ir postkomunistinėje Lietuvoje," in *Tarp Karlailio ir Klaipėdos: Visuomenės ir kultūros kritikos etiudai* (Klaipėdos Universiteto leidykla, 1997), 16–17.

11 Geoffrey Hosking, *The Awakening of the Soviet Union.* (Cambridge, MA: Harvard University Press, 1990), 23.

12 Maksimov notes further that "No urban literature of any distinction was published in Tvardovskiy's journal … Everything that was powerful in *Novy mir* was the peasants." John Glad, *Besedy v izgnanii: Russkoe Literaturnoe Zarubezhie* (Moskva: Izd-vo "Knizhnaiapalata", 1991), 13.

13 See Nikolai Mitrokhin's *Russkaia partiia. Dvizhenie russkikh natsionalistov SSSR, 1953–1985* (Moscow: Novoe literaturnoe obozrenie, 2003).

14 Vladislav Zubok, *Zhivago's Children: The Last Russian Intelligentsia* (Cambridge, MA: Belknap Press of Harvard University Press, 2009).

15 Aleksander Yakovlev became a historian after fighting in World War II, spent a year as an exchange student at Columbia University in 1958 and worked as head of the Department of Propaganda and Ideology of the CPSU from 1969 to 1973. He was Ambassador to Canada until 1983, where became a close friend of Prime Minister Pierre Trudeau, and developed a common understanding on a plan for reform with Mikhail Gorbachev, then Soviet Minister of Agriculture, during the latter's visit to Canada.

16 Aleksandr Yakovlev, "Protiv antiistorizma," *Literaturnaya gazeta* 46 (November 15, 1972), 4–5.

17 Alexander Yakovlev, interviewed by Yu. Solomonov, "Fashizm prost, kak palka, poetomu s nim tak slozhno borotsia," *Literaturnaya gazeta* (July 9, 1997). See also Yakovlev's memoirs *Sumerki* (Moscow: Materik, 2005), 341.

18 Anatoly Salutsky, "Aleksandr Zinovyev vs. Aleksandr Yakovlev," *Literaturnaya Gazeta* 50–51 (December 18, 2002), 15.

19 In "Fashizm prost, kak palka," Yakovlev relates Brezhnev's words on the issue: Why did you do this? Why did you not ask me first (raising his eyebrows)? And finally, putting a hand on his shoulder: "You drop this now, and that will be the end of the matter."

20 See John B. Dunlop, *The Faces of Contemporary Russian Nationalism* (Princeton, NJ: Princeton University Press, 1983), 60; Yitzhak M. Brudny, *Reinventing Russia: Russian Nationalism and the Soviet State, 1953–1991* (Cambridge, MA: Harvard University Press, 2000), 57.

21 *Sumerki*, 342.

22 Alexandr Yakovlev, interviewed by Yu. Solomonov, "Fashizm prost, kak palka, poetomu s nim tak slozhno borotsia," *Literaturnaya gazeta* (July 9, 1997).

23 Borys Lewytszkyj, *Politics and Society in Soviet Ukraine: 1953–1980* (Edmonton: CIUS Press, 1984), 147–48. Bohdan Nahaylo, "Ukrainian Dissent and Opposition after

Shelest," in Bohdan Krawchenko, ed. *Ukraine After Shelest* (Edmonton: Canadian Institute of Ukrainian Studies, 1983), 31.

24 Brudny, *Reinventing Russia*, 77.

25 In Lithuanian: "Dėl mano mirties kaltinkite tik santvarką," Łukasz Kamiński, "Gyvieji fakelai." Bernardinai.lt (January 20, 2010).

26 Arvydas Anušauskas, "KGB reakcija į 1972 m. įvykius," *Genocidas ir rezistencija* 1.13 (2003). Amanda Swain, "'Freedom for Lithuania' or 'Freedom for Hippies'? Nationalism, Youth Counterculture and De-Stalinization in Soviet Lithuania" (unpublished paper).

27 Tomas Remeikis, *The Lithuanian Phoenix: Studies and Essays* (Vilnius: Versus Aureus, 2009), 220.

28 Myroslav Shkandrij, "Literary Politics and Literary Debates in Ukraine 1971–81," in *Ukraine After Shelest*, 55–57.

29 Rimantas Kmita, *Ištrūkimas iš fabriko: modernėjanti lietuvių poezija XX amžiaus 7–9 dešimtmečiais* (Vilnius: Lietuvių literatūros ir tautosakos institutas, 2009), 280.

30 In Zita Kutraitė, ed. *Manau, kad ... Pokalbiai su Tomu Venclova* (Vilnius: Baltos lankos, 2000), 62.

31 Ibid.

32 In Zita Kutraitė, ed. "Apie miestą, kaimą, laisvę ir poeziją," *Akiračiai* 5/89 (1977), in *Manau, kad ... Pokalbiai su Tomu Venclova* (Vilnius: Baltos lankos, 2000), 24–25.

33 The well-known Lithuanian novels *Vilnius Poker* (1987) by Ričardas Gavelis (1952–2002) and *Tūla* (1993) by Jurgis Kunčinas (1947–2002) are among the rare exceptions that prove the rule, in the sense that they are profoundly concerned with urban thematic in the Soviet Lithuanian context. But while each was written during the late Soviet period, neither author received much recognition until the post-Soviet period.

34 See Chapter 1.

35 Antanas Venclova, Diary (May 22, 1967): 132. Venclovas House Museum Archives, Vilnius.

36 Laura J. Olson, *Performing Russia: Folk Revival and Russian Identity* (New York: RoutledgeCurzon, 2004).

37 For a more extensive description of the group, see Mingailė Jurkutė, "Ansamblis 'Lietuva': režimo įrankis ir nesėkmė," *Naujasis židinys-Aidai* 3 (2011): 151–57.

38 Henrikas Paulauskas, *Senovinių kupiškėnų vestuvių istorija* (Vilnius: Petro ofsetas, 2006), 28.

39 Algimantas Apanavičius, Interview by author. Audio recording. Vilnius, April 10, 2012. Algirdas Tarvydas, Interview by author. Audio recording. Vilnius, March 11, 2011.

40 For a collection of personal reminiscences by contemporaries, see A. Jasaitis and A. Kleniauskas, eds. *Tai bent vestuvės: Senovinių kupiškėnų vestuvių 40-mečiui* (Utena: Utenos Indra, 2006).

41 For more on the history of this group through the interwar, Soviet and post-Soviet periods see Jonė Žebrytė, "Dar kartą apie 'Senovines kupiškėnų vestuves' arba nuobodinė pasaka," in *Kupiškis: kultūra ir istorija*, 40–47 and, for comparison, Aušra Zabielienė, "Trejos kupiškėnų vestuvės," *Liaudies kultūra* 1 (2004): 29–33.

42 In Ainė Ramonaitė, "'Paralelinės visuomenės' užuomazgos sovietinėje Lietuvoje: katalikiškojo pogrindžio ir etnokultūrinio sąjūdžio simbiozė," in *Sąjūdžio ištakų beieškant: nepaklusniųjų tinklaveikos galia*, ed. Jūratė Kavaliauskaitė and Ainė Ramonaitė (Vilnius: Baltos lankos, 2011), 47.

43 Robertas Verba, *Čiutyta rūta* (Vilnius: Lietuvos kino studija, 1968).

44 Robertas Verba, *Senis ir žemė* (Vilnius: Lietuvos kino studija, 1965); Laimonas Tapinas, *LTSR nusipelnęs meno veikėjas, kino režisierius ir operatorius Robertas Verba* (Vilnius, 1977), 1.

45 The same motifs were echoed in another documentary by Verba entitled *Tales of Hundred Year Olds*. Robertas Verba, *Šimtamečių godos* (Vilnius: Lietuvos kino studija, 1969).

46 Bill Nichols, *Representing Reality: Issues and Concepts in Documentary* (Bloomington, IN: Indiana University Press, 1991), 42.

47 Rūta Oginskaitė, *Nuo pradžios pasaulio: Apie dokumentininką Verbą* (Vilnius: Aidai, 2010): [11].

48 Antanas Sutkus, "Fotografija – žmogaus dvasios metraštis," *Bernardinai.lt* (May 29, 2009).

49 Lev Anninskii, *Solntse v vetviakh: Ocherki o litovskoi fotografii* (Vilnius: Obshchestvo fotoiskusstva Litovskoi SSR, 1984).

50 During interviews with the author, Sutkus and Žvirgždas each noted that Steichen's *The Family of Man* and Cartier-Bresson's *People of Moscow* came to Lithuania in the form of catalogs from exhibitions of these series in Moscow in 1959 and 1958, respectively.

51 In Rūta Oginskaitė, "Nuo pradžios pasaulio: apie dokumentininką Robertą Verbą," (Vilnius: Aidai, 2010), 146. Algirdas Tarvydas, Interview by author. Audio recording. Vilnius, March 7, 2011.

52 Ainė Ramonaitė, "'Paralelinės visuomenės'," 33–58.

53 By 1972, the archives of the Philology Department were among the largest in the Soviet Union with more than 800,000 individual exponents. A five-volume compendium of folklore was published in 1968, and path breaking works of folklore studies were published in 1970 and 1971. Bronius Vaškelis, "The Assertion of Ethnic Identity Via Myth and Folklore in Soviet Lithuanian Literature," *Lituanus* 19.2 (Summer 1973): 16–27.

54 Algirdas Patackas, "Apie Romuvą, tėvyniškumą ir neperžengiamas ribas" [interviewed by Paulius Subačius], in *Pastogės Lietuva: pogrindžio, Sąjūdžio ir laisvės kronika* (Vilnius: Aidai, 2011), 26.

55 Ainė Ramonaitė, "'Paralelinės visuomenės'," 54.

56 See Laura Olson, *Performing Russia: folk revival and Russian identity* (New York: RoutledgeCurzon, 2004).

57 Nerija Putinaitė, *Nenutrūkusi styga. Prisitaikymas ir pasipriešinimas sovietų Lietuvoje* (Vilnius: Aidai, 2007), 289–90.

58 Arūnas Streikus. "Kierunki polityki pamięci na Litwie sowieckiej," *Politeja* 16 (2011): 281–307.

59 Arūnas Streikus, "Apie antikrikščioniškus sovietinių švenčių ir apeigų tikslus," *Naujasis židinys-Aidai* 10 (2003): 514–17.

60 See for example Frank Trentman's analysis of the "rambler's movement" in England between the wars, where he emphasizes that efforts to ascribe a concrete political motivation to this kind of grassroots movement often fail to grasp the complex cultural dynamics at play. "Civilization and Its Discontents: English Neo-Romanticism and the Transformation of Anti-Modernism in Twentieth-Century Western Culture," *Journal of Contemporary History* 29.4 (1994): 586.

61 Saulė Matulevičienė, "Iš pokalbių su Romualdu Ozolu: 7–8 dešimtmečio dvasinės erdvės," *Liaudies kultūra* 5 (2007): 45–53 at 48–49.

62 Saulė Matulevičienė, "Pogrindis, virtęs Pastoge. Saulės Matulevičienės pokalbis su Algirdu Patacku," *Liaudies kultūra* 1.118 (2008): 48.

63 One of the main preoccupations of the national communist leadership in Lithuania was to protect the agricultural sector from some of the most misguided reforms imposed by Khrushchev, which ultimately made Soviet Lithuanian agriculture far more productive than the Soviet average and a source of national pride. Vasinauskas once protested in an open letter against Khrushchev's proposals and managed to escape punishment thanks to his unrivalled reputation (his colleagues who signed the letter lost their jobs).

64 Vasinauskas was accompanied throughout the journey by the journalist Vladas Vaicekauskas, and on parts of it by film director Rimtautas Šilinis (Verba's former editor) and his cameraman Kornelijus Matuzevičius, the son of the poet and rather

influential cultural bureaucrat Eugenijus Matuzevičius and also – for a stretch – by the granddaughter of the influential writer and Soviet nomenklatura figure Juozas Baltušis, Akvilė Zavišaitė. The agronomer also wrote an account of the journey in a book which was not published at the time because he refused to apply the changes of the editor, and appeared in print only two decades later. Petras Vasinauskas, *Kelionė su arkliu po Lietuvą* (Vilnius: Logos, 1996).

65 For more on the power relations and changing ideological trends in the Lithuanian Writers Union, see Vilius Ivanauskas, "Intellectuals and Sovietization During Late Socialism: Shift from Indoctrination to National Processes (the Case of Writers in Soviet Lithuania)," forthcoming in *Europe-Asia Studies.*

66 Sigitas Geda, *Pėdos* (Vilnius: Vaga, 1966).

67 Sigitas Geda, *Strazdas* (Vilnius: Vaga, 1967).

68 Bronius Kutavičius (b. 1932) is considered the pioneer of Lithuanian minimalism.

69 Viktorija Daujotytė, "Bronius Kutavičius; pastovios preformos ir kintančios formos," in *Broniaus Kutavičiaus muzika: praeinantis laikas*, ed. Inga Jasinskaitė-Jankauskienė (Vilnius: Versus Aureus, 2008), 53.

70 Ibid., 51.

71 Marcelijus Martinaitis and Laima Sruoginis, *The Ballads of Kukutis* (Forest Grove, OR: Robert A. Davies, 1993). Translated by Laima Sruoginis.

72 Romualdas Granauskas, *Gyvenimas po klevu* [Life Under the Maple Tree] (Vilnius: Vaga, 1988), 20. First published in *Pergalė* 12 (1986): 5–64.

73 Romualdas Granauskas, Interview by author. Audio recording. Vilnius, June 3, 2011.

8 The rustic revolution

> We were deported not only from our homeland but from our language, customs, religion, respect for ourselves and our earth.
>
> Vytautas Landsbergis, 1990[1]

The popular movements that emerged throughout Central and Eastern Europe in the late 1980s continue to fascinate and perplex. It was an era of iconoclasm, marked by massive rallies, the burning of flags and the toppling of statues, broadcast to the astonishment of the entire world. And behind these sensational images, political transformation was driven by a deeper cultural process that scholars describe as the "return of memory," manifest in the lifting of censorship, the opening of sealed archives, and the telling of traumatic life-stories long suppressed. According to Tomas Venclova, the return of memory "brushed aside all social and individual distinctions and ensured a dramatic national consolidation that led Lithuania into independent existence."[2]

The mass publication of formerly suppressed memoirs of the deportees played a key role in this process. Alfred Senn's first-hand account of the period singles out the publication of the memoirs of Dalia Grinkevičiūtė (a child deportee whose memoirs are frequently compared to the diary of Ann Frank) as an event that "stunned the reading public and immediately took an important place in the collective memory of Lithuanians as an oppressed nation."[3] Dovilė Budrytė writes that the "political thaw ... instantly awakened memories of the displacement" and highlights the role of ceremonies commemorating the mass deportations.[4] The idea that the return of deportee memory contributed to the consolidation of national identity is by now a standard paragraph in high-school textbooks.[5]

In retrospect, however, it is clear that these profound changes of mass consciousness could not have occurred by themselves. Instead, political scientists like Mark Beissinger describe the process of nationalist mobilization as occurring in stages, where a long, quiet stage marked by the gradual accumulation of cultural capital is followed by an active stage when those resources are translated into collective political action. The "return of memory," just like the "power of the powerless," are phrases that were used to describe the final deployment of this symbolic capital to bring about political change.[6]

But like the "return of memory," the "power of the powerless" was partly a myth that reflected the utopian mindset of the times. In reality, power never left the stage, but was concentrated into the hands of the masters of discourse, the establishment intelligentsia who had been shaping Lithuanian memory throughout the Soviet period. As Gorbachev's policy of *glasnost'* enabled a more open and public discussion of previously forbidden topics, the role of the writers grew in strength and expanded in scope, building on their unsurpassed command of the language of public discourse that they themselves had created, encompassing non-literary areas such as environmentalism, social issues and politics through essays, opinion pieces and public speaking engagements.

This process was incarnated in the personal encounter of the former child deportee Dalia Grinkevičiūtė and Justinas Marcinkevičius, who not only helped to publish her seminal text, but also promoted and framed its reception through his own analysis and commentary. By weaving the deportee narratives into the background discourse of trauma and loss that was already strongly encoded in Soviet Lithuanian culture, Marcinkevičius and other leading members of the Soviet Lithuanian intelligentsia established a parallel between the trauma of deportation and the trauma of the various forms of physical and cultural displacements that characterized Soviet modernity in Lithuania, from collectivization to industrialization and from urbanization to Russification.

The notion that Lithuanians were all deportees, deported from their land, language and culture, came to be accepted as a self-evident basis for collective identification and political action. The social transformation and sense of solidarity that brought hundreds of thousands of people onto the streets was powerfully reinforced by mass rituals of return (*sugrįžimas*) and reburial of deportees who perished in the Soviet camps. In this context, the rustic turn and a specific discursive formation that represented urbanization, collectivization and deportation as a single trauma of displacement established a common denominator for Lithuanian national identity that dissolved the rift between the minority who suffered direct repressions, like the deportees and dissidents, and the majority who managed to accommodate themselves to the Soviet way of life.

The return of memory

Milan Kundera's aphorism that the "struggle of man against power is the struggle of memory against forgetting" was cited incessantly throughout the Soviet bloc in the late 1980s, as previously suppressed materials about the past were published in large-circulation newspapers, pamphlets and books.[7] In Lithuania the lifting of censorship and the first open criticism of official history unleashed an enormous wave of interest in "documentary" materials about the past, understood to mean "authentic" materials that were not tainted by Soviet ideology or censorship, especially concerning Lithuania's incorporation into the USSR, the post-war resistance and the deportations.[8]

Lithuanians of course had never "forgotten" about the deportations, as almost everyone had at least one relative who had been to the camps. And while the *Chronicles of the Catholic Church in Lithuania* and other dissident publications had only a small readership, they nonetheless provided an alternative source of information that was available to almost anybody who went looking for information. In this respect the return of memory must be understood rather as a mass phenomenon of a sudden and passionate interest in the past among the social mainstream.

Starting in 1987, Lithuanians began to queue early in the morning to buy the latest issue of *Komjaunimo tiesa*, the leading reformist newspaper that took the lead in printing documentary materials on history, and reached a phenomenal daily circulation of a half million issues in 1988.[9] History books and memoirs published at the time had circulations of 50,000–75,000 with the more popular reaching 100,000. For example, 90,000 copies of the memoirs of Juozas Urbšys, *Lithuania During the Fateful Years 1939–1940*, were published in 1989, followed by serial publication in the journal *Nemunas*. Adolfas Šapoka's *History of Lithuania*, written in the interwar period, was first serialized in *Kultūros barai* and then printed in book form with a circulation of 100,000.[10]

But it was the story of Dalia Grinkevičiūtė that had the greatest impact on popular opinion. The Lithuanian reading public was shocked by her lurid descriptions of suffering in the Gulag. Born to a middle-class family in Kaunas, Dalia Grinkevičiūtė had her childhood brought to an early end by war and deportation. A week before the German invasion, on the night of June 14–15, 1941, Grinkevičiūtė, her mother and brother were arrested by the NKVD and loaded onto cattle-cars bound for Siberia. Her father, a member of a right-wing nationalist party, *Tautininkai*, and a former high-ranking official in the independent Lithuanian government, was arrested the same night by the Soviet secret police and separated from the family.[11]

Grinkevičiūtė was destined for Trofimovsk, a virtually uninhabited settlement in northeastern Siberia. She and her fellow deportees were shipped north by riverboat to the mouth of the Lena River where it flows into the Laptev Sea. With inadequate shelter, miserly rations, and a murderous work-regime, most inmates died during the first winter. Dalia and her mother were among the few survivors, and they managed to relocate to a settlement further south.

In 1949, Dalia's mother was close to death, and the two risked their relative security and returned illegally to Kaunas by plane from Yakutsk. They lived in hiding with friends and family, often changing location. Now on the verge of death, Dalia's mother asked to go to their former house, even though this increased the risk of discovery. They did, and when Dalia's mother died, she had no alternative but to bury her in the cellar of their home, again to avoid detection and arrest. Shortly thereafter she was discovered, retried, sent to prison, and then back into exile.

Grinkevičiūtė wrote the first version of her memoirs in 1949–50, after she had escaped to Lithuania. She buried the manuscript in the yard of their house just before she was arrested in 1950, and the text was unearthed only in 1991, the year Lithuania regained its independence and several years after Grinkevičiūtė's death in December 1987. As a result, it was not her "childhood" memoirs that played such an important role during the popular movement, but a subsequent text that she wrote in the 1970s, when she was already a politically conscious dissident. This text, written in Russian and entitled *Litovskie ssylnye v Yakutie* (Lithuanian Exiles in Yakutsk), was first published in 1979 by the underground journal *Pamiat'* in Moscow. It was circulated through *samizdat*, and underwent continual mutation as it was manually copied and recopied. It was eventually smuggled abroad and published in French and English.

Sometime in the early 1980s, Grinkevičiūtė rewrote the 1979 version into Lithuanian. Aldona Šulskytė, her roommate and friend and a member of a repressed family herself, assisted in the writing process, not only in terms of editing and recopying but also carrying the manuscript on her person or hiding it at times when Grinkevičiūtė was being interrogated or when the apartment was searched by the police. Grinkevičiūtė called this last text the basic or fundamental version of her testimony. It was this version of her memoirs that would emerge into open discourse and exercise such a powerful effect on Soviet Lithuanian society.[12]

Unlike the other versions of her testimony, none of which has a title, this last manuscript has what appears to be the beginning of a title. The word "Our" is followed by ten dots, which led some to speculate that she intended to call it *Mūsų mažoji žemė* (*Our Small Land*), as an ironic reference to the title of Leonid Brezhnev's memoirs *Nasha malaya zemlya*. But while the reference to Brezhnev is speculative, the epigraph just below the title: "Their Innocence Was Their Guilt," was taken from the epic poem *Blood and Ashes* by Justinas Marcinkevičius. In the poem, this phrase serves as a refrain to a highly moving narrative of traumatic experience, as the villagers of Pirčiupiai were being herded into a barn and set on fire.

Like most Lithuanians living in the LSSR at the time, Grinkevičiūtė was a great admirer of the works of Marcinkevičius, especially *Mindaugas, Mažvydas* and *Katedra*, the trilogy of historical dramas that had gained the status of a national epic. She had never met him before but trusted him implicitly, hoping that he would help bring her own writing to Lithuanians. "I know that you will understand me," read a little note attached to the notebook which Marcinkevičius took into his hands.[13]

Marcinkevičius had indeed developed an incredible rapport with his readers. His many poems and other literary works were more than just popular and memorized by schoolchildren, but enjoyed a truly cult status. He gave innumerable and always well-attended public readings, where the audience, mostly but by no means only women, was regularly reduced to tears. For example, Aldona Liobytė describes the mood of one such poetry reading in 1980 which she attended: " ... archaic farm wells, hearts, God, a horse, and ladies with a tear in their eyes ... overall it was sorrowful, cozy, elevated."[14]

By the same token, Marcinkevičius's status meant that the gap between the two in terms of social standing was immense, so Grinkevičiūtė had prepared a special pretext to justify a meeting. She called him several times, proposing to give him some precious artefacts of Bishop Motiejus Valančius, one of the leaders of the first Lithuanian national awakening of the late nineteenth century.[15] This ruse was necessary because Grinkevičiūtė's status as a dissident and a former deportee meant that she still lived on the margins of society. And even though the deportees would soon be elevated to the status of national heroes themselves, the establishment intelligentsia continued to look upon them and upon dissidents with considerable irony and even disdain.[16]

Gender and professional status also raised barriers in what was still a highly parochial society. The great prestige accorded to professional writers in Soviet Lithuania had a negative side in the derision shown to amateur writers who were not part of the club and jeered as "graphomaniacs." Amateur female writers were the subject of special scorn, and were most often referred to as "scribbling women."[17]

Nevertheless, by July 16, 1987, Grinkevičiūtė had secured her appointment and traveled from the small townlet of Laukuva where she resided to Vilnius. During the same trip, she also visited Kazys Saja, a well-known playwright with whom she had been corresponding for some time, along with his wife Zita Mažeikaitė. The couple agreed to retype Grinkevičiūtė's memoirs, and they distributed the manuscript informally as they prepared it for publication. Grinkevičiūtė died in December 1987, several months before the first instalment of her memoirs was published in the August 1988 issue of the monthly journal *Pergalė*.

Her testimony had a strong impact on the reading public. "Until now we have read nothing so horrifying on this subject," stated the writer Vytautas Martinkus.[18] Saulius Žukas described the text as the source of the "moral rejuvenation" of the Lithuanian nation.[19] Professional writers like Juozas Aputis called on their peers to "put down their pen" and "give their place to deportee literature and memoirs."[20] However, the mass publication of other deportee memoirs that came in 1989 did not dislodge the professional writers from their positions of social influence.

In fact, the encounter of Grinkevičiūtė and Marcinkevičius shows how the social and moral role of the Soviet Lithuanian literary elite was only enhanced by the free publication of formerly repressed works. Indeed, the Soviet Lithuanian reading public was first exposed to Grinkevičiūtė's memoirs through their citation in an article written by Marcinkevičius about his encounter with her and his own experience of reading her text.[21]

Although *glasnost'* was gaining speed, deportee memoirs were still subject to censorship, but nothing could prevent Marcinkevičius from citing Grinkevičiūtė's manuscript in his own work. In effect, the citation of her work in his published article broke the taboo and cleared the way for the publication of the full text a few months later. By using his status to confer legitimacy and status on Grinkevičiūtė as an ex-deportee as well as a woman writer, Marcinkevičius also confirmed his own status as the custodian and voice of the nation's collective memory, which now came to embrace the experience of the deportees.

In the article, Marcinkevičius alludes to the anecdotes that used to circulate about how some deportees did quite well for themselves in Siberia as farmers and had to be forced to return to Lithuania, an ironic and repeated "dekula-kization." By contextualizing the reception of Grinkevičiūtė's testimony against the background of social stereotypes, the article pre-emptively addresses potential sources of scepticism, before asking how such an injustice could have been allowed to happen, and by extension how it could be allowed to pass without remorse or repentance, thus turning the ethical gaze squarely on contemporary Lithuanian society.

The text then turns to the testimony itself, choosing to reproduce a fragment of Grinkevičiūtė's manuscript that represents the experience of displacement as a defining aspect of Lithuanian identity:

> Trofimovsk Island now is empty and uninhabited again. During storms the waves of the Laptev Sea with enormous force are beating against its shore and are persistently destroying it. When in 1949 the last deportees were transported for fishing to other places the waves already started destroying the end of the joint grave and it started disintegrating. There is no doubt that all the corpses have already been washed away long ago. In what seas and oceans are they still travelling and searching for the path to their far away homeland?[22]

Marcinkevičius closes by articulating a path for social redemption. Although Lithuanians have up to now neglected the memory of the deportees, and did not do enough to make amends to the survivors, they could now, at least "take in their souls, which is their memory." As a postscript he calls for the construction of a monument to the victims of Stalinism. By recounting the steps of his own coming to terms with the person of Grinkevičiūtė and with her testimony, Marcinkevičius set the pattern for the popular reception of her work, and launched the process of appropriating deportee texts into the collective memory of the nation.

Two lives: a tragic symmetry

Marcinkevičius' article puts the focus on the crimes of Stalin and the victims of Stalinism. But the confrontation with the past during the popular movement quickly went beyond de-Stalinization to reject the Soviet period as a whole. And this repudiation of the past raised a number of difficult questions: who precisely were the victims of the Soviet regime? Was it only those who were deported, imprisoned, or killed? Those mobilized into the army, forced to work in a specific place, or prevented from working in a chosen profession? And who was to blame? Beyond the police and security forces responsible for political repressions, should the list include government officials, party members, and members of *Komsomol*? And what about leading members of the official intelligentsia like Marcinkevičius?

Indeed, the tragic symmetry of the life stories of Grinkevičiūtė and Marcinkevičius dramatically illustrates the deep social divide between the deportees and mainstream Soviet Lithuanian society. The two were born less than three years apart, but their social origins were starkly different. Marcinkevičius was born to a poor farmer in a small village, and the Bible was practically the only book to which he was exposed in his early childhood. Grinkevičiūtė, meanwhile, was born in Kaunas into the intelligentsia family of a high government official. As an upper-middle class city girl, she went to one of the best schools in the country, the Aušra girl's gymnasium. The household was cultured, and Dalia was constantly exposed to music, books and the theatre.

The arrival of Soviet power would change their fates irrevocably. Grinkevičiūtė lost everything, and was sent as a fourteen-year-old child to probable death. Marcinkevičius witnessed the trauma of war and the brutal guerrilla war in the countryside. But with the help of good grades in school and Soviet educational policies that promoted the entry of workers and peasants to institutions of higher education, he was able to enter Vilnius University and study literature. In 1949, the year when Grinkevičiūtė escaped from the Gulag and was hiding in Kaunas, forced secretly to dig the earth with her own hands to bury her mother in the basement of their former family home, Marcinkevičius and his cohort were literally singing in the streets of Vilnius.

As Marcinkevičius and the Generation of 1930 assumed leading positions among the new Soviet Lithuanian cultural elite after Stalin's death, Grinkevičiūtė was released from prison, but still forbidden to travel west of the Ural Mountains. In 1954 she started her medical education in Omsk, and after Khrushchev's amnesty of 1956 was finally allowed to return to Lithuania. She obtained a medical degree from Kaunas University in 1960 and took up a job in the hospital of the small provincial townlet of Laukuva. Grinkevičiūtė was bitter but not broken by the experience of exile and was outspoken in her criticism of the regime. She became an active participant in the Soviet dissident movement, which meant that she was subject to regular police surveillance and harassment by the authorities for the rest of her life.

In principle, Grinkevičiūtė could well have viewed Marcinkevičius as a representative of the regime that ruined her life. And yet, by entrusting her manuscript to him shortly before her death, she not only secured the transmission of her memory to subsequent generations, but symbolically bridged the gap between those who cooperated with the regime and those who were brutally repressed. For Grinkevičiūtė, Marcinkevičius commanded tremendous moral authority, due to the emotional power of his literary works and their ability to communicate the experience of trauma. In the last years of the Soviet Union, the Soviet Lithuanian intelligentsia would transform this symbolic capital into a force for political change.

The author's authority

Marcinkevičius, Maldonis, Martinaitis, Geda and many other leading members of the official intelligentsia were active leaders of the popular movement, making key speeches at mass rallies and mobilizing the populace through their literary works and political essays.[23] They were admired, applauded, cheered and adored. No longer "engineers of human souls," they now stepped forward as spokespeople for the nation and were seen as the guardians of the Lithuanian language, culture and collective memory.

This kind of public authority did not arise out of nowhere. Throughout the 1960s and 1970s, their role as the translators of official ideology and values into the cultural vernacular was developed through a nation-wide system of speaking engagements. Factories, schools, libraries and the pervasive network of "culture palaces" organized readings of recent works by Soviet Lithuanian writers on a weekly and monthly basis.[24] These sorts of events were very popular, and contributed to the public influence of writers as a group.

The social power of the cultural intelligentsia was entrenched in the cityscape of the nation's capital. The most prestigious address in the city, known as the Bishop's Palace in the fourteenth century and the Officer's House of the Red Army after World War II (and the President's Palace in the post-Soviet era), was symptomatically converted into the Palace of Artists in the 1960s. In the early 1980s, the closing ceremonies of the Spring of Poetry festival came to be held in the Great Cathedral, by this point converted into a museum, but which still retained its aura as the most important site of Lithuanian spirituality since the thirteenth century when it was transformed from a pagan into a Christian temple.

The establishment writers were also a cohesive group with significant organizational resources. In 1986, the Writers' Union had 216 members, of whom 45 percent (97) were members of the Communist Party of Lithuania. The Communist Party organization of the Writers' Union used its authority to hold open meetings which were the vanguard of *glasnost'* in the republic, radically expanding the envelope of acceptable political discussions. In the political discourse of the time, a threshold was passed on April 4, 1988 at one of the meetings organized in the Palace of Artists. The delegates passed a number of resolutions on strengthening the role of Lithuanian and limiting that of Russian in public life and education that would have been unthinkable just a year or two before.[25]

On May 5, 1988, Maldonis addressed the Central Committee of the Lithuanian Communist Party in his capacity of Writers' Union board chairman. Copies of his speech which criticized the falsification of history and Moscow's control over cultural issues in Lithuania were widely circulated in manuscript form, copied by hand and passed around. The popular movement was initiated and driven by many members of the creative and technical intelligentsia, but the leading role of the writers was recognized. For example, the geographer Česlovas Kudaba (1934–93), a leading member of *Sąjūdis* whose own

writings on ecology and nature were extremely influential at the time and who would be one of the signatories of the act of independence, asserted that the writers proved to be "the most courageous and ahead of the rest. We all trusted them."[26]

As recalled by contemporaries, the speeches of writers delivered at public gatherings, conferences, and party meetings unfailingly expressed precisely *those words* that the audience was expecting to hear; the very words that they intuited would be and should be pronounced. They spoke with an intonation that conveyed as much emotional affect as the speeches of deportees, whose gravitas derived from the tragic nature of their biographies rather than any particular skill with words. Indeed, the "wolves of discourse" had the self-confidence to speak publically that few could match. Their speeches were constantly relayed by the mass media and were frequently transcribed, copied and circulated by hand.[27]

In an essay published at the height of the popular movement in 1988, Vytautas Martinkus describes the role of the writer in the following exalted terms:

> The writer, without even wanting it, is called upon to atone for the sins of others. He is the defender of the sober mind, of philosophical thinking and, of course, honesty. We now have the situation under our skies like that described by Nikolai Chernyshevsky, more than 100 years ago in Russia, when literature was the concentrated essence of the nation's intellectual life. As a result, the writer has the duty to be interested in such matters which in other countries have come to belong to the competence of specialists in other branches of intellectual activity. Thus, to rephrase the great Russian critic, I would say that while England could easily manage without, for example, C. P. Snow, I cannot imagine how Lithuania could manage without, for example, Justinas Marcinkevičius.[28]

Of course, not all agreed with this sentiment. In 1986, Algirdas Patackas, the aforementioned participant in the hiker's' movement, was imprisoned for editing a *samizdat* journal. He lost his job and upon his release in 1987 had to work as a laborer, though he soon entered politics and would later become a signatory of the act of independence. For people like Patackas, who risked his career and wellbeing to engage in active opposition to the Soviet regime, the Soviet Lithuanian writers were seen as conformists: "Marcinkevičius was never our man. People who lived, in those times, an independent life, would never let him into their company."[29]

Vytautas Ališauskas, a Catholic philosopher who like Patackas lost his job due to anti-Soviet activities and became active in the popular movement, was even more outspoken in his criticism: "All those lines about goodness, spirituality and nature made my stomach turn," he recalls, referring to the sublime pastoralism of Marcinkevičius' late poetry. "The regime was doing what it needed to do, and all that was fully incorporated in it. To use the Soviet expression," he said, "it was opium for the masses."[30]

For Patackas, Ališauskas, and other dissidents who adopted a principled stance against Soviet power, the true face of resistance and authority was not the writer who gave expression to the sorrows of the nation in the Soviet press, but the fighter or dissident who continued to fight or the survivor who refused to taint his honor with collaboration. A similar position was held by the tragic and talkative figure of Justinas Mikutis (1922–88), an eccentric Gulag survivor who became something of an icon and a cult figure among some creative and dissident circles in Vilnius, and who was extremely critical of figures like Marcinkevičius and other establishment intellectuals who joined and, from their point of view, co-opted the popular movement after the initial, most dangerous steps had been taken by the dissidents.[31]

Indeed, the first public demonstration in Vilnius to seize upon the opening provided by Moscow's policy of *glasnost'* was organized on August 23, 1987 by Antanas Terleckas, Vytautas Bogušis, Petras Cidzikas and Nijolė Sadūnaitė, dissidents who identified with the Lithuanian Freedom League (*Lietuvos laisvės lyga*) – well before *Sąjūdis* was founded on June 3, 1988. They called on Lithuanians to meet at the Adam Mickiewicz monument next to St. Ann's Church in Vilnius to commemorate the 48th anniversary of the Molotov–Ribbentrop Pact. The Vilnius rally coincided with demonstrations in the other two Baltic capitals of Tallinn and Riga.

The rallies of August 23, 1987 in each Baltic capital were relatively small, attended by a few thousand people at most.[32] In Lithuania at that time, the *Lietuvos laisvės lyga* and the dissidents were viewed by many as strange eccentrics or dangerous radicals for their uncompromising insistence on full independence.[33] Instead, it would be *Sąjūdis*, led primarily by prominent members of the official intelligentsia, rather than dissidents, who would mobilize the population and organize the truly mass rallies that began in 1988.

Thus, when Grinkevičiūtė approached Marcinkevičius for assistance in July 1987, just weeks before the rally at the Mickiewicz monument, she provided him with the means to reinforce his status as a national leader at a critical moment, when the dissident and official wings of the intelligentsia were effectively vying for leadership of the popular movement. For the Lithuanian mainstream, Marcinkevičius and his peers had ceased to be identified with the Soviet system, and they successfully asserted their collective role as the voice of the authentic Lithuanian nation.[34]

We are all deportees

The Soviet Lithuanian intelligentsia played a key role in ensuring that deportation became the key trope for describing all forms of suffering and oppression under Soviet rule, under the Russian Empire, and even earlier. They methodically subjected the very idea of deportation to metaphorical expansion synchronically and diachronically to include all living Lithuanians and Lithuanians throughout history, and not only individual Lithuanians but all aspects of Lithuanian

Figure 8.1 Rally to mark signing of Molotov–Ribbentrop Pact. Surveillance photo
taken by the LSSR KGB. Vilnius, August 23, 1987
LYA, f. 1771, ap. 270, b. 182, l. 63. Courtesy of ELTA.

Figure 8.2 Algirdas Sabaliauskas, *Justinas Marcinkevičius at a meeting of Sąjūdis.*
Vingis Park, Vilnius, June 11, 1989
Courtesy of LCVA.

identity. Even Lithuanians who emigrated to the West were identified as deportees. In the opening article for the literary "Deportee Archive" in *Pergalė*, Liudvikas Gadeikis encouraged members of the émigré community to contribute their testimonies.[35]

In another issue of *Pergalė* published that year, Viktorija Daujotytė wrote that Lithuanians had been driven from their homeland during the Teutonic Crusades, and deported again during the partitions of Poland. Deportation was systematized as a means to defeat the rebellions of 1794, 1830 and 1863, peaking in the unprecedented Soviet deportations of 1940–41 and 1945–53, with only the twenty-year period of independence between the wars and the 200 years following the Battle of Grunwald as historical moments of reprieve. In line with Marcinkevičius' presentation of Grinkevičiūtė, Daujotytė constructs the moment of return from deportation as opening the possibility of moral redemption: "The poems of the deportees are approaching us like an iceberg of pain from the Laptev sea, not yet fully emerged. Deportee poems are resurfacing from oblivion and desecration like white bones from the land of eternal frost."[36]

Marcinkevičius would continue the process of abstracting the experience of deportation into the more general concept of displacement in public discourse. At a session of the Supreme Council of the LSSR, he made a call to declare Lithuanian the state language and to restore other key symbols of Lithuanian statehood: "Our language has experienced much abuse, discrimination and injustice. It is now returning home as if from deportation."[37] Similarly, Daujotytė also wrote of the Lithuanian language and culture as having been deported: "Together with people, many words which were dear to Lithuanians were deported: God, God's mother, Homeland Lithuania, Cross, Crucifix, prayer, Easter, Christmas, holy hymns were deported."[38] The metaphor of displacement was absolutely central to the rhetoric of *Sąjūdis*, as Vytautas Landsbergis made clear in a speech delivered in 1990: "We were deported not only from our homeland but from our language, customs, religion, respect for ourselves and our earth."[39]

The return of memory through the discourse of displacement had a deep political, social and cultural impact. It imbued the referent of the past with a palpable reality and a concrete, meaningful relationship to the present that could inform and drive political action. The emphasis was on investing specific symbols and sites with a deeply felt meaning. Pierre Nora described the emergence of such places over time as *lieux de mémoire*, the historical significance of which is measured in both cognitive and, more importantly, affective dimensions.

The discourse of displacement was reinforced and channelled into performative rituals of personal transformation through mass rallies and ceremonies of commemoration. Contemporary observers frequently commented on the performative nature of the politics of *Sąjūdis*, echoing that of the ethnocultural movement. Vytautas Kavolis wrote in 1991 of how the rituals of the popular movement revealed a "Baroque popular culture" and a "theatrical cast of mind":

only in Lithuania are there processions in the tens of thousands carrying crosses across the country to the Hill of Crosses. ... Only in Lithuania can young men in the guise of medieval knights march in to defend the Parliament building against Soviet tanks. ... This occurs against a backdrop of almost daily celebrations of all conceivable memorial days, numerous re-inaugurations of destroyed monuments, reburials of exhumed bodies of Siberian deportees.[40]

The *sodyba* or homestead of artist Vilius Orvidas (1952–92) provides a vivid example of the syncretic nature of the discourse of displacement. Starting in the 1970s, Orvidas began to gather stones and trees from villages destroyed during the times of forced urbanization and arranged them into art forms on his farmstead in northwestern Lithuania (Samogitia) not far from the town of Salantai. He hung trees upside down, carved stones and turned the farmstead into a combination of installation, sanctuary, museum and archive.

His "relics," as Orvidas called them, came to comprise an eclectic collection of sculptures, crosses and stones, old tree trunks placed next to wild vegetation and cultivated plants, and even an old Soviet tank. In the mid-1980s, the site became a highly symbolic magnet for all sorts of individuals who were discontented or looking for alternatives to the mainstream – from intellectuals and students to drug addicts, folk music enthusiasts, punks and other subcultures – a common meeting place, a destination for pilgrimages.[41]

The act of making pilgrimages had its origins in the ethnocultural movement of the 1960s and 1970s, assumed a new dimension in late 1986 when Lithuanians took advantage of the lifting of restrictions to visit the distant sites of the Gulag system. This mass social phenomenon of bringing back the remains of perished deportees was interpreted as a "return" (*sugrįžimas*) – a spontaneous, grass-roots movement driven by individual families who took advantage of Gorbachev's liberal reforms to go to Siberia to recover the remains of their loved ones.

Made for television documentary films like *Lithuania Between Past and Future* (Antanas Maciulevičius, 1990) and *The Return* (Petras Abukevičius, Vytautas Damaševičius, 1990) among many others documented the commemorative rituals of Gulag deportees and their descendants during the twilight of the USSR.[42] In *Lithuania between Past and Future*, for example, scenes of people digging up graves in Siberia and coffins draped in Lithuanian flags at the airport in Vilnius are framed by an extended discussion by ethnographer Norbertas Vėlius, among others, on the mythology and culture of the ancient Lithuanians. "Lithuanians are inseparable from their land. Even after death they return to their homeland ... They could never understand a person who voluntarily chooses to live outside of his home country."[43] The ritual of return is thus contextualized in the framework of deeply rooted myths and beliefs. The cinematic representation of pilgrimages to Siberia to recover the remains of ancestors for reburial in the homeland of Lithuania disseminated the denaturing effects of displacement on identity to a broad audience of viewers.

Figure 8.3 Viktoras Kapočius. Remains of deceased deportees returned to Lithuania from Krasnoyarsk. Kėdainiai military airfield, July 28, 1989
LCVA. 0-127561.

Figure 8.4 Viktoras Kapočius. Commemoration of June 1941. Deportations at the Naujoji Vilnia train station. Vilnius, June 14, 1989. Return of remains from the Gulag
LCVA. 0-127417.

This phenomenon of reburial was not unique to the Baltics, and has parallels throughout the post-communist world. In a study of what she calls the "politics of dead bodies," cultural anthropologist Katherine Verdery describes how the remains of persons persecuted by the communist regimes have been disinterred and reburied with elaborate ceremony as a means of "giving new contours to the past through revising genealogies and rewriting history."[44]

When the deportee memoirs began to be published *en masse* in 1988, and the phenomenon of *sugrįžimas* reached its peak in 1989 with televised mass ceremonies of reburial, the narratives and images of deportation and return were received against the background of the pre-existing discourse of traumatic displacement, which had already drawn an explicit equivalence between the minority experience of deportation and the other forms of displacement experienced by the majority.

In December 1991, when the Soviet Union finally collapsed, Martinaitis summed up the attachment of Lithuanians to the land as a counterpoint or response to the trauma of deportation:

> The earth was turned during the years of collectivization; during the years of melioration, there were attempts to eliminate our relationship with the earth using politics, science, school and literature. In the end, we were all deportees; collectivization was deportation.[45]

By equating these two forms of displacement with specific reference to the modernization and socialist enlightenment agenda ("politics, science, school and literature") of the postwar regime, Martinaitis drew the minority of Lithuanians who had actually been sent to the Gulag into the same category as the majority of Lithuanians who had not, but who had experienced various other forms of social, cultural or physical displacement in the context of Soviet-style modernization.

The mass rites of reburial gave all Lithuanians, including those who were actively repressed and those who had accommodated themselves to the regime, or even benefited from it to some extent, the opportunity to identify with the deportees. Collectivization, urbanization and Russification were seen as one with the trauma of deportation. In spite of the potential for a clash between the "two nations" of Soviet Lithuania, the cohesion of the popular movement was maintained through the performative identification of the majority of Lithuanians with the trauma of displacement.

Notes

1 Vytautas Landsbergis, speech delivered at a public meeting. In *Tremtinys* 6.21 (May 1990).
2 Tomas Venclova, "A Fifth Year of Independence: Lithuania, 1922 and 1994," *East European Politics and Societies* 9 (1995): 344.
3 Alfred Senn, *Lithuania Awakening* (Berkeley, CA: University of California Press, 1990), 45.

4 Dovilė Budrytė, "Coming to Terms with the Past: Memories of Displacement and Resistance in the Baltic States," in *Historical Injustice and Democratic Transition in Eastern Asia and Northern Europe: Ghosts at the Table of Democracy*, ed. Kenneth Christie and Robert Cribb (London: RoutledgeCurzon, 2002), 126.

5 In a Lithuanian literary history for high school students, Viktorija Daujotytė underscores how much Grinkevičiūtė's testimony contributed to the spread of popular movement. Viktorija Daujotytė and Elena Bukelienė, *Lietuvių literatūra 1940–1997* (Kaunas: Šviesa, 1997), 27.

6 Mark Beissinger, *Nationalist mobilization and the collapse of the Soviet State* (Cambridge: Cambridge University Press, 2002). Václav Havel and John Keane, *The Power of the Powerless: Citizens against the State in Central-Eastern Europe* (Armonk, NY: M. E. Sharpe, 1985).

7 Milan Kundera, *The Book of Laughter and Forgetting* (New York: A. A. Knopf, 1980); Geoffrey Hosking, *The Awakening of the Soviet Union* (Cambridge, MA: Harvard University Press, 1990).

8 Saulė Matulevičienė, "Dokumentinė literatūra: pokario ir tremties atsiminimai" [Documentary Literature: Memoirs of the Post-war Period and the Deportations], in *Naujausioji lietuvių literatūra*, ed. Giedrius Viliūnas (Vilnius: Alma Littera, 2003), 319–45.

9 *Lietuvos rytas*, the successor of *Komjaunimo tiesa*, now has a circulation of about 60,000 and is still the most popular subscription daily.

10 Liudas Truska, "Origins of the Lithuanian Reform Movement *Sąjūdis*" *13 January 1991 in Lithuania in the Context of the Recent Research* (Vilnius: Vilnius Pedagogical University, 2006), 158. By way of comparison, the average history book published during the late Soviet period before *Sąjūdis* would have a circulation of about 20,000 copies, while history books published in the post-Soviet period rarely surpass 10,000 copies and are most printed in runs of 1,000 or 2,000.

11 Juozas Grinkevičius died of starvation in October of 1943 in a prison in the Ural Mountains.

12 For more on Grinkevičiūtė's memoirs, see Jūra Avižienis, "Performing Identity: Lithuanian Memoirs of Siberian Deportation and Exile," in Marcel Cornis-Pope, ed. *History of the Literary Cultures of East-Central Europe: Junctures and Disjunctures in the 19th and 20th Centuries* (Amsterdam: Benjamins, 2010), 504–14. Jerilyn Sambrooke, "Narratives of Identity: A Postcolonial Reading of Dalia Grinkevičiūtė's *Lithuanians by the Laptev Sea*," in Violeta Davoliūtė and Tomas Balkelis, eds. *Maps of Memory: Trauma, Identity and Exile in Deportation Memoirs from the Baltic States* (Vilnius: LTTI, 2012): 90–103. Violeta Davoliūtė, "Deportee Memoirs and Lithuanian History: the Double Testimony of Dalia Grinkevičiūtė," *Journal of Baltic Studies* 36.1 (2005): 51–68.

13 Daujotytė, Viktorija and Elena Bukelienė, *Lietuvių literatūra: 1940–1997* (Kaunas: Šviesa, 1997). Aldona Šulskytė recalls that Grinkevičiūtė, with whom she lived as a roommate, had an immense appreciation for the literary works of Marcinkevičius and that she would sometimes refer to him as "the King." Aldona Šulskytė, Interview by author. Personal interview, August 12, 2003, Laukuva.

14 R.Z. Saukienė, ed. *Šmaikščioji rezistentė Aldona Liobytė: publicistika, laiškai, atsiminimai* (Vilnius: Lietuvos rašytojų sąjungos leidykla, 1995), 178.

15 Viktorija Daujotytė-Pakerienė, "Ugnies maiše nepaslėpsi," in *Lietuviai prie Laptevų jūros: Atsiminimai, miniatiūros, laiškai*, ed. A. Šulskytė (Vilnius: Lietuvos rašytojų sąjungos leidykla, 1997), 22.

16 Tomas Venclova said in 1990 that "dissidents were considered unessential by the Lithuanian intelligentsia. They were considered fanatics, hollow or even mentally ill since they had a different opinion." In "Sakau karčią tiesą" (I tell a bitter truth), *Atgimimas* 24 (1990). Liudas Truska offers a more moderate assessment: "From my personal experience I can state that intellectuals disdained dissidents and looked

upon them with a slight irony." Liudas Truska, "Origins of the Lithuanian Reform Movement *Sąjūdis*," in *13 January 1991 in Lithuania in the Context of the Recent Research*, ed. Vygandas Vareikis (Vilnius: Vilnius Pedagogical University, 2006), 158.

17 The proper place of women was seen as the listeners of the delivery of literature read by men in literary evenings, poetry and prose readings and lectures. Judita Vaičiūnaitė, a famous Lithuanian poet, was told straightforwardly by her editor Albinas Žukauskas that she was too beautiful to be a good poet. Ula Vaičiūnaitė, "Išaugusios viena iš kitos," *Moteris* 7 (2008): 44–49. Vytautė Žilinskaitė recalls how her male colleagues constantly reprimanded her for writing humourous pieces because "real humour" is for men and not women to write. Interview by author. Audio recording. Vilnius, October 11, 2011, July 9, 2013.

18 Vytautas Martinkus, "Rašytojo žodis: mitas ar tikrovė?" *Literatūra ir menas* 39 (September 24, 1988): 2–3.

19 Saulius Žukas, "Nepasitikėk vieškeliais," *Literatūra ir menas* 40 (October 1, 1988): 5.

20 Juozas Aputis, "Tautos gedulo diena," *Pergalė* 6 (1989), 7.

21 Justinas Marcinkevičius, "Reabilituota – 1970 metais," *Literatūra ir menas* 22 (May 18, 1988): 2–3.

22 Ibid., 3.

23 Other prominent figures include Vytautas Bubnys, Romas Gudaitis, Virgilijus Čepaitis, Kazys Saja, Petras Dirgėla, Vytautas Petkevičius and others.

24 The Fictional Literature Propaganda Bureau of the Lithuanian Writers Union published pamphlets for each venue such as, for example, the reading room of the Vilnius Screw Factory, which included a year-long schedule of public readings. See Lietuvos TSR Rašytojų sąjungos grožinės literatūros propogandos biuras, Vilniaus grąžtų gamyklos klubas, *Literatūros panorama* (Vilnius, 1978–79).

25 Truska, "Origins of the Lithuanian Reform Movement *Sąjūdis*," 171.

26 Česlovas Kudaba, "Pokalbis apie Sąjūdį" (Conversation about Sąjūdis), *Akiračiai* 10 (1988). Ibid., 173.

27 Vytautas Martinkus, "Sąjūdžio eseistika: rašytojai literatūros ir politikos kryžkelėje (1998)," in *Literatūra ir paraliteratūra: straipsniai ir esė* (Vilnius: Lietuvos rašytojų sąjungos leidykla, 2003), 56–65.

28 Vytautas Martinkus, "Rašytojo žodis: mitas ar tikrovė?" *Literatūra ir menas* 39 (September 24, 1988): 3.

29 Saulius Šaltenis, "Pokalbis su K. Saja ir A. Patacku," *Šiaurės Atėnai* (July 3, 1991).

30 "Justino Marcinkevičiaus darna," *Naujasis židinys-Aidai* 4 (2003): 155–60.

31 Vaidotas Žukas, "Justinas Mikutis – laisvas žmogus nelaisvoje aplinkoje," *Bernardinai. lt* (April 26, 2012).

32 Alfred Senn writes that 2,000 showed up in Tallinn, 5,000 in Riga, while the Vilnius rally was attended by 500 core participants and about 2,000 passersby who showed varying degrees of interest. *Lithuania Awakening*, 20.

33 Vytas S. Vardys and Judith B. Sedaitis, *Lithuania: The Rebel Nation* (Boulder, CO: Westview Press, 1997), 110.

34 Efforts to prove otherwise have met with disappointment: " … if we were looking for the roots of *Sąjūdis* in the networks of dissidents we would have to state with sadness that these networks in Lithuania were especially narrow and could not explain in any way the total mobilization of society in 1988." Ainė Ramonaitė, "'Paralelinės visuomenės' užuomazgos sovietinėje Lietuvoje: katalikiškojo pogrindžio ir etnokultūrinio sąjūdžio simbiozė," in *Sąjūdžio ištakų beieškant: nepaklusniųjų tinklaveikos galia*, ed. Jūratė Kavaliauskaitė and Ainė Ramonaitė (Vilnius: Baltos lankos, 2011), 33.

35 Liudvikas Gadeikis, "Tremties archyvas" (Archive of Deportation), *Pergalė* 1 (1989): 185.

36 Viktorija Daujotytė, "Paskutinis laisvės prieglobstis" (The Last Shelter of Freedom), *Pergalė* 12 (1989): 178–83.

37 Justinas Marcinkevičius, "Tartum grįžtumėm iš tremties" (As though we were returning from deportation). Speech delivered at a session of the Supreme Council of the LSSR, 18 November 1988. *Pažadėtoji žemė. (The Promised Land)* (Vilnius: Lietuvos rašytojų sąjungos leidykla, 2009), 40–45.
38 Daujotytė, "Paskutinis laisvės prieglobstis," 178.
39 Vytautas Landsbergis, speech delivered at a public meeting. In *Tremtinys* 6.21 (May 1990).
40 Vytautas Kavolis, "The Second Lithuanian Revival: Culture as Performance," *Lituanus* 37.2 (Summer 1991): 57–58.
41 For more on Vilius Orvidas, see, Daina Parulskienė, ed., *Kitoks: Vilius Orvidas* (Vilnius: Dialogo kultūros institutas, 2003); Dangė Čebatariūnaitė, "Vilius Orvidas ir jo mito logika," *Naujasis židinys-Aidai* 6 (June 2004): 251–53.
42 Petras Abukevičius and Vytautas Damaševičius, dir. *Sugrįžimas*, LKS, 1990. Antanas Maciulevičius, dir. *Lietuva tarp praeities ir ateities*, LKS, 1990. During the time of popular movement, filming and chronicling became a national obsession. Established directors like Robertas Verba as well as amateurs took thousands of meters of footage of various commemoratives public rituals and events. To this day these materials remain poorly documented and organized. Conversation with staff of the Mažvydas National Library, January 2012.
43 In Antanas Maciulevičius, dir. *Lietuva tarp praeities ir ateities*, LKS, 1990.
44 Katherine Verdery, *The Political Lives of Dead Bodies: Reburial and Postsocialist Change* (New York: Columbia University Press, 1999), 40.
45 Marcelijus Martinaitis. Interview conducted by Dana Šiaudinytė. "Žemė mus išgelbės" (The Land Will Save Us), *Vakarinės naujienos* (2 December 1991): 5.

Epilogue
Memory's many returns

The collapse of the Soviet Union and the emergence of independent states in its place, like the collapse of the Russian Empire in the heat of the Great War seventy years earlier, have provoked another great movement of peoples. Millions of former Soviet citizens, mostly but not only ethnic Russians, suddenly found themselves living in a "foreign" land, and sought to return "home."[1] From Lithuania alone, tens of thousands emigrated to Russia in the 1990s.

But if tens of thousands left Lithuania towards the East, hundreds of thousands moved West in search of opportunity.[2] From 1992 to 2012, the population decreased by nearly 700,000, with most of the émigrés consisting of relatively young Lithuanians of working age. This precipitous drop represents one fifth of the population that inhabited the territory upon the declaration of independence, roughly the same drop as occurred between 1939 and 1945 as a proportion of the total population, and considerably greater in absolute terms (699,000 compared to 500,000).[3]

The effects of mass displacement in the twenty-first century on Lithuanian collective identity are sure to be significant, but may not become apparent for several years or even decades from now. Meanwhile, memories of the twentieth century continue to wash upon Lithuanian shores as earlier waves of émigrés and their descendants – including Lithuanians, Jews and Poles – return to their "lost and forgotten homeland," looking to connect with their memories or the stories they inherited from parents and grandparents who once lived on this territory.

The renowned American critic Stephen Greenblatt, for example, travelled to Vilnius in the late 1990s, the city from which his grandparents had emigrated a hundred years earlier.[4] Like many other visitors of Jewish descent, he was dismayed to find little or no trace of the great seventeenth-century synagogue, or any other monument that could relate the cityscape before his eyes to the family lore of *Vilne* he heard as a child.[5] Instead of the synagogue, he found an elementary school built in its place. Walking further, he came across what he describes as "a recent memorial of Žemaitė, a noblewoman who turned away from the dominant Polish culture to write in the vernacular of the Lithuanian peasants." Greenblatt supposes the statue of Žemaitė was constructed during the "the post-Soviet celebration of collective identity and the

Figure 9.1 Jonas Ohman, *Statue of Žemaitė*. Vilnius, 2012

Figure 9.2 Jonas Ohman, *Statue of Vilnius Gaon*. Vilnius, 2012

ideology of romantic nationalism," and he marvels at how "statues of Lithuanian generals, poets, statesmen, folk heroes, and intellectuals are springing up everywhere," now in the late twentieth century just as must have been the case in the late nineteenth century.[6]

The monuments noted by Greenblatt do indeed "stake a Lithuanian claim to the city," as he puts it, but they were mostly erected during the Soviet, not the post-Soviet period. For example, the (only) memorial to Žemaitė in Vilnius was installed in 1970 by Algimantas and Vytautas Nasvytis, the twin brother architects who designed the Neringa Café, while the statue itself was sculpted by Petras Aleksandravičius in 1950. The "celebration of national identity" that Greenblatt describes began with the establishment of independence in 1918 and never really stopped during the Soviet period.

By the time the return of memory had reached its peak in 1989, the Lithuanian character of the city had long been taken for granted, the "Vilnius Question" resolved once and for all – at least on the surface. If anything, the post-Soviet period has witnessed a deeper reflection among some Lithuanian intellectuals about their arrival in the city after the war and the contingency of its Lithuanian character, as in the following passage from Marcelijus Martinaitis's essay "Vilnius, My Village."

> After the war we traveled to [Vilnius] in lorries decorated with birch tree branches singing: "We will rebuild the city of Gediminas ... " But we did not *know* this city at all until the time when our children had all but grown up, until we ourselves started reading the memoirs of old Vilnius residents, looking for family names, faces, drawings, pictures, city plans, old street names, places where palaces, sanctuaries, old defence fortifications had been built.[7]

Indeed, the first monuments erected in Vilnius during the post-Soviet era were focussed on commemorating the deportations and other atrocities committed during the Soviet and Nazi occupations, including the Holocaust, something that was impossible during the Soviet era. During Soviet times, the specific character of the Holocaust as the genocide of the Jews was ignored.[8]

Pace Greenblatt, the historical monument located closest to the site of the Great Synagogue is not that of Žemaitė, but that of the Vilna Gaon, erected in 1997 to commemorate the 200th anniversary of the death of the celebrated Jewish rabbi and scholar. The Vilna Gaon Lithuanian State Jewish Museum was established in 1989, and the first official admission of Lithuanian involvement in the Holocaust was made in 1990. In 1994, September 23 was declared the National Memorial Day for the Genocide of Lithuanian Jews, and it has been commemorated every year since.

On March 1, 1995, Algirdas Brazauskas delivered an address to the Israeli Knesset as the President of Lithuania where he openly admitted the involvement of Lithuanians in the Holocaust, asked for forgiveness and promised to bring war criminals to justice. Efforts at reconciliation were institutionalized in 1998, when President Valdas Adamkus established the International Commission for the Evaluation of the Crimes of the Nazi and Soviet Occupation Regimes in Lithuania, with a mandate to establish the truth of the crimes of the Nazi and Soviet regimes, to commemorate the victims, and to educate the public.[9]

However, these steps could all be described as "top-down" initiatives or the work of a minority of committed activists, which had a limited impact on the attitudes of the population at large. As increasing numbers of visitors like Greenblatt arrived from abroad to visit the cities and towns in Lithuania where their Jewish ancestors had lived, they were shocked to see that, outside of Vilnius and Kaunas where some limited measures had been taken, cemeteries and memorial sites were completely neglected, overgrown with grass and weeds, sometimes without even a plank showing the way to the site of a mass killing.

The almost complete lack of information concerning Lithuania's Jewish past stood in stark contrast to the memorial detail about the ethnic Lithuanian heritage throughout the landscape – a legacy of the folk revival and the ethnographic movement of the 1960s and 1970s. Regional tourist guides from the 1990s carefully document the location and cultural significance of every ancient stone or brook of folkloric significance, but contain relatively little to suggest that entire communities of Jews have ever lived in this or that town.

The "return of memory" of the late 1980s in Lithuania was indeed selective, conditioned by the "rustic turn." After decades of participation in folk revivals and reading Soviet Lithuanian literature representing the trauma of deracination, Lithuanians became acutely aware of how Sovietization had cut off their ties from their traditional way of life in the countryside. The deportations, collectivization and urbanization came to be seen in the single light of displacement, consolidating the collective identity of Lithuanians as a community of trauma, a nation of deportees, with a correspondingly fierce, autochthonous sense of attachment to the land.

This approach to collective identity has proven ill-adapted to the demands of building a democratic polity in an independent state. It obstructs social reflection on the experience of other groups and it leaves many blank spots in the memory of the Soviet period, notably where Lithuanians were not so much the victims, as the agents of history. In recent years, Lithuania has witnessed the emergence of a more aggressive brand of nationalism, which peaked along with the economic hardships that came in the wake of the financial crisis of 2009. The country is hardly unique in this respect, as political populism has been on the rise across the continent. Nonetheless, the upsurge of anti-cosmopolitan sentiment provoked Tomas Venclova in July 2010 to write a searing critique of post-Soviet Lithuanian society, and especially its cultural elite, rehearsing old Soviet-era debates between the cultural nativists and the cosmopolitans.[10]

Based on an extended parallel to *The Clouds* of Aristophanes, in which the farmer Strepsiades burns down the "thinkery" of Socrates, Venclova complains of the parochialism of Lithuanian society in which he, like Socrates in his burning thinkery, is suffocating.

> For at least fifty years ... Lithuania has lacked a normal, Socratic, intellectual culture. Our people are accustomed to thinking exclusively in ethnic

categories and have lost the desire and ability to realize there are other categories and other kinds of values, sometimes even more important ones. A primitive, unreflecting nationalism has come to the fore: I would call it a Strepsiadesian cult of one's own *deme*, the desire to immortalize isolation and provinciality. The fact that Lithuania has always been – although it is no longer – an agrarian society of small farmers strengthens this kind of nationalism.[11]

The article provoked a heated and often bitter debate, in which Venclova was in turn accused of elitism, arrogance and a lack of standing to make such critical remarks, given his privileged and protected status as the son of a high Soviet official who was insulated from the brutal experience suffered by the majority of the population during the postwar period, and later as an émigré in the USA.[12]

Indeed, the passing of the collective euphoria that attended the collapse of the USSR has uncovered long-standing fissures in Lithuanian society, which never went through a strict policy of lustration, or process of historical reconciliation that could have laid to rest the steady stream of accusations and mutual suspicions that continue to hang over any discussions of the past. While there has been a considerable amount of academic and some social debate over the active collaboration of the few, it is the passive accomodation of the many to Soviet rule that remains a painful issue.

While few would find fault with the decision taken the majority of Lithuanians at one point or another in the late 1940s to the early 1950s to make the best of the inevitability of Soviet rule, it is the equally incontrovertible fact that Lithuanian society, culture and identity as they exist today were shaped and formed by nearly fifty years of Sovietization that is so difficult to accept. As poet and critic Vytautas Rubavičius writes, Lithuanians eschew naming the Soviet experience as their own, as something they "have all lived through and accumulated, and which is now expressed in various cultural forms."[13]

It is clearly impossible that a half-century of development under Soviet rule could have gone without leaving a trace, but this is the impression created by that strand of Lithuanian historical discourse which views the period of occupation as an abyss, as an abnormal gap between two periods of normality. Ironically, the urge to make a radical break with the Soviet past suits those who were always against the Soviet regime, and wanted to bury its every trace, as well as those who were most intimately implicated in the regime and wanted to cover their traces.

The problem with this approach to the past, which remembers the Soviet period only through the commemoration of the regime's victims, is that it also had the effect of wiping out any appreciation for the everyday dimension of life under the Soviets, and thus any sensibility towards the social and cultural legacy of that period in the present, aside from the platitude that "old Soviet ways" of doing things must be overcome.

Martinaitis had already reflected on this issue in a 1993 essay. Even while he acknowledges the importance of the rustic turn to the rejuvenation and healing of Lithuanian collective identity ("The village of Lithuania is return-ing and will be returning for a long time, as if from deportation. Not only from distant Siberia but also from the deportations that took place within Lithuania. For what were these collectivizations, meliorizations and cement houses if not deportation?"), he warns against the mirage of the "Lithuanian utopia":

> The rites, celebrations and cutoms that have returned to us from past epochs represent a kind of utopia, a model of the ideal life registered in traditional culture, which we can restore through discourses of myth, religion and ethnic culture ... And in this way we are gripped by the conviction that we can return and become the same as we were some fifty or more years ago, before the catastrophe. We hear a lot now from the lips of protestors and politicians about this fixed, mythological time, which was ended by the occupations.[14]

Since then, Lithuanian memory of the Soviet period appears to have reached a point similar to German memory in the 1970s, when calls were made for an increased attention to *Alltagsgeschichte*, or the history of everyday life.[15] In order to be able to talk about the Third Reich not as an exception but as an integral part of history, and thus for individuals to take responsibility for what has occurred, it was argued that Germans had to stop viewing their past as external and separate from their own experience, and to mobilize their private and family memories of the period. Martinaitis himself produced a fascinating example of this kind of personal exploration in his 2009 memoirs, *We Lived.*[16]

Indeed, it was a commonplace among German historians in the late 1970s that personal stories and reminiscences had to be evoked and told as means of overcoming the "quasi-hypnotic paralysis" that most Germans had with regard to the Nazi past.[17] Scholars recognized that the focus of *Alltagsgeschichte* on the "normality" of life under Nazi rule carried the risk of romanticizing the past or indulging in nostalgia, but argued that, when properly done, it enabled a thematic detachment (*Verfremdung*) as the basis for a new apprehension of the past.[18]

It was, perhaps, only with the recent passing of key members of the Generation of 1930 that Lithuanian society has been offered an opportunity to develop a similar sense of detachment from the Soviet period. In the summer of 2010, for example, thousands of Lithuanians came out to mourn the passing of Algirdas Brazauskas, the last communist leader of Soviet Lithuania and the first leader of a Soviet republic to cut ties with the Com-munist Party of the Soviet Union. The political controversy that Brazauskas provoked during his life followed him into the grave, as the Catholic Church refused to admit his corpse into the Great Cathedral of Vilnius for the mass that he expressly requested in his last testament.

Nonetheless, after his death, public television showed historical documentaries that focussed on the turning points of his life, his family and career, which resonated with many Lithuanians whose life stories did not fit into the prevailing narrative of national resistance and martyrdom. The passing of Brazauskas – by no means an ordinary Lithuanian – nonetheless triggered a natural attentiveness to the everyday aspects of life during Soviet times that had been "forgotten" and repressed. It served as a reminder that life stories from this period are meaningful, even if they were not particularly heroic or tragic.[19]

The death of Justinas Marcinkevičius in 2011, on the other hand, was commemorated unambiguously as the passing of a national hero. The pathos of newspaper headlines proclaiming "The Nation Grieves the Loss of its Shepherd" or "The Death of the Poet Leaves the Nation Orphaned" was reinforced by the timing of his death on February 16, the anniversary of the declaration of Lithuanian independence in 1918. Crowds of Lithuanians braved the cold and wet snow, walking several kilometers after the mass held in the Great Cathedral to accompany Marcinkevičius' body to its final resting place in the Antakalnis Military Cemetery.

Lingering reservations that some may have felt about Marcinkevičius as a cog in the Soviet cultural machine were at least temporarily overwhelmed by the myth of the poet – the myth that Marcinkevičius himself was instrumental in devising. Media commentary focussed on his leadership role during *Sąjūdis*, the awakening of national consciousness, and the power with which he kindled a love and nostalgia for the scents, sounds and bygone ways of the village. Virtually no attention was paid to his earlier works, composed in the late 1950s and early 1960s, of his education in postwar Vilnius and rise to the peak of the cultural establishment, or the enthusiasm with which he and his peers developed the core narrative of Soviet Lithuanian modernity that they would later tear apart.

Since the late Soviet era it has been something of a cliché that Marcinkevičius and the Generation of 1930 provided a bridge of living memory to the repressed past of the interwar period, an essential resource for the revival of national identity. But their lives offer more than that. The story of their arrival in Vilnius after World War II, of upward social mobility, the passage into modernity and their transformation into Soviet Lithuanian subjects – stories that they themselves told and which represent the experience of generations of Lithuanians – provide a map towards the misplaced memory of how Lithuania became was it actually is today.

Notes

1 In fact, the return of ethnic Russians from the non-Russian republics to the RSFSR had already begun in the mid-1970s, reversing a centuries-long pattern of population expansion into the non-Russian peripheries of the Russian Empire. The process of return was merely accelerated, dramatically, by the collapse of the Soviet Union. Nearly 7 million people migrated to the RSFSR between 1989 and 2004. Timothy Heleniak, "An Overview of Migration in the Post-Soviet Space," in

Cynthia J. Buckley, Blair A. Ruble, and Erin T. Hofmann. Eds. *Migration, Homeland, and Belonging in Eurasia* (Washington, DC: Woodrow Wilson Center Press, 2008), 29–67.

2 Still, a small but growing number of ethnic Lithuanians are migrating East for work and business. See Violeta Davoliūtė, "Lithuania and the New West–East Migration," *OIKOS: Lithuanian Migration & Diaspora Studies* 6.2 (2008): 73–80.

3 Statistics Lithuania www.stat.gov.lt records the departure of 472,627 individuals from 1994 to 2012 and a natural decrease of the population during the same period of 142,895. Immigration to Lithuania remains small but has increased steadily from 1,664 individuals in 1994 to 19,843 in 2012, for a total of 115,893 during that period.

4 Greenblatt reflects on this experience in an article entitled "Racial Memory and Literary History," where he argues against national models of literary history and against nationalism in general. *PMLA* 116.1 (Jan. 2001): 48–63.

5 Indeed, as discussed in Chapter 3, the Great Synagogue was damaged during the war, and demolished in 1950.

6 Stephen Greenblatt, "Racial Memory and Literary History," *PMLA* 116.1 (Jan 2001): 55.

7 Marcelijus Martinaitis, "Vilniau, kaime mano … " *Literatūra ir menas* (April 20, 2007): 2–22.

8 Memorials and monuments raised at mass killing sites during Soviet times generally noted the sacrifice made by "Soviet citizens," including at the Paneriai (Ponary) site near Vilnius, where some 70,000 Jews, 20,000 Poles and 8,000 Russians were killed.

9 For more on the progress of Jewish–Lithuanian relations in the post-Soviet period, see Violeta Davoliūtė, "The Prague Declaration of 2008 and its Repercussions in Lithuania: Historical Justice and Reconciliation," *Lituanus* 57.3 (Fall 2011): 49–62.

10 Tomas Venclova, "Aš dūstu" www.bernardinai.lt/straipsnis/2010-07-14-tomas-venclova-asdustu/47325, accessed on May 10, 2013.

11 www.bernardinai.lt/straipsnis/2010-07-14-tomas-venclova-as-dustu/47325. Last accessed May 10, 2013.

12 Romas Gudaitis, "Kai legenda dūsta (atsakymas T. Venclovai)," *delfi.lt* (July 26, 2010); Krescencijus Stoškus, "Dar kartą apie T. Venclovą: poliai, kuriems nelemta vienas kito suprasti," *delfi.lt* (April 28, 2011).

13 Vytautas Rubavičius, "A Soviet Experience of Our Own: Comprehension and the Surrounding Silence," in *Baltic Postcolonialism*, ed. Violeta Kelertas (Amsterdam: Rodopi), 86.

14 Marcelijus Martinaitis, "Lietuviška utopija," *Kultūros barai* 8–9 (1993): 3.

15 Geoff Eley, "Labor History, Social History, 'Alltagsgeschichte': Experience, Culture, and the Politics of the Everyday. A New Direction for German Social History?" *The Journal of Modern History* 61.2 (1989), 297–343.

16 Marcelijus Martinaitis, *Mes gyvenome: biografiniai užrašai* (Vilnius: Lietuvos rašytojų sąjungos leidykla, 2009).

17 Thomas Elsaesser, *Fassbinder's Germany: History, Identity, Subject* (Amsterdam: Amsterdam University Press, 1996), 143.

18 Alf Lüdtke, *The History of Everyday Life: Reconstructing Historical Experiences and Ways of Life* (Princeton, NJ: Princeton University Press, 1995), 12.

19 Leonidas Donskis, "A. Brazauskas ir kita Lietuva," *IQ. The Economist partneris Lietuvoje* (July 1, 2010), www.delfi.lt/news/ringas/lit/ldonskis-a-brazauskas-ir-kita-lietuva.d?id=34032157.

Appendix
Biographies of people interviewed for this book

Apanavičius, Algimantas (b. 1935), composer. Born in Marijampolė district. Graduated from the Lithuanian Conservatory in Vilnius in 1961. Worked at the Lithuanian film studios since 1960 with the most prominent filmmakers and script writers. Composed music for about 150 films, including Vytautas Žalakevičius' *Nobody Wanted to Die.*

Areška, Vitas (b. 1927), literary critic, writer, professor. Born to a family of poor farmers in Rokiškis district. Moved to Vilnius in 1945, graduated from the Vilnius Pedagogical Institute in 1952, received a doctorate from the Institute of World Literature in Moscow in 1964. Joined the Writers' Union in 1971. Held numerous distinguished academic and administrative posts.

Baltakis, Algimantas (b. 1930), poet, critic, translator, one of the three key members of the Generation of 1930 along with Marcinkevičius and Maldonis. Born to the family of a poor village organ player in the Utena district. Moved to Kaunas in 1937. Graduated from the Faculty of Lithuanian Philology of Vilnius University in 1954. Joined the Writers' Union in 1955, held various positions on the editorial board of *Pergalė* since 1956, including editor-in-chief (1964–76/1985–90).

Brėdikis, Vytautas (b. 1930), architect, pedagogue, professor at Vilnius Academy of Art. Born in Biržai to a lower middle class Lithuanian family. Moved to Vilnius in 1949 to study at the Department of Architecture at the Vilnius Art Institute. Worked from 1955 at the Urban Planning Institute in Vilnius, since 1958 a member of the Soviet Lithuanian Union of Architects. Co-architect of the Lazdynai residential district in Vilnius (together with Vytautas Čekanauskas and others), which was awarded a Lenin Prize in 1974.

Bubnys, Vytautas Jurgis (b. 1932), writer, pedagogue, public figure, politician. Born in Prienai district, graduated from Vilnius Pedagogical Institute. Member of the Lithuanian Soviet Writers' Union since 1958, member of various editorial boards. One of the founding members of Sąjūdis, 1992–96 member of the Lithuanian parliament.

Granauskas, Romualdas (b. 1939) prose writer, playwright, an influential public figure during the popular movement. Born to a poor farmer's family in Samogitia, Granauskas had little formal education and held jobs ranging from construction worker to locksmith and high-school teacher. He worked on the editorial boards of *Nemunas* from 1968 to 1970, after which he devoted himself to writing novels and plays.

Katilius, Ramūnas (b. 1935), physicist. Born in Kaunas to a family of Lithuanian gymnasium teachers, raised in Marijampolė. Graduated in 1959 from the Faculty of Physics and Mathematics, Vilnius University. Worked at the Lithuanian Academy of Sciences from 1962 to 1966, later in Moscow at the USSR Academy of Sciences. Close friend of Joseph Brodsky, Tomas Venclova.

Lankauskas, Romualdas (b. 1932), prose writer, playwright and artist. Born in Klaipėda, graduated from Vilnius University in Russian philology in 1953. Worked as an editor for literary journals. Belonged to the non-conformist branch of the Writers' Union.

Lukšas, Gytis (b. 1946), film director. Born in Kaunas to Romualdas Lukšas, a theatre set designer. Graduated from the Moscow Institute of Cinematography in 1971, then worked at the Lithuanian Film Studio. Interacted closely with the key protagonists of the "Rustic turn" – Sigitas Geda, Marcelijus Martinaitis, Juozas Aputis and others, contributed to the exploration of ethnic identity in the Lithuanian cinema (*Vakar ir visados*). Chair of the Lithuanian Filmmaker's Union since 1991.

Marcinkevičius, Justinas (1930–2011), poet, playwright, public figure, one of the three key members of the Generation of 1930 along with Baltakis and Maldonis. Born to a family of poor farmers in the Prienai district. Graduated from the Prienai Gymnasium in 1949, and Vilnius University, Faculty of Lithuanian Philology in 1954. Joined the Writers' Union in 1955, was Secretary of the Board from 1959 to 1960 and Deputy Chairman from 1960 to 1965. Joined the Communist Party in 1957. Rose to become Lithuania's most popular poet and a cult figure by the eighties. A leading member of *Sąjūdis*, he withdrew from politics after Lithuania gained independence.

Martinaitis, Marcelijus (1936–2013), poet, writer, public figure. Born to a family of poor farmers in the Raseiniai district. Initially studied engineering in Kaunas, then graduated from Vilnius University, Faculty of Lithuanian Philology in 1964. Worked as a journalist in the 1960s, taught at Vilnius University since the 1980s. Elected to Parliament in 1989, prominent member of Sąjūdis.

Mikelinskas, Jonas (b. 1922), prose writer, public figure. Born to a family of farmers in the Pasvalys district. Taken as a forced laborer to Germany during World War II, entered Vilnius University and graduated in French Philology in 1952. A member of the Writers' Union since 1960. Active participant of the first public debates about the participation of Lithuanians in the Holocaust and their collective guilt (especially with Tomas Venclova).

Nasvytis, Algimantas (b. 1928), architect. Born in Kaunas to the family of a military doctor of gentry origin. Graduated from the State Art Institute of Lithuania (now Vilnius Academy of Art) in 1952. From 1960 worked at the Urban Planning Institute. Best-known works include the Neringa cafe and hotel in Vilnius (1960), detailed zoning plans for Vilnius (1971–79), Seimas Palace (1982), Lithuanian National Drama Theatre (1982), Hotel Lietuva (1983), White Bridge across Neris (1995). Active in *Sąjūdis* and later minister of construction and urban development.

Nasvytis, Vytautas (b. 1928), architect. Born in Kaunas to the family of a military doctor of gentry origin. Graduated from the State Art Institute of Lithuania (now Vilnius Academy of Art) in 1952. Artist of the Lithuanian pavilion of the USSR Agricultural exhibition in Moscow in 1952. Taught at the Art Institute in Vilnius from 1953, chief architect at the Lithuanian urban planning institute in Vilnius since 1962. Co-designer with his brother Algimantas of many famous architectural objects such as the Neringa cafe and hotel, the LSSR Supreme Council (parliament building) and others. Politically active during the time of *Sąjūdis*, later a member of the Vilnius city council.

Paleckis, Vincas Justas (b. 1942), journalist, diplomat and politician. Born in Samara, then called Kuybyshev, the city to which his father's family had been evacuated upon the Nazi invasion in 1941. Moved to Vilnius in 1945. Graduated in journalism from Vilnius University in 1964, worked as a correspondent for *Komjaunimo tiesa*. Studied at the Diplomatic Academy in Moscow from 1966 to 1969, then worked as a Soviet diplomat with postings to Switzerland and the GDR. Returned to Vilnius to work in the Central Committee of the Communist Party of Lithuania until December 1989 when he renounced his Communist Party membership. Member of the Lithuanian Parliament until 1992, served as a Lithuanian Ambassador to the UK, Portugal and Ireland, and Deputy Minister of Foreign Affairs. Elected to the European Parliament in 2004.

Pocius, Algirdas (1930), journalist, prose writer, public figure. Born to family of well-off farmers in Samogitia, graduated in Lithuanian Philology from the Klaipėda Pedagogical Institute in 1951. Worked as a radio correspondent and editor in Klaipėda and Šiauliai before moving to Vilnius in 1955. Joined the Writers' Union in 1956, Secretary of the Board from 1963 to 1981, Deputy Chairman from 1981 to 1986. Joined the Communist Part in 1960, member of the Lithuanian Social Democratic Party since 1990. Member of Parliament from 1992 to 1996.

Rakauskas, Romualdas (b. 1941), photographer, one of the key founders of the distinct school of Lithuanian photography during the late 1950s–1960s. Born in Akmenė, studied journalism at Vilnius University. One of the key initiators of the "rustic turn" in photography.

Reimeris, Vacys (b. 1921), poet, influential member of Soviet Lithuanian cultural nomenclatura. Born to a poor family in Kuršėnai district, Samogitia. During World War II moved to Russia, and was mobilized to the army. Joined Soviet Lithuanian Writers' Union in 1947, held many influential posts in the Union as sat on various editorial boards.

Saja, Kazys (b. 1932), playwright, novelist, public figure. Born to a family of poor farmers in the Pasvalys district, orphaned and raised by relatives. Studied in Klaipėda and Kaunas before graduating in Lithuanian philology from the Vilnius Pedagogical Institute in 1958. A member of the Writers' Union. Active in the politics of *Sąjūdis*, signatory to the Act of the Re-Establishment of the State of Lithuania.

Šilinis, Rimtautas Vladislovas (b. 1937), documentary filmmaker. Born in Utena to a family of agronomists and doctors. Graduated from Vilnius University in history and philology. Joined the Lithuanian Film Studio as an editor in 1965, started to produce films in 1966 and remained in the industry for four decades.

Sluckis, Mykolas (1928–2013), prose writer, influential Soviet Lithuanian Writers' Union official. Born in Panevėžys to a poor Jewish family, which perished in the Holocaust. He was attending a pioneer camp in Palanga when the Nazis invaded and was evacuated to the USSR. Returned to Lithuania in 1944, graduated in Russian Philology from Vilnius University in 1951. Claimed that since childhood his dream was to become a Lithuanian writer. Joined the Writers' Union, served as Secretary of the Board from 1959. After independence withdrew from the public scene.

Šulskytė, Aldona (1930–2008), teacher, poet, dissident. Her father fought in the Lithuanian wars of independence and served as a police officer for the inter-war republic. He was arrested by the Soviets in 1945 and deported, while Šulskytė went into hiding with her mother and sister. She later became a close friend and roommate of Dalia Grinkevičiūtė. The two lived in Laukuva, and Šulskytė was indirectly involved in dissident activities, hiding Grinkevičiūtė's manuscript from the authorities. After Grinkevičiūtė's death, Šulskytė maintained a memorial exposition of her life and works in their house.

Sutkus Antanas (b. 1939), photographer, co-founder of the Lithuanian Photography Art Society in 1969, one of the "founding fathers" of the national school of Lithuanian art photography after the war. Born in a village in the Kaunas district. Graduated in journalism from Vilnius University in 1964, active photographer since 1958 when he began his studies. Served as its Chairman from 1980 to 1989.

Tarvydas, Algirdas (b. 1940), film director, photographer, cameraman. Born in Kaunas. Worked with a team of filmmakers on the official documentary series on Soviet life in the LSSR called "Soviet Lithuania." Worked with Robertas Verba on *Šimtamečių godos* (1969) and *Čiūtyta rūta* (1968).

Veisaitė, Irena (b. 1928), literary and theatre critic, public figure. Cousin of Aleksandras Shtromas. Born in Kaunas and studied at the Sholom Aleichem Gymnasium in Kaunas 1934–41. Parents perished in the Kaunas Ghetto. Graduated from the Salomėja Nėris high school in Vilnius in 1947, and from Moscow State University in 1954 in German language and literature. Defended her dissertation at Leningrad State University in 1963. Taught at the Vilnius Pedagogical University from 1953. Long-term President of the Open Society in Lithuania Foundation.

Venclova, Tomas (b. 1937), scholar, poet, dissident and human rights activist. Born in Klaipėda, the son of Antanas Venclova, a writer, the first Soviet Minister of Culture in Lithuania and author of the words of the Soviet Lithuanian national anthem. The family moved to Vilnius in 1946 and Tomas graduated from Vilnius University, Department of Lithuanian Philology in 1960. Became a dissident in the late 1960s, denied entry to the Lithuanian Writers' Union in 1975. Co-founder of the Lithuanian Helsinki Movement in 1976, emigrated to the USA in 1977, later became a Professor at Yale University.

Žilinskaitė Vytautė (b. 1930), poet, humourist, acadaimed writer of children's literature. Born in Kaunas to a family of educated professionals. Her father was a passionate Vilnius patriot and the head of the Kaunas section of the Union for the Liberation of Vilnius. Žilinskaitė's family moved to Vilnius just before WWII and she stayed there throughout the war. Although her father was repressed after the war, she entered Vilnius University in 1950, aided perhaps by her athletic achievements as a member of the LSSR national volleyball team. Studied journalism, wrote for a number of literary journals and joined the Writers' Union in 1963.

Zingeris, Markas (1947), writer, poet, playwright, journalist. Born in the Prienai district, graduated from Vilnius University in journalism in 1971. Taught philosophy in Kaunas from 1971 to 1976, then worked for the State Historical Museum. Member of the Writers' Union since 1990. Director of the Vilna Gaon State Jewish Museum since 2005.

Žvirgždas, Stanislovas (b. 1941), photographer. Born in the Prienai district and studied history at Vilnius University in 1960–61, but expelled and imprisoned in the Moldavian SSR until 1965 for participating in an event in which the banned Lithuanian flag was raised. In 1972 he studied photography at the University of Popular Art in Moscow and thereafter worked as a photographer. Chairman of the Lithuanian Union of Photographers since 1996.

Bibliography

Abukevičius, Petras and Vytautas Damaševičius. Dir. *Sugrįžimas*. LKS, 1990.

Adomaitis, Regimantas. "Sąjūdis ateina iš toli" [*Sąjūdis* comes from afar]. Vilnius: Margi raštai, 2008.

Agarin, Timofei. "Demographic and Cultural Policies of the Soviet Union in Lithuania from 1944 to 1956. A Post-Colonial Perspective." In *The Sovietization of the Baltic States, 1940–1956*, edited by Olaf Mertelsmann, 111–25. Tartu: KLEIO Ajalookirjanduse Sihtasutus, 2003.

Alantas, V. "Tautinės kultūros problemos." *Vairas* 1 (1940).

Amal'rik, Andrei. *Will the Soviet Union Survive Until 1984?* New York: Harper & Row, 1970.

Andriušis, Pulgis. "Grąžinkim garbę senamiesčiui!" *Į laisvę* 47 (August 16, 1941): 5.

Ankersmit, Frank R. "The Sublime Dissociation of the Past: Or How to Be(come) What One Is No Longer." *History and Theory* (October 2001): 295–323.

Anninskii, Lev. *Solntse v vetviakh: Ocherki o litovskoi fotografii*. Vilnius: Obshchestvo fotoiskusstva Litovskoi SSR, 1984.

Antanavičiūtė, Rasa. "Stalininis penkmetis: Vilniaus viešųjų erdvių įprasminimo darbai 1947–52 m" [The First Five Years Under Stalin: The Signification of Public Spaces in Vilnius, 1947–52]. *Menotyra* 16.3–4 (2009): 150–69.

Anušauskas, Arvydas. *The Anti-Soviet Resistance in the Baltic States*. Vilnius: Du Ka, 1999.

——. "KGB reakcija į 1972 m. įvykius." *Genocidas ir rezistencija* 1.13 (2003).

Apanavičius, Algimantas. Interview by author. Audio recording. Vilnius, April 10, 13, 2012.

Aputis, Juozas. "Tautos gedulo diena." *Pergalė* 6 (1989): 7.

Arad, Yitzhak. *Ghetto in Flames: The Struggle and Destruction of the Jews in Vilna in the Holocaust*. Jerusalem: Yad Vashem, Martyrs' and Heroes' Remembrance Authority, 1980.

Arendt, Hannah. *The Origins of Totalitarianism*. New York: Harcourt Brace, 1951.

Areška, Vitas. Interview by author. Audio recording. Vilnius, June 3, 2011.

Avižienis, Jūra. "Performing Identity: Lithuanian Memoirs of Siberian Deportation and Exile." In Marcel Cornis-Pope, ed. *History of the Literary Cultures of East-Central Europe: Junctures and Disjunctures in the 19th and 20th Centuries*. Amsterdam: Benjamins, 2010, 504–14.

Baliukevičius, Lionginas. *Partizano Dzūko dienoraštis*. Entry on November 10, 1948, Vilnius: LGGRTC, 2006.

Baliukonytė, Onė. "Ir pats stipresnis." [Interview with Algimantas Baltakis] *Moksleivis* 2 (1980): 14–15.

Baliutytė, Elena. "The Evolution of Eduardas Mieželaitis' Creative Work from the 1960s to the 1980s: From Prometheanism to Quixoticism." In *Baltic Memory: Processes of Modernisation in Lithuanian, Latvian and Estonian Literature of the Soviet Period*, edited by Elena Baliutytė and Donata Mitaitė, 177–87. Vilnius: Institute of Lithuanian Literature and Folklore, 2011.

Balkelis, Tomas. "Ethnicity and Identity Memoirs of Children Deportees," 1941–52, *Lituanus* 51.3 (Fall 2005): 40–74.

——. "War, Ethnic Conflict and the Refugee Crisis in Lithuania, 1939–40," *Contemporary European History* 16.6 (2007): 461–77.

——. *The Making of Modern Lithuania*. London: Routledge, 2010.

——. "Turning Citizens into Soldiers: Baltic Paramilitary Movements after the Great War." In *War in Peace: Paramilitary Violence after the Great War, 1917–1923*, edited by Robert Gerwarth and John Horn, 126–45. Oxford: Oxford University Press, 2012.

Balkelis, Tomas and Violeta Davoliūtė. *A Study on How the Memory of Crimes Committed by Totalitarian Regimes is Dealt with in Lithuania*. Vilnius: KKTC, 2009.

Baltakis, Algimantas. *Požeminės upės (Underground rivers)*. Vilnius: Vaga, 1967.

——. *Keliaujantis kalnas: Eilėraščiai*. Vilnius: Vaga, 1967.

——. *Poetų cechas*. Vilnius: Vaga, 1975.

——. *Gimiau pačiu laiku: iš dienoraščių, 1960–1997*. Vilnius: Tyto alba, 2008.

——. Interview by author. Audio recording. Vilnius, October 14, 2007, February 22, 2010, March 8, 2011.

Beauvoir, Simone de. *Tout Compte Fait*. Paris: Gallimard, 1972.

Becirevic, Edina. "Bosnia's 'Accidental' Genocide," *TRI* 470 (5 October 2006).

Becker, Charles S., Joshua Mendelsohn and Kseniya Benderskaya. *Russian Urbanization in the Soviet and Post-Soviet Eras*. London: International Institute for Environment and Development (IIED), 2012.

Beissinger, Mark. *Nationalist Mobilization and the Collapse of the Soviet State*. Cambridge: Cambridge University Press, 2002.

Benediktas [*pseud*]. "Naujojo Vilniaus istorija," *Vilniaus balsas* (10 July 1940).

Benjamin, Walter and Gary Smith. *Moscow Diary*. Cambridge, MA: Harvard University Press, 1986.

Berger, John. *And Our Faces, My Heart, Brief as Photos*. New York: Vintage Books, 1984.

Bieliauskas, Alfonsas, J. Jakaitienė, Justas V. Paleckis, and M. Tamošiūnas. *Taurios širdies žmogus: Atsiminimai apie Justą Paleckį*. Vilnius: Vaga, 1987.

Binkis, Kazys. *100 pavasarių*. Kaunas: Niola, 1923.

Bitoun, Pierre. *L'Equivoque Vichyssoise*. Paris, INRA, 1986.

Blum, Alain, Marta Craveri, and Valérie Nivelon. *Déportés en URSS récits d'Européens au goulag*. Paris: Autrement, 2012.

Boterbloem, Kees. *The Life and Times of Andrei Zhdanov, 1896–1948*. Montreal: McGill-Queen's University Press, 2004.

Brazauskas, Algirdas. *Ir tuomet dirbome Lietuvai: faktai, atsiminimai, komentarai*. Vilnius: Knygiai, 2007.

Brazdžionis, Bernardas. *Kunigaikščių miestas*. Kaunas: Sakalas, 1939.

Brėdikis, Vytautas. "Kelionių žavesys ir skurdas (b)." Manuscript, chapter from unpublished memoirs. Vilnius, 2013.

——. Interview by author. Audio recording. Vilnius, March 12, 2013.

Briedis, Laimonas. *Vilnius, City of Strangers*. Vilnius: Baltos Lankos, 2008.

Brio, Valentina. *Poetry and Poetics of the City: Wilno–Vilne–Vilnius.* Moscow: New Literary Observer Press, 2008.

Brubaker, Rogers. *Nationalism Reframed: Nationhood and the National Question in the New Europe.* Cambridge: Cambridge University Press, 1996.

Brudny, Yitzhak M. *Reinventing Russia: Russian Nationalism and the Soviet State, 1953–1991.* Cambridge, MA: Harvard University Press, 1998.

Bubnys, Arūnas. *Vokiečių okupuota Lietuva, 1941–1944.* Vilnius: LGGRTC, 1998.

——. *Nazi Resistance Movement in Lithuania 1941–1944.* Vilnius: Vaga, 2003.

Bubnys, Vytautas. *Alkana žemė: Romanas.* Vilnius: Vaga, 1971.

——. Interview by author. Audio recording. Vilnius, November 7, 2012.

Budrytė, Dovilė. "Coming to Terms With the Past: Memories of Displacement and Resistance in the Baltic States." In *Historical Injustice and Democratic Transition in Eastern Asia and Northern Europe: Ghosts at the Table of Democracy,* edited by Kenneth Christie and Robert Cribb. London: RoutledgeCurzon, 2002.

Burauskaitė, Birutė, ed. *Lietuvos gyventojų genocidas.* Vilnius: Represijų Lietuvoje tyrimo centras, 1992.

Burinskaitė, Kristina. "KGB prieš buvusius politinius kalinius ir tremtinius." *Genocidas ir rezistencija* 2.24 (2008): 121–26.

Burrin, Philippe. "Vichy." In Pierre Nora, ed., *Les Lieux de mémoire vol. 1.* Paris: Gallimard, 1992, 181–204.

Čaplinskas, Antanas Rimvydas. *Vilnius Streets: History, Street Names, Maps.* Vilnius: Charibde, 2000.

Čebatariūnaitė, Dangė. "Vilius Orvidas ir jo mito logika." *Naujasis židinys-Aidai* 6 (June 2004): 251–53.

——. "Ideologija fizinėje erdvėje: butų interjerai sovietinėje Lietuvoje 'atšilimo' laikotarpiu." *Naujasis židinys-Aidai* 8 (August 2006): 329–38.

Čepaitienė, Rasa. "Tarybinės sostinės konstravimas J. Stalino epochoje: Minsko ir Vilniaus atvejai." In *Nuo Basanavičiaus, Vytauto Didžiojo iki Molotovo ir Ribbentropo: atmintis ir atminimo kultūrų transformacijos XX – XXI a.,* edited by Alvydas Nikžentaitis, 171–224. Vilnius: LII, 2011.

Čepėnas, Pranas. *Naujųjų laikų lietuvos istorija.* Chicago, IL: Kazio Griniaus fondas, 1977.

Cicėnas, Jeronimas. *Vilnius tarp audrų* [Vilnius Between the Storms]. Chicago, IL: Terra, 1953.

——. "Susitikimai su Kaziu Boruta." *Atsiminimai.* Vilnius: Lietuvos rašytojų sąjungos leidykla, 2005, 126.

Clark, Katerina. *The Soviet Novel: History As Ritual.* Chicago, IL: University of Chicago Press, 1981.

——. "Socialist Realism and the Sacralizing of Space." In *The Landscape of Stalinism: The Art and Ideology of Soviet Space,* edited by Dobrenko E.A., and Eric Naiman, 3–18. Seattle, WA: University of Washington Press, 2003.

——. *Moscow, the Fourth Rome: Stalinism, Cosmopolitanism, and the Evolution of Soviet Culture, 1931–1941.* Cambridge, MA: Harvard University Press, 2011.

Clark, Katerina, E.A. Dobrenko, Andrei Artizov, and Oleg V. Naumov. *Soviet Culture and Power: A History in Documents, 1917–1953.* New Haven, CT: Yale University Press, 2007.

Clark, Terry D. and Jovita Pranevičiūtė. "Perspectives on Communist Successor Parties: The Case of Lithuania." *Communist and Post-Communist Studies* 41 (2008): 443–64.

Crossman, R.H.S., and Arthur Koestler. *The God That Failed.* New York: Harper, 1950.

Daniliauskas, A. *Lietuvos miesto gyventojų materialinė kultūra XX a.* Vilnius: Mokslas, 1978.

Daugirdaitė, Solveiga. "1965-ųjų akimirkos su Simone de Beauvoir ir Jeanu Pauliu Sartre'u." *Colloquia* 21 (2008): 96–113.

Daujotytė, Viktorija. "Paskutinis laisvės prieglobstis." *Pergalė* 12 (1989): 178–83.

———. "Bronius Kutavičius: pastovios preformos ir kintančios formos." In *Broniaus Kutavičiaus muzika: praeinantis laikas,* edited by Inga Jasinskaitė-Jankauskienė. Vilnius: Versus Aureus, 2008.

Daujotytė, Viktorija and Elena Bukelienė. *Lietuvių literatūra (1940–1997).* Kaunas: Šviesa, 1997.

Daujotytė-Pakerienė, Viktorija. "Ugnies maiše nepaslėpsi." In *Lietuviai prie Laptevų jūros: atsiminimai, miniatiūros, laiškai,* edited by A. Šulskytė. Vilnius: Lietuvos rašytojų sąjungos leidykla, 1997.

David-Fox, Michael. "Multiple Modernities vs. Neo-Traditionalism: On Recent Debates in Russian and Soviet History." *Jahrbücher für Geschichte Osteuropas* 54.4 (2006): 535–55.

Davoliūtė, Violeta. "Deportee Memoirs and Lithuanian History: the Double Testimony of Dalia Grinkevičiūtė." *Journal of Baltic Studies* 36.1 (2005): 51–68.

———. "The Popular Movement and Postmodernism: Reflections on the Cinema of Sąjūdis." *Athena: Philosophical Studies* 3 (2007): 124–34.

———. "Lithuania and the New West-East Migration." *OIKOS: Lithuanian Migration & Diaspora Studies* 6.2 (2008): 73–80.

———. "Mūsų kursas buvo ypatingas – daug poetų, daug savižudžių" [Our Year was Special: Many Poets, Many Suicides. Interview with Justinas Marcinkevičius]. *Kultūros Barai* 2 (March 2011): 43–46.

———. "The Prague Declaration of 2008 and its Repercussions in Lithuania: Historical Justice and Reconciliation." *Lituanus* 57.3 (Fall 2011): 49–62.

Davoliūtė, Violeta and Tomas Balkelis, eds. *Maps of Memory: Trauma, Identity and Exile in Deportation Memoirs from the Baltic States.* Vilnius: LTTI, 2012.

Deak, Istvan. "How to Construct a Productive, Disciplined, Monoethnic Society: The Dilemma of East Central European Governments, 1914–56." In *Landscaping the Human Garden: Twentieth-Century Population Management in a Comparative Framework,* edited by Amir Weiner, 205–17. Stanford, CA: Stanford University Press, 2003.

Dieckmann, Christoph. *Deutsche Besatzungspolitik in Litauen 1941–1944.* Göttingen: Wallstein, 2011.

Dieckmann, Christoph and Saulius Sužiedėlis. *The Persecution and Mass Murder of Lithuanian Jews during Summer and Fall of 1941: Sources and Analysis.* Vilnius: Margi raštai, 2006.

Dobrenko, E.A., and Eric Naiman. *The Landscape of Stalinism: The Art and Ideology of Soviet Space.* Seattle, WA: University of Washington Press, 2003.

Donskis, Leonidas. "A. Brazauskas ir kita Lietuva." *IQ. The Economist partneris Lietuvoje* (July 1, 2010), www.delfi.lt/news/ringas/lit/ldonskis-a-brazauskas-ir-kita-lietua.d? id=34032157.

———. "Miesto likimas komunistinėje ir postkomunistinėje Lietuvoje." In *Tarp Karlailio ir Klaipėdos: visuomenės ir kultūros kritikos etiudai.* Klaipėda: Klaipėdos Universiteto leidykla, 1997, 3–23.

Drąsutytė, Roberta. *Senyvo amžiaus moterų trauminių prisiminimų rekonstrukcija.* Unpublished M.A. thesis, VDU, Department for Social Work, 2012.

Drazdauskas, Valys. "Rytoj važiuoju į Vilnių!" *Kultūros barai* 12 (2001): 77–82.

Drėmaitė, Marija. "Šiaurės modernizmo įtaka 'lietuviškajai architektūros mokyklai' 1959–69 m." *Menotyra* 18.4 (2011): 308–28.

——. "Sovietmečio paveldas Vilniaus architektūroje: tarp lietuviškumo ir sovietiškumo." In *Naujasis Vilniaus perskaitymas: didieji Lietuvos istoriniai pasakojimai ir daugiakultūris miesto paveldas.* 2009, 79–103.

——. "'Negražaus' Vilniaus vaizdai: industrinio miesto ikonografija XIX a. antroje pusėje – XX a. pradžioje." *Naujasis židinys-Aidai* 7 (2009): 232–36.

——. "Naujas senasis Vilnius: senamiesčio griovimas ir atstatymas 1944–59 metais." In *Atrasti Vilnių: skiriama Vladui Drėmai*, edited by Giedrė Jankevičiūtė, 183–201. Vilnius: Lietuvos dailės istorikų draugija, Vilniaus dailės akademijos leidykla, 2010.

Dundulienė, Pranė. *Senieji lietuvių šeimos papročiai* [Ancient customs of the Lithuanian family]. Vilnius: Mokslo ir enciklopedijų leidybos institutas, 2002.

Dunham, Vera S. *In Stalin's Time: Middleclass Values in Soviet Fiction.* Cambridge: Cambridge University Press, 1976.

Dunlop, John B. *The Faces of Contemporary Russian Nationalism.* Princeton, NJ: Princeton University Press, 1983.

Eberhart, Piotr. *Ethnic Groups and Population Changes in Twentieth-Century Central-Eastern Europe: History, Data, and Analysis.* Armonk, NY.: M. E. Sharpe, 2003.

Eidintas, Alfonsas. *Žydai, lietuviai ir holokaustas.* Vilnius: Vaga, 2002.

——. *Antanas Smetona ir jo aplinka.* Vilnius: Mokslo ir enciklopedijų leidybos centras, 2012.

Eisenstadt, S.N. *From Generation to Generation: Age Groups and Social Structure.* London: Routledge and Kegan Paul, 1956.

Eley, Geoff. "Labor History, Social History, 'Alltagsgeschichte': Experience, Culture, and the Politics of the Everyday—a New Direction for German Social History?" *The Journal of Modern History* 61.2 (1989): 297–343.

Elie, Marc. *Les Anciens Détenus Du Goulag: Libérations Massives, Réinsertion Et Réhabilitation Dans L'URSS Poststalinienne, 1953–1964.* Paris: Ecole des Hautes Etudes en Sciences Sociales, 2007.

Elsaesser, Thomas. *Fassbinder's Germany: History, Identity, Subject.* Amsterdam: Amsterdam University Press, 1996.

Elsuwege, Peter V. *From Soviet Republics to EU Member States: A Legal and Political Assessment of the Baltic States' Accession to the EU.* Leiden: Martinus Nijhoff Publishers, 2008.

Epstein, Mikhail, Alexander Genis, and Slobodanka Vladiv-Glover. *Russian Postmodernism: New Perspectives on Post-Soviet Culture.* Edited and translated by Slobodanka Vladiv-Glover. New York: Berghahn Books, 1999.

Fitzpatrick, Sheila. "Ascribing Class: The Construction of Social Identity in Soviet Russia." *Journal of Modern History* 65.4 (December 1993): 745–70.

——. *Everyday Stalinism: Ordinary Life in Extraordinary Times: Soviet Russia in the 1930s.* Oxford: Oxford University Press, 2000.

Fitzpatrick, Sheila and Robert Gellately. *Accusatory Practices: Denunciation in Modern European History, 1789–1989.* Chicago, IL: University of Chicago Press, 1997.

Foreign Relations of the United States (1945) *Diplomatic Papers: The Conference of Berlin (the Potsdam Conference)*, Washington, DC: U.S. G.P.O, 1960: 1511.

Fowkes, Ben. "The National Question in the Soviet Union under Leonid Brezhnev: Policy and Response." In *Brezhnev Reconsidered*, edited by Edwin Bacon and Mark Sandle, 68–89. Houndmills and Basingstoke: Palgrave Macmillan, 2002.

Furst, Juliane. *Late Stalinist Russia: Society Between Reconstruction and Reinvention.* London: Routledge, 2006.

Gadeikis, Liudvikas. "Tremties archyvas" [Archive of Deportation], *Pergalė* 1 (1989): 185.

Gaškaitė, Nijolė. *Pasipriešinimo istorija: 1944–1953 metai*. Vilnius: Aidai, 1997.

Gaškaitė-Žemaitienė, Nijolė, ed. *Partizanai apie pasaulį, politiką ir save. 1944–1956 m. partizanų spaudos publikacijos*. Vilnius: Lietuvos gyventojų genocido ir rezistencijos tyrimo centras, 1998.

Gatrell and N. Baron, eds. *Warlands: Population Resettlement and State Reconstruction in the Soviet–East European Borderlands, 1945–50*. Basingstoke: Palgrave Macmillan, 2009.

Gavelis, Ričardas. *Vilnius Poker*. Translated by Elizabeth Novickas. Rochester, NY: Open Letter, 2009.

Geda, Sigitas. *Pėdos*. Vilnius: Vaga, 1966.

——. *Strazdas*. Vilnius: Vaga, 1967.

Girnius, Juozas. "Idėjiniai nacionalsocializmo pagrindai." *Į laisvę* 63 (September 4, 1941): 3.

Girnius, Kęstutis. "Pasipriešinimas, prisitaikymas, kolaboravimas." *Naujasis židinys-Aidai* 5 (1996): 268–79.

Glad, John. *Besedy v izgnanii: Russkoe literaturnoe zarubezhie*. Moskva: Izd-vo Knizhnaiapalata, 1991.

Gorsuch, Anne E. *All This Is Your World: Soviet Tourism at Home and Abroad After Stalin*. Oxford: Oxford University Press, 2011.

Goskomstat SSSR. *Demograficheskiy yezhegodnik SSSR 1990*. Moscow: Finansy i statistika, 1991.

Granauskas, Romualdas. *Duonos valgytojai* [The Bread Eaters]. Vilnius: Vaga, 1975.

——. *Gyvenimas po klevu* [Life Under the Maple Tree]. Vilnius: Vaga, 1989.

——. Interview. *Vakarinės naujienos* (2 October 1992).

——. Interview by author. Audio recording. Vilnius, June 3, 2011.

Greenblatt, Stephen. Introduction to "The Forms of Power and the Power of Forms in the Renaissance." *Genre* 15 (1982): 5.

——. "Racial Memory and Literary History." *PMLA* 116.1 (Jan. 2001): 48–63.

Greimas, Algirdas J. and Saulius Žukas. *Iš arti ir iš toli: literatūra, kultūra, grožis*. Vilnius: Vaga, 1991.

Grikevičius, Almantas. *Laikas eina per miestą*. Vilnius: LKS, 1966.

Grinkevičiūtė, Dalia. *Lietuviai prie Laptevų jūros: atsiminimai, miniatiūros, laiškai*, edited by A. Šulskytė. Vilnius: Lietuvos rašytojų sąjungos leidykla, 1997.

Gross, Jan Tomasz. *Revolution from Abroad: The Soviet Conquest of Poland's Western Ukraine and Western Belorussia*. Princeton, NJ: Princeton University Press, 1988.

——. "Social Consequences of War: Preliminaries to the Study of Imposition of Communist Regimes in East Central Europe." *East European Politics and Societies* 3.2 (Spring 1989): 198–214.

——. *Neighbours: The Destruction of the Jewish Community in Jedwabne, Poland*. New York: Penguin Books, 2001.

Grossman, Vasilii S., Anna Aslanyan, Robert Chandler, and Elizabeth Chandler. *Everything Flows*. London: Harvill Secker, 2010.

Grunskis, Eugenijus. *Lietuvos gyventojų trėmimai, 1940–1941 ir 1945–1953 metais*. Vilnius: Lietuvos istorijos institutas, 1996.

Grybas, Vladas. "Vilnius." *Pergalė* 11 (1948): 53–54.

Grybkauskas, Saulius, Česlovas Laurinavičius and G. Vaskela. *Sovietinė nomenklatūra ir pramonė Lietuvoje 1965–1985 metais*. Vilnius: Lietuvos Istorijos instituto leidykla, 2011.

Gudaitis, Romas, "Kai legenda dūsta (atsakymas T.Venclovai)." delfi.lt (July 26, 2010).

Gustaitis, Motiejus. "Vilnius." *Baras* 4 (1925): 5.

Halfin, Igal. "Looking into the Oppositionists's Soul: Inquisition Communist Style." *Russian Review* 60.3 (2001): 316–39.

Hedin, Astrid. "Stalinism as Civilization: New Perspectives on Communist Regimes." *Political Studies Review* 2 (2004): 166–84.

Heidegger, Martin. "Building, Dwelling, Thinking." In *Poetry, Language, Thought*, translated by Albert Hofstadter. New York: Harper Colophon Books, 1971.

Hellbeck, Jochen. *Revolution on My Mind: Writing a Diary Under Stalin*. Cambridge, MA: Harvard University Press, 2006.

Heynickx, Rajesh, Tom Avermaete, and Luc Vints. *Making a New World: Architecture & Communities in Interwar Europe*. Leuven: Leuven University Press, 2012.

Hoffman, David. *Peasant Metropolis: Social Identities in Moscow, 1929–1941*. Ithaca, NY: Cornell University Press, 1994.

Hosking, Geoffrey A. *The Awakening of the Soviet Union*. Cambridge, MA: Harvard University Press, 1990.

Idzelis, Augustine. "Industrialization and Population Change in the Baltics." *Lituanus* 30.2 (Summer 1984): 26–42.

Indriūnas, Algimantas. *Nelegalios karjeros metai*. Vilnius: Gairės, 2005.

Iriye, Akira. *Cultural Internationalism and World Order*. Baltimore, MD: Johns Hopkins University Press, 1997.

Ivanauskas, Vilius. "Intellectuals and Sovietization During Late Socialism: Shift from Indoctrination to National Processes (the Case of Writers in Soviet Lithuania)." Unpublished manuscript, 2011.

Jasaitis, Algimantas and Andrius Kleniauskas, eds. *Tai bent vestuvės: "Senovinių kupiškėnų vestuvių 40-mečiui."* Utena: Utenos Indra, 2006.

Jokūbonis, Gediminas. *Kai žaidė angelai: atsiminimai*. Vilnius: Vilniaus dailės akad. leidykla, 2009.

Judelevičius, Dovydas. "Apie žodžius, laiką ir save." *Pergalė* 9 (1962): 144–56.

———. "Tau viską reikės atrasti iš naujo." *Literatūra ir menas* (10 February 1966).

Judelevičius, Dovydas, A. Rabačiauskaitė, Jonas Lankutis, R. Pakalniškis *et al.* "Literatūrinis *Pergalės* antradienis." *Pergalė* 2 (1966): 181–83.

Judt, Tony. "The Past is Another Country: Myth and Memory in Post-war Europe." *Daedalus* 21.4 (Fall 1992): 83–114.

Jurašienė, Aušra-Marija. "The Problem of Creative Artistic Expression in Contemporary Lithuania." *Lituanus* 22.3 (Fall 1976): 28–54.

Jurkutė, Mingailė. "Ansamblis 'Lietuva': režimo įrankis ir nesėkmė." *Naujasis židinys-Aidai* 3 (2011): 151–57.

Kamiński, Łukasz. "Gyvieji fakelai." *Bernardinai.lt* (January 20, 2010).

Kalyvas, Stathis N. "The Urban Bias in Research on Civil Wars." *Security Studies* 13.3 (Spring 2004): 160–90.

———. *The Logic of Violence in Civil War*. Cambridge: Cambridge University Press, 2006.

Karka, Mykolas. "Kuriame naują Lietuvą." In *Taurios širdies žmogus*. Vilnius: Vaga, 1987, 162–63.

Katilius, Ramūnas. Interview by author. Audio recording. Vilnius, April 5, 6, 2012.

Kaubrys, Saulius. *National Minorities in Lithuania: An Outline*. Vilnius: Vaga, 2002.

Kavolis, Vytautas. "The Second Lithuanian Revival: Culture as Performance." *Lituanus* 37.2 (Summer 1991): 52–64.

———. *Žmogus istorijoje*. Vilnius: Vaga, 1994.

Keliuotis, Juozas. "Politikos etika." *Naujoji Romuva* 12 (1931): 273.

——. "Senieji ir jaunieji." *Naujoji Romuva* 147 (1933): 860.

Kersten, Krystyna. "Forced Migration and the Transformation of Polish Society in the Post-war Period." In *Redrawing Nations: Ethnic Cleansing in East-Central Europe, 1944–1948*, edited by Phillip Ther and Anna Siljak, 75–86. Oxford: Rowman and Littlefield, 2001.

Kiaupa, Zigmantas, Jūratė Kiaupienė, and Albinas Kuncevičius. *The History of Lithuania Before 1795*. Vilnius: Lithuanian Institute of History, 2000.

Khlevniuk, Oleg. *Politbiuro. Mekhanismy politicheskoi vlasti v 1930-e gody*. Moscow: Rosspen, 1996.

Klumbys, Valdemaras. *Lietuvos kultūrinio elito elgsenos modeliai sovietmečiu*. Unpublished dissertation, Vilnius, 2009.

Kmita, Rimantas. *Ištrūkimas iš fabriko: modernėjanti lietuvių poezija XX amžiaus 7–9 dešimtmečiais*. Vilnius: Lietuvių literatūros ir tautosakos institutas, 2009.

——. "Nature and Politics: Lithuanian Poetry of the Soviet Period." In *Baltic Memory*, edited by Elena Baliutytė and Donata Mitaitė, 163–176. Vilnius: Institute of Lithuanian Literature and Folklore, 2011.

Koivunen, Pia. "The 1957 Moscow Youth Festival: Propagating a New, Peaceful Image of the Soviet Union." In *Soviet State and Society under Nikita Khrushchev*, edited by Melanie Iliac and Jeremny Smith, 66–85. London: Routledge, 2009.

Konovalov, Nikolai. "Soshestvie bogov," *Izvestia* 274 (November 19, 1959): 4.

Korsakas, Kostas. Stenogram of a speech delivered on October 27, 1945 at the First Convention of the Soviet Lithuanian Writers Union. *Pirmasis Lietuvos Tarybinių rašytojų suvažiavimas, October 25–28, 1945*. Lithuanian Archive of Literature and Arts, f. 34, a. 1, b. 1.

Kotkin, Stephen. *Magnetic Mountain: Stalinism as a Civilization*. Berkeley, CA: University of California Press, 1995.

——. "Modern Times: The Soviet Union and the Interwar Conjuncture." *Kritika: Explorations in Russian and Eurasian History* 2.1 (Winter 2001): 111–64.

Krasauskaitė, Aistė J. *Juoda ir balta: prisiminimai apie Stasį Krasauską*. Vilnius: Tyto Alba, 2004.

Krawchenko, Bohdan ed. *Ukraine After Shelest*. Edmonton: Canadian Institute of Ukrainian Studies, 1983.

Krikščiūnas, Jonas, (Jovaras). Stenogram of a speech delivered on October 27, 1945 at the First Convention of the Soviet Lithuanian Writers Union. *Pirmasis Lietuvos Tarybinių rašytojų suvažiavimas, October 25–28, 1945*. Lithuanian Archive of Literature and Arts, f. 34, a. 1, b. 1, 56.

Kruk, Herman and Benjamin Harshav. *The Last Days of the Jerusalem of Lithuania: Chronicles from the Vilna Ghetto and the Camps, 1939–1944*. New Haven, CT: YIVO Institute for Jewish Research, 2002.

Kubilius, Vytautas. *Lithuanian Literature*. Vilnius: Vaga, 1997.

——. *Neparklupdyta mūza: lietuvių literatūra vokietmečiu*. Vilnius: Lietuvių literatūros ir tautosakos institutas, 2001.

Kubilius, Vytautas, Janina Žėkaitė, and Jūratė Sprindytė. *Dienoraščiai 1945–1977*. Vilnius: Lietuvių literatūros ir tautosakos institutas, 2006.

Kudaba, Česlovas. "Pokalbis apie Sąjūdį." *Akiračiai* 10 (1988).

Kunčinas, Jurgis. *Tūla*. Vilnius: Lietuvos Rašytojų sąjungos leidykla, 1993.

Kundera, Milan. *The Book of Laughter and Forgetting*. New York: A.A. Knopf, 1980.

Kutraitė, Zita, ed. *Manau, kad … Pokalbiai su Tomu Venclova*, Vilnius: Baltos lankos, 2000.

Kvietkauskas, Mindaugas. "Triūsas savo sode." Interview with Justinas Marcinkevičius. *Metai* 3 (2000): 98–102.

Labūnaitis, Vytautas K. "Gyvenimas be žydų." *Naujoji lietuva* 10 (9 July 1941): 2.

Labūnaitis, Vytautas. "Mūsų tautos priešai." *Naujoji lietuva* 16 (12 July 1941): 4.

Lakačauskaitė, Regina. "Miestiečio butas Sovietų Lietuvoje: ideologijos atspindžiai gyvenamojoje erdvėje." *Naujasis židinys-Aidai* 1–2 (2010): 13–22.

Landsbergis, Vytautas. Speech delivered at a public meeting. In *Tremtinys* 6.21 (May 1990).

Lankauskas, Romualdas. Interview by author. Audio recording. Vilnius, October 11, 2010.

Lankutis, Jonas. "Ginčas dėl gyvenimo prasmės." *Pergalė* 2 (1962): 137–45.

———. "Žmogus ir dinozauras." *Pergalė* 2 (1966): 89–100.

Lankutis, Jonas, ed. *Literatūrinio gyvenimo kronika, 1940–1960.* Vilnius: Vaga, 1970.

Lapinskienė, Alma. *Vilniaus kultūrinis gyvenimas 1900–1940.* Vilnius: Lietuvių literatūros ir tautosakos institutas, 1998.

———. *Vilniaus kultūrinis gyvenimas, 1939–1945.* Vilnius: Lietuvių literatūros ir tautosakos institutas, 1999.

Laučkaitė, Laima. "Vilniaus sostapilis kaip miesto ikona XX amžiaus pradžioje." *Naujasis Židinys* 7 (2009): 225–31.

Lebedys, Jurgis. *Mikalojus Daukša.* Vilnius: Valstybinė grožinės literatūros leidykla, 1963.

Levin, Dov. *Fighting Back: Lithuanian Jewry's Armed Resistance to the Nazis, 1941–1945.* New York: Holmes & Meyer, 1985.

Lewandowska, Stanisława. *Życie codzienne Wilna w latach II wojnyświatowej.* Warsaw: Neriton, 1997.

Lewin, Moshe. *The Soviet Century.* London: Verso, 2005.

Lewytszkyj, Borys. *Politics and Society in Soviet Ukraine: 1953–1980.* Edmonton: CIUS Press, 1984.

Liekis, Šarūnas. *1939: The Year That Changed Everything in Lithuania's History.* Amsterdam: Rodopi, 2010.

LTSR rašytojų sąjungos grožinės literatūros propagandos biuras. *Literatūros panorama: Vilnius, 1977–1978 m.m.* Vilnius: Lietuvos Aklųjų draugijos centrinė biblioteka, 1977.

———. *Literatūros panorama: Vilnius, 1978–1979 m.m.* Vilnius: Vilniaus gražtų gamyklos klubas, 1978.

Lipphardt, Anna. *Vilne. Die Juden aus Vilnius nach dem Holocaust. Eine transnationale Beziehungsgeschichte.* Paderborn: Schöningh, 2010.

Lovell, Stephen, ed. *Generations in Twentieth Century Europe.* Basingstoke: Palgrave Macmillan, 2007.

Lüdtke, Alf. *The History of Everyday Life: Reconstructing Historical Experiences and Ways of Life.* Princeton, NJ: Princeton University Press, 1995.

Lukšas, Gytis. Interview by author. Audio recording. Vilnius, August 2, 2012.

Lygo, Emily. *Leningrad Poetry 1953–1975: The Thaw Generation.* Bern: P. Lang, 2010.

Maciuika, Benedict. "Contemporary Social Problems in the Collectivized Lithuanian Countryside." *Lituanus* 22.3 (Fall 1976): 5–27.

Mackonis, Jonas. *Boružės odisėjos.* Vilnius: Tyto Alba, 2003.

Maciulevičius, Antanas, dir. *Lietuva tarp praeities ir ateities,* LKS, 1990.

Mačiulis, Algimantas. *Architektai Algimantas ir Vytautas Nasvyčiai.* Vilnius: Vilniaus dailės akademijos leidykla, 2007.

Mačiulis, Dangiras. "Vytauto Didžiojo metų (1930) kampanijos prasmė." *Lituanistica* 2.46 (2001): 54–75.

——. *Valstybės kultūros politika Lietuvoje 1927–1940 metais.* Vilnius: Lietuvos istorijos institutas, 2005.

——. "Apie dvi propagandines kampanijas 20 a. Lietuvoje." *Inter-studia humanitatis* 9 (2009): 119–38.

——. "Vilniaus vaizdinys Vilnių vaduojančioje Lietuvoje" [The Picture of Vilnius in the Period when Lithuania was yearning to retake Vilnius]. *Acta litteraria comparative* 4 (2009): 80–97.

Mansbach, Stephen A. "Modernist Architecture and Nationalist Aspiration in the Baltic: Two Case Studies." *Journal of the Society of Architectural Historians* 65.1 (March 2006): 92–111.

Marcevičienė, Marija, ed. *Atmintis: tremtinių atsiminimų rinkinys.* Kaišiadorys: Kaišiadorių muziejus, 2003.

Markevičienė, Jūratė. "Vilniaus kultūros paveldo apsauga Lietuvos Respublikos (1939–40), Sovietų Sąjungos okupacijos bei aneksijos pradžios (1940–41 ir 1944–45) ir nacistinės Vokietijos okupacijos (1941–44) laikotarpiu." In *Vilniaus kultūrinis gyvenimas 1939–1945*, edited by Alma Lapinskienė, 142–75. Vilnius: LTTI, 1999.

Marcinkevičius, Justinas. *Dvidešimtas pavasaris: poema.* Vilnius: valstybinė grožinės literatūros leidykla, 1956.

——. *Kraujas ir pelenai: herojinė poema.* Vilnius: Valstybinė grožinės literatūros leidykla, 1960.

——. *Pušis, kuri juokėsi: apysaka.* Vilnius: Valstybinė grožinės literatūros leidykla, 1961.

——. *Donelaitis.* Vilnius: Valstybinė grožinės literatūros leidykla, 1964.

——. *Siena: Miesto Poema.* Vilnius: Vaga, 1965.

——. *Mediniai tiltai.* Vilnius: Vaga, 1966.

——. *Mažvydas: trijų dalių giesmė.* Vilnius: Vaga, 1977.

——. *Dienoraštis be datų.* Vilnius: Vaga, 1981.

——. "Reabilituota – 1970 metais." *Literatūra ir menas* 22 (May 18, 1988): 2–3.

——. "Tartum grįžtumėm iš tremties." Speech delivered at a session of the Supreme Council of the LSSR, 18 November 1988. *Pažadėtoji žemė.* Vilnius: Lietuvos rašytojų sąjungos leidykla, 2009, 40–45.

——. Interview by author. Audio recording. Vilnius, January 3, 2010.

Martinaitis, Marcelijus. *Kukučio baladės.* Vilnius: Vaga, 1977.

——. Interview conducted by Dana Šiaudinytė. "Žemė mus išgelbės." *Vakarinės naujienos,* December 1991, 5.

——. "Lietuviškos utopijos." *Kultūros barai* 8–9 (1993): 3.

——. "Vilniau, kaime mano … " *Literatūra ir menas* (April 20, 2007): 2–22.

——. "Eduardas Mieželaitis, bet ne tas." In *Eduardas Mieželaitis: Post scriptum.* Vilnius: Lietuvos rašytojų sąjungos leidykla, 2008.

——. *Mes gyvenome: biografiniai užrašai.* Vilnius: Lietuvos rašytojų sąjungos leidykla, 2009.

——. Interview by author. Audio recording. Vilnius, November 12, 2008.

Martinaitis, Marcelijus and Laima Sruoginis. *The Ballads of Kukutis.* Forest Grove, OR: Robert A. Davies, 1993.

Martinkus, Vytautas. "Rašytojo žodis: mitas ar tikrovė." *Literatūra ir menas* 39 (September 24, 1988): 2–3.

——. "Sąjūdžio eseistika: rašytojai literatūros ir politikos kryžkelėje (1998)." In *Literatūra ir paraliteratūra: straipsniai ir esė.* Vilnius: Lietuvos rašytojų sąjungos leidykla, 2003.

Matulevičienė, Saulė. "Dokumentinė literatūra: pokario ir tremties atsiminimai" [Documentary Literature: Memoirs of the Post-war Period and the Deportations]. In *Naujausioji lietuvių literatūra*, edited by Giedrius Viliūnas, 319–45. Vilnius: Alma Littera 2003.

——. "Iš pokalbių su Romualdu Ozolu: 7–8 dešimtmečio dvasinės erdvės." *Liaudies kultūra* 5 (2007): 45–53.

——. "Pogrindis, virtęs Pastoge. Saulės Matulevičienės pokalbis su Algirdu Patacku." *Liaudies kultūra* 1.118 (2008): 43–51.

Matulytė, Margarita. *Nihil Obstat: Lietuvos fotografija sovietmečiu*. Vilnius: Vilniaus Dailės akademijos leidykla, 2011.

Mazower, Mark. "Reconstruction: The Historiographical Issues." *Past and Present*, Supplement 6 (2011): 17–28.

Merkelis, Aleksandras. *Antanas Smetona: jo visuomeninė, kultūrinė ir politinė veikla* [Antanas Smetona: His civic, cultural and political activity]. New York: Amerikos lietuvių tautinė sąjunga, 1964.

Merkys, Vytautas. *Atminties prošvaistės*. Vilnius: Versus Aureus, 2009.

Mertelsmann, Olaf, ed. *The Sovietization of the Baltic States, 1940–1956*. Tartu: KLEIO Ajalookirjanduse Sihtasutus, 2003.

Mieželaitis, Eduardas. *Tėviškės vėjas*. Vilnius: Valstybinė grožinės literatūros leidykla, 1946.

——. *Mano lakštingala*. Vilnius: Valstybinė grožinės literatūros leidykla, 1956.

——. *Autoportretas; Aviaeskizai: Dvi Knygos*. Vilnius: Vaga, 1962.

——. *Žmogus*. Vilnius: Valstybinė grožinės literatūros leidykla, 1962.

——. "Medžio grimasos." *Nemunas* 3 (1970): 10–12.

Mikelinskas, Jonas. Interview by author. Audio recording. Vilnius, June 17, 2011.

Mikeš, Vítězslav. "The Phenomenon of Bronius Kutavičius and Sigitas Geda." Presentation delivered at the 43rd International conference of Baltic Musicologists (Tribute to 80th Anniversary of Bronius Kutavičius). Vilnius, September 12, 2012.

Mikučianis, Vladislovas. *Norėjau dirbti Lietuvoje*. Vilnius: Vilniaus dailės akademijos leidykla, 2001.

Misiūnas, Romuald J. and Rein Taagepera. *The Baltic States, Years of Dependence, 1940–1990*. Berkeley, CA: University of California Press, 1993.

Mitaitė, Donata. "Kelios Alfonso Maldonio archyvo pasiūlytos temos." *Lituanistica* 55.3–4 (2009): 144–52.

Mitrokhin, Nikolai. *Russkaia partiia. Dvizhenie russkikh natsionalistov SSSR, 1953–1985*. Moscow: Novoe literaturnoe obozrenie, 2003.

Mosse, George L. *The Nationalization of the Masses: Political Symbolism and Mass Movements in Germany from the Napoleonic Wars through the Third Reich*. New York: New American Library, 1977.

Mulevičius, Leonas. "Agrarinis klausimas Lietuvoje 1905 metų revoliucijos išvakarėse," *Lietuvos istorijos metraštis, 1975 metai* (1976): 5–21.

Mulevičiūtė, Jolita. *Modernizmo link. Dailės gyvenimas Lietuvos Respublikoje 1918–1940*. Kaunas: Nacionalinis M.K. Čiurlionio dailės muziejus, 2001.

Nahaylo, Bohdan. "Ukrainian Dissent and Opposition after Shelest." In *Ukraine After Shelest*, edited by Bohdan Krawchenko, 30–54. Edmonton: Canadian Institute of Ukrainian Studies, 1983.

Naiman, Eric. "On Soviet Subjects and the Scholars Who Make Them." *Russian Review* 60.3 (2001): 307–15.

Naimark, Norman. *Fires of Hatred: Ethnic Cleansing in Twentieth-Century Europe.* Cambridge, MA: Harvard University Press, 2001.

——. *Stalin's Genocides.* Princeton, NJ: Princeton University Press, 2010.

Nasvytis, Algimantas. Interview by author. Audio recording. Vilnius, May 12, 2012.

Nasvytis, Vytautas. Interview with author. Audio recording. Vilnius, June 3, 2012.

Nichols, Bill. *Representing Reality: Issues and Concepts in Documentary.* Bloomington, IN: Indiana University Press, 1991.

Nora, Pierre. *Rethinking France: Les Lieux De Mémoire, Space.* London: University of Chicago Press, 2006.

——. "Reasons for the current upsurge in memory," *Eurozine.com* (April 19, 2002).

Oginskaitė, Rūta. *Nuo pradžios pasaulio: Apie dokumentininką Verbą.* Vilnius: Aidai, 2010.

Ohman, Jonas. *The Hitmen.* Documentary film. Vilnius, 2009.

Olson, Laura J. *Performing Russia: Folk Revival and Russian Identity.* New York: RoutledgeCurzon, 2004.

Parulskienė, Daina, ed. *Kitoks: Vilius Orvidas.* Vilnius: Dialogo kultūros institutas, 2003.

Paleckis, Justas. Stenogram of a speech delivered on October 2, 1946 at a meeting of the Soviet Lithuanian Writers Union. *LTSR Rašytojų visuotinio susirinkimo stenogramos ir rezoliucija*, Lithuanian Archive of Literature and Arts, f. 34, ap. 1, b. 20, 112.

——. (Palemonas). "Vilnius." *Pergalė* 7 (1949): 6.

Paleckis, Vincas Justas. Interview by author. Audio recording. Vilnius, April 4 and 10, 2012.

Pétain, Philippe. *Actes et Ecrits.* Paris: Flammarion, 1974.

Petkevičius, Vytautas. *Žydi bičių duona.* Vilnius: Valstybinė grožinės literatūros leidykla, 1963.

Petrulis, Vaidas. "The Modern Movement in Lithuania: Cultural and Political Encounters." *Docomomo Journal* 37 (September 2007): 68–71.

——. "Erdvinės lietuvių tautinio stiliaus politikos projekcijos 1918–39 m." In *Meno istorija ir kritika 4. Menas ir tapatumas*, 35–48. Kaunas: Vytauto didžiojo universiteto leidykla, 2008.

——. "Architektūros politikos apraiškos Lietuvos tarpukario (1918–40 m.) periodikoje: tarp reprezentacijos ir socialinio teisingumo." *Urbanistika ir architektūra* 33.2 (2009): 126–34.

Paulauskas, Henrikas. *Senovinių kupiškėnų vestuvių istorija: faktai ir prisiminimai.* Vilnius: Petro ofsetas, 2006.

Pilkington, Hilary. *Russia's Youth: A Nation's Constructors and Constructed.* London: Routledge, 1994.

Pocius, Algirdas. Interview by author. Personal interview. Vilnius, September 22, 2008; Rubikiai, July 3, 2010.

Pocius, Mindaugas. *Kita mėnulio pusė: Lietuvos partizanų kova su kolaboravimu 1944–1953 metais.* Vilnius: Lietuvos istorijos institutas, 2009.

Putinaitė, Nerija. *Nenutrūkusi styga. Prisitaikymas ir pasipriešinimas sovietų Lietuvoje* [The Unbroken String: Accommodation and Resistance in Soviet Lithuania]. Vilnius: Aidai, 2007.

——. "The Good vs. 'the Own': Moral Identity of (Post)Soviet Lithuania." *Studies of East European Thought* 60 (2008): 261–78.

Rakauskas, Romualdas. Interview by author. Personal interview. Vilnius, May 23, 2012.

Ramonaitė, Ainė. "'Paralelinės visuomenės' užuomazgos sovietinėje Lietuvoje: katali-kiškojo pogrindžio ir etnokultūrinio sąjūdžio simbiozė." In *Sąjūdžio ištakų beieškant:*

nepaklusniųjų tinklaveikos galia, edited by Jūratė Kavaliauskaitė and Ainė Ramonaitė, 33–58. Vilnius: Baltos lankos, 2011.

Reiber, Alfred J. *Forced Migration in Central and Eastern Europe, 1939–1950.* London: Frank Cass, 2000.

Reid, Susan E. "Modernizing Socialist Realism in the Khrushchev Thaw. The struggle for a 'Contemporary Style' in Soviet art." In *The Dilemmas of De-Stalinization: Negotiating Cultural and Social Change in the Khrushchev Era,* edited by Polly Jones, 209–30. London: Routledge, 2006.

Remeikis, Thomas. *Opposition to Soviet Rule in Lithuania, 1945–1980.* Chicago, IL: Institute of Lithuanian Studies Press, 1980.

——. *The Lithuanian Phoenix: Studies and Essays, 1940–1990.* Vilnius: Vytautas Magnus University, the Lithuanian Emigration Institute, 2009.

Reimeris, Vacys. Interview by author. Audio recording. Vilnius, April 12, 2012.

Richmond, Yale. *Cultural Exchange and the Cold War: Raising the Iron Curtain.* University Park, PA: Pennsylvania University Press, 2003.

Richter, Klaus. "Anti-Semitism, "Economic Emancipation, and the Lithuanian Cooperative Movement before World War I." *Quest. Issues in Contemporary Jewish History* 3 (July 2012): 182–97.

Ritter, Rudiger. "Prescribed Identity. The Role of History for the Legitimization of Soviet Rule in Lithuania." In *The Sovietization of the Baltic States, 1940–1956,* edited by Olaf Mertelsmann, 85–110. Tartu: KLEIO Ajalookirjanduse Sihtasutus, 2003.

Ro'i, Yaacov. 'The Transformation of Historiography on the "Punished Peoples."' *History and Memory* 21. 2 (Fall/Winter 2009): 150–76.

Rolf, Malte. "A Hall of Mirrors: Sovietizing Culture under Stalinism." *Slavic Review* 68.3 (Fall 2009): 601–30.

Rowell, S.C. *Lithuania Ascending: A Pagan Empire Within East-Central Europe, 1295–1345.* Cambridge: Cambridge University Press, 1994.

Rubavičius, Vytautas. "A Soviet Experience of Our Own: Comprehension and the Surrounding Silence." In *Baltic Postcolonialism,* edited by Violeta Kelertas, 83–104. Amsterdam: Rodopi 2006.

Rupas, V. and L. Vaitekūnas. *Lietuvos kaimo gyventojai ir gyvenvietės.* Vilnius: Mintis, 1980.

Saja, Kazys. "Lietuvos Antigonė," *Lietuvos aidas* (October 7, 1995), 5.

——. Interview by author. Audio recording. Vilnius, November 28, 2012.

Salutsky, Anatoly. "Aleksandr Zinovyev vs. Aleksandr Yakovlev." *Literaturnaya Gazeta* 50–51 (December 18, 2002): 15.

Šaltenis, Saulius. "Pokalbis su K. Saja ir A. Patacku." *Šiaurės Atėnai* (July 3, 1991).

Sambrooke, Jerilyn. "Narratives of Identity: A Postcolonial Reading of Dalia Grinkevičiūtė's *Lithuanians by the Laptev Sea.*" In *Maps of Memory: Trauma, Identity and Exile in Deportation Memoirs from the Baltic States,* edited by Violeta Davoliūtė and Tomas Balkelis, 90–103. Vilnius: LTTI, 2012.

Sauka, Donatas. *Fausto amžiaus epilogas.* Vilnius: Tyto alba, 1998.

Saukienė, R.Z. ed. *Šmaikščioji rezistentė Aldona Liobytė: publicistika, laiškai, atsiminimai.* Vilnius: Lietuvos rašytojų sąjungos leidykla, 1995.

Savickas, Augustinas. *Žalia tyla.* Vilnius: Tyto Alba, 2002.

Schlögel, Karl. "The Comeback of the European Cities." *International Review of Sociology/Revue Internationale de Sociologie* 16.2 (2006): 471–85.

——. "Orte Und Schichten Der Erinnerung. Annaherungen an Das Ostliche Europa." *Osteuropa* 58.6 (2008): 13.

Schmitt, Carl. *Theory of the Partisan: A Commentary on the Concept of the Political.* Berlin: Duncker & Humboldt, 1963.

Schull, Joseph. "What is Ideology? Theoretical Problems and Lessons from Soviet-Type Societies." *Political Studies* 40 (1992): 728–41.

Scott, James C. *Domination and the Arts of Resistance: Hidden Transcripts.* New Haven, CT: Yale University Press, 1990.

Šeinius, Ignas. "Lietuviškos dvasios beieškant" [Looking for the Lithuanian Spirit]. In *Vairas* 12 (December 1932): 302.

Senn, Alfred E. *The Great Powers, Lithuania and the Vilna Question 1920–1928.* Leiden: E. J. Brill, 1967.

——. *Lithuania Awakening.* Berkeley, CA: University of California Press, 1990.

——. *Lithuania 1940: Revolution from Above.* Amsterdam: Rodopi, 2007.

Šepetys, Lionginas. *Neprarastoji karta.* Vilnius: Lietuvos rašytojų sąjungos leidykla, 2005.

——. *Ar galėjau.* Vilnius: Lietuvos rašytojų sąjungos leidykla, 2011.

Šešelgis, Kazys. *Lietuvos urbanistikos istorijos bruožai. Nuo seniausių laikų iki 1918 m.* [History of urban development in Lithuania, from ancient times till 1918]. Vilnius: Mokslo ir enciklopedijų leidykla, 1996.

Shkandrij, Myroslav. "Literary Politics and Literary Debates in Ukraine 1971–81." In *Ukraine After Shelest*, edited by Bohdan Krawchenko, 55–72. Edmonton: Canadian Institute of Ukrainian Studies, 1983.

Šiaučiūnaitė-Verbickienė, Jurgita and Larisa Lempertienė. *Jewish Space in Central and Eastern Europe: Day-to-day History.* Newcastle: Cambridge Scholars Publishing, 2007.

Šilinis, Rimtautas. *Ar nuneši mane jauną.* Vilnius: LKS, 1975.

——. Interview by author. Audio recording. Vilnius, August 2, 2012.

Sinyavsky, Andrei. *On Socialist Realism.* New York: Pantheon Books, 1960.

Slezkine, Yuri. "The USSR As a Communal Apartment, or How a Socialist State Promoted Ethnic Particularism." *Slavic Review* 53.2 (1994): 414–52.

Sluckis, Mykolas. Interview by author. Audio recording. Vilnius, November 10, 2008.

Solntseva, L.P. and M.V. Iunisov, eds. *Samodeiatel'noe khudozhestvennoe tvorchestvo v SSSR: Ocherki istorii. Konets 1950-x-nachalo 1990-x godov.* St Petersburg: Dmitrii Bulanin, 1999.

Smetona, Antanas. *Rinktiniai raštai* [Collected Works]. Alfonsas Eidintas, ed. Kaunas: Menta, 1990.

Smith, Anthony D. *Myths and Memories of the Nation.* Oxford: Oxford University Press, 1999.

——. "Culture, Community and Territory: The Politics of Ethnicity and Nationalism." *International Affairs* 72.3 (July 1996): 445–58.

Snyder, Timothy. *The Reconstruction of Nations.* New Haven, CT and London: Yale University Press, 2004.

——. "Memory of sovereignty and sovereignty over memory: Poland, Lithuania and Ukraine, 1939–99." In *Memory and Power in Post-War Europe: Studies in the Presence of the Past*, edited by Jan-Werner Müller. Cambridge: Cambridge University Press, 2002.

Sprindytė, Jūratė. "The Symbolic Capital of Ideologically Untainted Writers: Estonian, Latvian and Lithuanian Small Novels." In *Baltic Memory: Processes of Modernisation in Lithuanian, Latvian and Estonian Literature of the Soviet Period*, edited by Elena Baliutytė and Donata Mitaitė, 83–96. Vilnius: Institute of Lithuanian Literature and Folklore, 2011.

Sruoga, Balys. "Vilniaus ir Kauno visuomeninė sanveika." *Vairas* 4 (1940): 347.

Statiev, Alexander. *The Soviet Counterinsurgency in the Western Borderlands.* Cambridge: Cambridge University Press, 2010.

Stravinskienė, Vitalija. *Tarp gimtinės ir Tėvynės: Lietuvos SSR gyventojų repatriacija į Lenkiją (1944–1947, 1955–1959 m.).* Vilnius: Lietuvos istorijos institutas, 2011.

Stražas, A.S. "From Auszra to the Great War: The Emergence of the Lithuanian Nation." *Lituanus* 42.4 (Winter 1996): 34–73.

Streikus, Arūnas. *Sovietų valdžios antibažnytinė politika Lietuvoje, 1945–1990.* Vilnius: LGGRTC, 2002.

——. "Apie antikrikščioniškus Sovietinių švenčių ir apeigų tikslus." *Naujasis židinys-Aidai* 10 (2003): 514–17.

——. "Kierunki polityki pamięci na Litwie sowieckiej." *Politeja* 16 (2011): 281–307.

Stone, Daniel. *The Polish-Lithuanian State, 1386–1795.* Seattle, WA: University of Washington Press, 2001.

Stoškus, Krescencijus. "Dar kartą apie T. Venclovą: poliai, kuriems nelemta vienas kito suprasti." delfi.lt (April 28, 2011).

Šulskytė, Aldona. Interview by author. Personal interview. August 12, 2003, Laukuva.

Štromas, Aleksandras. "Official Soviet Ideology and the Lithuanian People." In *Mind against the Wall: Essays on Lithuanian Culture Under Soviet Occupation,* edited by Silbajoris, Rimvydas. Chicago, IL: Institute of Lithuanian Studies Press, 1983.

Šukys, Aurimas. *Alternative Activity of Intellectuals in Soviet Lithuania, 1956–1988.* Unpublished dissertation. Vytautas Magnus University, Institute of Lithuanian History: Kaunas, 2012.

Sutkus, Antanas. *Sartre & Beauvoir, Cinq jours en Lituanie.* Latresne: Le Bord de L'Eau, 2005.

——. Interview by author. Audio recording. Vilnius, May 3, 9 and 14, 2012.

Sutzkever, Abraham. *Vilner Geṭo, 1941–1944.* Paris: Aroysgegebn durkh dem Farband fun di Vilner in Frankraykh, 1946.

Sužiedėlis, Saulius. "Language and Social Class in Southwestern Lithuania before 1864." *Lituanus* 27.3 (Fall 1981): 35–58.

——. "The Historical Sources for Antisemitism in Lithuania and Jewish-Lithuanian Relations during the 1930s." In *The Vanished World of Lithuanian Jews,* edited by Alvydas Nikžentaitis, Stefan Schreiner and Darius Staliūnas, 119–54. Amsterdam: Rodopi, 2004.

——. *Historical Dictionary of Lithuania.* Lanham, MD: Scarecrow Press, 2011.

Sventickas, Valentinas. *Paskui pėsčią paukštį.* Vilnius, Vaga, 1988.

——. "Išsaugoti – žmones, kūrybą, Lietuvą: poetą Justiną Marcinkevičių kalbina Valentinas Sventickas 2005.III.3" [Interview with Justinas Marcinkevičius]. *Literatūra ir menas* 3039 (11 March 2005).

Tamošaitis, Jonas. "Kaip augs miestai." *Pergalė* 10 (1962): 140.

Tamošaitis, Mindaugas. *Didysis apakimas: lietuvių rašytojų kairėjimas 4-ajame XX dešimtmetyje.* Vilnius: Gimtasis žodis, 2010.

Tapinas, Laimonas. *LTSR nusipelnęs meno veikėjas, kino režisierius ir operatorius Robertas Verba.* Vilnius, 1977.

Tarvydas, Algirdas. Interview by author. Audio recording. Vilnius, March 7, 2011.

Ther, Philipp and Ana Siljak, eds. *Redrawing Nations: Ethnic Cleansing in East-Central Europe, 1944–48.* Oxford: Rowman and Littlefield Publishers, 2001.

Therborn, Göran. "Eastern Drama. Capitals of Eastern Europe, 1830s-2006: an Introductory Overview." *International Review of Sociology* 16.2 (2006): 209–42.

Thum, Gregor. *Uprooted: How Breslau Became Wrocław During the Century of Expulsions*. Princeton, NJ: Princeton University Press, 2011.

Tininis, Vytautas. *Sniečkus: 33 metai valdžioje*. Lietuvos karo akademija, Vilnius, 2000.

Toleikis, Vytautas. "Lietuvos čigonai nacių okupacijos metais." In *Totalitarinių režimų nusikaltimai Lietuvoje: karo belaisvių ir civilių gyventojų žudynės Lietuvoje*. Edited by Christoph Dieckmann, Vytautas Toleikis and Rimantas Zizas. Vilnius: Margi raštai, 2005, 55–72.

Tolz, Vera. "Cultural Bosses as Patrons and Clients: The Functioning of the Soviet Creative Unions in the Post-war Period." *Contemporary European History* 11.1 (2002): 87–105.

Tornau, Ūla. "Socialistinio miesto vizijos taikymas Lietuvoje: pokarinis Vilnius." In *Europos erdvė: naujausios žinios apie genius loci*. Vilnius: Tarptautinės dailės kritikų asociacijos Lietuvos sekcija, 2004, 13–16.

Trentmann, Frank. "Civilization and Its Discontents: English Neo-Romanticism and the Transformation of Anti-Modernism in Twentieth-Century Western Culture." *Journal of Contemporary History* 29.4 (1994): 583–625.

Trimonis, Rytis. *Vladas Grybas*. Vilnius: Vaga, 1989.

Truska, Liudas. *Emigracija iš Lietuvos 1868–1914*. LTSR Akademijos darbai ser. A, 1, no. 10 (1961): 71–85.

——. *Lietuva 1938–1953 metais*. Kaunas: Šviesa, 1995.

——. "Origins of the Lithuanian Reform Movement Sąjūdis." In *13 January 1991 in Lithuania in the Context of the Recent Research*. Vilnius: Vilnius Pedagogical University, 2006.

——. "Ilgas kelias į Vilnių." *Kultūros barai* 5 (2010): 58–65.

Truska, Liudas and Vygantas Vareikis. *Holokausto prielaidos: antisemitizmas Lietuvoje XIX antroji pusė – 1941 m. birželis/The Preconditions for the Holocaust: Anti-Semitism in Lithuania (Second Half of the 19th Century – June 1941)* (Totalitarinių režimų nusikaltimai Lietuvoje/The Crimes of Totalitarian Regimes in Lithuania. Volume 1: *Nacių okupacija/The Nazi Occupation*). Vilnius: Margi raštai, 2004.

Tumas-Vaižgantas, Juozas. "Lietuviai miestuose." *Tėvynės sargas* 10 (1899).

Tyla, Antanas. "Lietuvos valstiečių istorijos bruožai, 1795–1861." *Lietuvių atgimimo istorijos studijos* 4 (1993): 25–28.

Vaičiūnas, Petras. "Mes grįžom į Vilnių." *Tiesa* 162 (July 13, 1946): 1.

——. *Laisvės keliais*. Vilnius: Vaga, 1991, 492–93.

Vaičiūnaitė, Ula. "Išaugusios viena iš kitos." *Moteris* 7 (2008): 44–49.

Vaičiūnienė, Teofilija. *Taurios širdies žmogus*. Vilnius: Vaga, 1987.

Vaiseta, Tomas. *Nuobodulio visuomenė: vėlyvojo sovietmečio Lietuva (1964–1984)*. Unpublished Dissertation. Vilnius, 2012.

Vaitekūnas, S. *Lietuvos gyventojai per du tūkstantmečius*. Vilnius: Mokslo ir enciklopedijų leidybos institutas, 2006.

Vardys, Stanley. "The Partisan Movement in Post-war Lithuania." *Lituanus* 15.1 (Spring 1969): 8–40.

Veisaitė, Irena. Interview by author. Personal interview. Vilnius, September 22, 2009.

Vasinauskas, Petras. *Kelionė su arkliu po Lietuvą*. Vilnius: Logos, 1996.

Vaskela, Gediminas. "The Land Reform of 1919–40: Lithuania and the Countries of East and Central Europe," *Lithuanian Historical Studies* 1 (1996): 116–32.

Vaškelis, Bronius. "The Assertion of Ethnic Identity Via Myth and Folklore in Soviet Lithuanian Literature." *Lituanus* 19.2 (Summer 1973): 16–27.

Venclova, Antanas. "Amžinasis mūsų miestas: giesmė apie Vilnių." *Pergalė* 2 (1944): 3–6.

——. Diary. *Venclovas House Museum Archives*. Vilnius.

Venclova, Tomas. *Raketos, planetos ir mes*. Vilnius: Valstybinė grožinės literatūros leidykla, 1962.

——. "Apie miestą, kaimą, laisvę ir poeziją." *Akiračiai* 5.89 (1977). In *Manau, kad. Pokalbiai su Tomu Venclova*, edited by Zita Kutraitė, 24–25. Vilnius: Baltos lankos, 2000.

——. "Sakau karčią tiesą," *Atgimimas* 24 (1990).

——. "A Fifth Year of Independence: Lithuania, 1922 and 1994." *East European Politics and Societies* 9 (1995): 344–67.

——. *Vilnius: A Personal History*. Riverdale-on-Hudson, NY: Sheep Meadow Press, 2009.

——. Interview by author. Audio recording. Vilnius, June 22, 2009.

——. "Lithuanian Dissent in the Context of Central and Eastern Europe: 1953–80." *Lituanus* 55.2 (Summer 2009): 38–50.

——. "Vilnius: The City as Object of Nostalgia." *Kultūros Barai* (September 2009), www.eurozine.com/articles/2010-07-27-venclova-en.html.

——. "Aš dūstu." www.bernardinai.lt/straipsnis/2010-07-14-tomas-venclova-asdustu/ 47325, accessed on 10 May 2013.

Verba, Robertas. *Senis ir žemė*. Directed by Robertas Verba. Vilnius: Lietuvos kino studija, 1965.

——. *Ciūtyta rūta*. Directed by Robertas Verba. Vilnius: Lietuvos kino studija, 1968.

——. *Šimtamečių godos*. Vilnius: Lietuvos kino studija, 1969.

Verdery, Katherine. *The Political Lives of Dead Bodies: Reburial and Postsocialist Change*. New York: Columbia University Press, 1999.

Viola, Lynne. *The Unknown Gulag: The Lost World of Stalin's Special Settlements*. Oxford: Oxford University Press, 2007.

Vitkevičienė, Marija. "Dėmės baltame chalate" [Stains on a White Robe]. *Artojas* 67 (11 June 1974): 3–4.

Vosylius, Jonas. *Literatūra 1940–1960: dokumentų rinkinys*. Vilnius: Academia, 1991.

Walker, Barbara. "Kruzhok Culture: the Meaning of Patronage in the Early Soviet Literary World." *Contemporary European History* 11.1 (February 2002): 117–23.

Weeks, Theodore. "Russification and the Lithuanians, 1863–1905." *Slavic Review* 60.1 (Spring 2001): 96–114.

——. "A Multi-ethnic City in Transition: Vilnius' Stormy Decade, 1939–49." *Eurasian Geography and Economics* 47.2 (2006): 153–75.

——. "Population Politics in Vilnius 1944–47: A Case Study of Socialist-Sponsored Ethnic Cleansing." *Post-Soviet Affairs* 23.1 (2007): 76–95.

——. "Remembering and Forgetting: Creating a Soviet Lithuanian Capital. Vilnius, 1944–49." *Journal of Baltic Studies* 39.4 (2008): 517–33.

Weiner, Amir. *Making Sense of War: The Second World War and the Fate of the Bolshevik Revolution*. Princeton, NJ: Princeton University Press, 2002.

——. *Landscaping the Human Garden: Twentieth-Century Population Management in a Comparative Framework*. Stanford, CA: Stanford University Press, 2003.

——. "The Empires Pay a Visit: Gulag Returnees, East European Rebellions, and Soviet Frontier Politics." *The Journal of Modern History* 78 (June 2006): 333–76.

Werth, Paul W. "From Resistance to Subversion: Imperial Power, Indigenous Opposition, and Their Entanglement." *Kritika: Explorations in Russian and Eurasian History* 1.1 (Winter 2000): 21–43.

Werner, Michael and Bénédicte Zimmermann. "Beyond Comparison: *Histoire Croisée* and the Challenge of Reflexivity." *History and Theory* 45 (February 2006): 30–50.

Williams, Raymond. *The Country and the City.* London: Chatto and Windus, 1973.
——. *Marxism and Literature.* Oxford: Oxford University Press, 1977.
Winston, Victor H. "Observations on the Population of Vilnius: The Grim Years and the 1942 Census." *Eurasian Geography and Economics* 47.2 (2006): 176–203.
Worobec, Christine. *Peasant Russia: Family and Community in the Post-Emancipation Period.* Princeton, NJ: Princeton University Press, 1991.
Yakovlev, Aleksandr. "Protiv antiistorizma." *Literaturnaya gazeta* 46 (15 November 1972): 4–5.
——. *Sumerki.* Moscow: Materik, 2005.
Zabielienė, Aušra. "Trejos kupiškėnų vestuvės." *Liaudies kultūra* 1 (2004): 29–33.
Zassoursky, Yassen. "Whitman's Reception and Influence in the Soviet Union." In *Walt Whitman of Mickle Street: A Centennial Collection,* edited by Geoffrey M. Sill, 42–49. Knoxville, TN: University of Tennessee Press, 1994.
Žebrytė, Jonė. "Dar kartą apie 'Senovines kupiškėnų vestuves' arba nuobodinė pasaka." *Kupiškis: kultūra ir istorija* (2007): 40–47.
Žepkaitė, Regina. *Vilniaus istorijos atkarpa: 1939–1940.* Vilnius: Mokslas, 1990.
Žilinskaitė, Vytautė. Interview by author. Audio recording. Vilnius, October 11, 2011, July 9, 2013.
Zingeris, Markas. Interview by author. Audio recording. Vilnius, June 18, 2012.
Zubkova, E.I.U. *Pribaltika i Kreml', 1940–1953.* Moscow: ROSSPEN, 2008.
Zubok, Vladislav. "Soviet Policy Aims at the Geneva Conference." In *Cold War Respite: The Geneva Conference of 1955,* edited by Gunter Bischof and Saki Dokrill, 55–74. Baton Rouge, LA: 2006.
——. *Zhivago's Children: The Last Russian Intelligentsia.* Cambridge, MA: Belknap Press of Harvard University Press, 2009.
Žukas, Saulius. "Nepasitikėk vieškeliais." *Literatūra ir menas* 40 (October 1, 1988): 5.
Žukas, Vaidotas. "Justinas Mikutis – laisvas žmogus nelaisvoje aplinkoje." *Bernardinai.lt.* (April 26, 2012).
Žukauskas, Albinas. "Miestai ar didkaimiai?" *Literatūra ir menas* 6.1 (January 1962): 1.
Žvirgždas, Stanislovas. Interview by author. Personal Interview. Vilnius, May 16, 2012.

Index